Mometrix
TEST PREPARATION

I0878901

TerraNova® NEXT
Grade 8 Reading and Language Test Prep Guide

Written and edited by the Mometrix Test Preparation Team
Printed in the United States of America

TABLE OF CONTENTS

Introduction

Thank you for purchasing this resource! You have made the choice to prepare yourself for a test that could have a huge impact on your future, and this guide is designed to help you be fully ready for test day. Obviously, it's important to have a solid understanding of the test material, but you also need to be prepared for the unique environment and stressors of the test, so that you can perform to the best of your abilities.

For this purpose, the first section that appears in this guide is the **Success Strategies**. We've devoted countless hours to meticulously researching what works and what doesn't, and we've boiled down our findings to the most impactful steps you can take to improve your performance on the test. We start at the beginning with study planning and move through the preparation process, all the way to the testing strategies that will help you get the most out of what you know when you're finally sitting in front of the test.

We recommend that you start preparing for your test as far in advance as possible. However, if you've bought this guide as a last-minute study resource and only have a few days before your test, we recommend that you skip over the first two Success Strategies since they address a long-term study plan.

If you struggle with **test anxiety**, we strongly encourage you to check out our recommendations for how you can overcome it. Test anxiety is a formidable foe, but it can be beaten, and we want to make sure you have the tools you need to defeat it.

Strategy #1 – Plan Big, Study Small

There's a lot riding on your performance. If you want to ace this test, you're going to need to keep your skills sharp and the material fresh in your mind. You need a plan that lets you review everything you need to know while still fitting in your schedule. We'll break this strategy down into three categories.

Information Organization

Start with the information you already have: the official test outline. From this, you can make a complete list of all the concepts you need to cover before the test. Organize these concepts into groups that can be studied together, and create a list of any related vocabulary you need to learn so you can brush up on any difficult terms. You'll want to keep this vocabulary list handy once you actually start studying since you may need to add to it along the way.

Time Management

Once you have your set of study concepts, decide how to spread them out over the time you have left before the test. Break your study plan into small, clear goals so you have a manageable task for each day and know exactly what you're doing. Then just focus on one small step at a time. When you manage your time this way, you don't need to spend hours at a time studying. Studying a small block of content for a short period each day helps you retain information better and avoid stressing over how much you have left to do. You can relax knowing that you have a plan to cover everything in time. In order for this strategy to be effective though, you have to start studying early and stick to your schedule. Avoid the exhaustion and futility that comes from last-minute cramming!

Study Environment

The environment you study in has a big impact on your learning. Studying in a coffee shop, while probably more enjoyable, is not likely to be as fruitful as studying in a quiet room. It's important to keep distractions to a minimum. You're only planning to study for a short block of time, so make the most of it. Don't pause to check your phone or get up to find a snack. It's also important to **avoid multitasking**. Research has consistently shown that multitasking will make your studying dramatically less effective. Your study area should also be comfortable and well-lit so you don't have the distraction of straining your eyes or sitting on an uncomfortable chair.

The time of day you study is also important. You want to be rested and alert. Don't wait until just before bedtime. Study when you'll be most likely to comprehend and remember. Even better, if you know what time of day your test will be, set that time aside for study. That way your brain will be used to working on that subject at that specific time and you'll have a better chance of recalling information.

Finally, it can be helpful to team up with others who are studying for the same test. Your actual studying should be done in as isolated an environment as possible, but the work of organizing the information and setting up the study plan can be divided up. In between study sessions, you can discuss with your teammates the concepts that you're all studying and quiz each other on the details. Just be sure that your teammates are as serious about the test as you are. If you find that your study time is being replaced with social time, you might need to find a new team.

Strategy #2 – Make Your Studying Count

You're devoting a lot of time and effort to preparing for this test, so you want to be absolutely certain it will pay off. This means doing more than just reading the content and hoping you can remember it on test day. It's important to make every minute of study count. There are two main areas you can focus on to make your studying count.

Retention

It doesn't matter how much time you study if you can't remember the material. You need to make sure you are retaining the concepts. To check your retention of the information you're learning, try recalling it at later times with minimal prompting. Try carrying around flashcards and glance at one or two from time to time or ask a friend who's also studying for the test to quiz you.

To enhance your retention, look for ways to put the information into practice so that you can apply it rather than simply recalling it. If you're using the information in practical ways, it will be much easier to remember. Similarly, it helps to solidify a concept in your mind if you're not only reading it to yourself but also explaining it to someone else. Ask a friend to let you teach them about a concept you're a little shaky on (or speak aloud to an imaginary audience if necessary). As you try to summarize, define, give examples, and answer your friend's questions, you'll understand the concepts better and they will stay with you longer. Finally, step back for a big picture view and ask yourself how each piece of information fits with the whole subject. When you link the different concepts together and see them working together as a whole, it's easier to remember the individual components.

Finally, practice showing your work on any multi-step problems, even if you're just studying. Writing out each step you take to solve a problem will help solidify the process in your mind, and you'll be more likely to remember it during the test.

Modality

Modality simply refers to the means or method by which you study. Choosing a study modality that fits your own individual learning style is crucial. No two people learn best in exactly the same way, so it's important to know your strengths and use them to your advantage.

For example, if you learn best by visualization, focus on visualizing a concept in your mind and draw an image or a diagram. Try color-coding your notes, illustrating them, or creating symbols that will trigger your mind to recall a learned concept. If you learn best by hearing or discussing information, find a study partner who learns the same way or read aloud to yourself. Think about how to put the information in your own words. Imagine that you are giving a lecture on the topic and record yourself so you can listen to it later.

For any learning style, flashcards can be helpful. Organize the information so you can take advantage of spare moments to review. Underline key words or phrases. Use different colors for different categories. Mnemonic devices (such as creating a short list in which every item starts with the same letter) can also help with retention. Find what works best for you and use it to store the information in your mind most effectively and easily.

Strategy #3 – Practice the Right Way

Your success on test day depends not only on how many hours you put into preparing, but also on whether you prepared the right way. It's good to check along the way to see if your studying is paying off. One of the most effective ways to do this is by taking practice tests to evaluate your progress. Practice tests are useful because they show exactly where you need to improve. Every time you take a practice test, pay special attention to these three groups of questions:

- The questions you got wrong
- The questions you had to guess on, even if you guessed right
- The questions you found difficult or slow to work through

This will show you exactly what your weak areas are, and where you need to devote more study time. Ask yourself why each of these questions gave you trouble. Was it because you didn't understand the material? Was it because you didn't remember the vocabulary? Do you need more repetitions on this type of question to build speed and confidence? Dig into those questions and figure out how you can strengthen your weak areas as you go back to review the material.

Additionally, many practice tests have a section explaining the answer choices. It can be tempting to read the explanation and think that you now have a good understanding of the concept. However, an explanation likely only covers part of the question's broader context. Even if the explanation makes perfect sense, **go back and investigate** every concept related to the question until you're positive you have a thorough understanding.

As you go along, keep in mind that the practice test is just that: practice. Memorizing these questions and answers will not be very helpful on the actual test because it is unlikely to have any of the same exact questions. If you only know the right answers to the sample questions, you won't be prepared for the real thing. **Study the concepts** until you understand them fully, and then you'll be able to answer any question that shows up on the test.

It's important to wait on the practice tests until you're ready. If you take a test on your first day of study, you may be overwhelmed by the amount of material covered and how much you need to learn. Work up to it gradually.

On test day, you'll need to be prepared for answering questions, managing your time, and using the test-taking strategies you've learned. It's a lot to balance, like a mental marathon that will have a big impact on your future. Like training for a marathon, you'll need to start slowly and work your way up. When test day arrives, you'll be ready.

Start with the strategies you've read in the first two Success Strategies—plan your course and study in the way that works best for you. If you have time, consider using multiple study resources to get different approaches to the same concepts. It can be helpful to see difficult concepts from more than one angle. Then find a good source for practice tests. Many times, the test website will suggest potential study resources or provide sample tests.

Practice Test Strategy

If you're able to find at least three practice tests, we recommend this strategy:

Untimed and Open-Book Practice

Take the first test with no time constraints and with your notes and study guide handy. Take your time and focus on applying the strategies you've learned.

Timed and Open-Book Practice

Take the second practice test open-book as well, but set a timer and practice pacing yourself to finish in time.

Timed and Closed-Book Practice

Take any other practice tests as if it were test day. Set a timer and put away your study materials. Sit at a table or desk in a quiet room, imagine yourself at the testing center, and answer questions as quickly and accurately as possible.

Keep repeating timed and closed-book tests on a regular basis until you run out of practice tests or it's time for the actual test. Your mind will be ready for the schedule and stress of test day, and you'll be able to focus on recalling the material you've learned.

Strategy #4 – Pace Yourself

Once you're fully prepared for the material on the test, your biggest challenge on test day will be managing your time. Just knowing that the clock is ticking can make you panic even if you have plenty of time left. Work on pacing yourself so you can build confidence against the time constraints of the exam. Pacing is a difficult skill to master, especially in a high-pressure environment, so **practice is vital**.

Set time expectations for your pace based on how much time is available. For example, if a section has 60 questions and the time limit is 30 minutes, you know you have to average 30 seconds or less per question in order to answer them all. Although 30 seconds is the hard limit, set 25 seconds per question as your goal, so you reserve extra time to spend on harder questions. When you budget extra time for the harder questions, you no longer have any reason to stress when those questions take longer to answer.

Don't let this time expectation distract you from working through the test at a calm, steady pace, but keep it in mind so you don't spend too much time on any one question. Recognize that taking extra time on one question you don't understand may keep you from answering two that you do understand later in the test. If your time limit for a question is up and you're still not sure of the answer, mark it and move on, and come back to it later if the time and the test format allow. If the testing format doesn't allow you to return to earlier questions, just make an educated guess; then put it out of your mind and move on.

On the easier questions, be careful not to rush. It may seem wise to hurry through them so you have more time for the challenging ones, but it's not worth missing one if you know the concept and just didn't take the time to read the question fully. Work efficiently but make sure you understand the question and have looked at all of the answer choices, since more than one may seem right at first.

Even if you're paying attention to the time, you may find yourself a little behind at some point. You should speed up to get back on track, but do so wisely. Don't panic; just take a few seconds less on each question until you're caught up. Don't guess without thinking, but do look through the answer choices and eliminate any you know are wrong. If you can get down to two choices, it is often worthwhile to guess from those. Once you've chosen an answer, move on and don't dwell on any that you skipped or had to hurry through. If a question was taking too long, chances are it was one of the harder ones, so you weren't as likely to get it right anyway.

On the other hand, if you find yourself getting ahead of schedule, it may be beneficial to slow down a little. The more quickly you work, the more likely you are to make a careless mistake that will affect your score. You've budgeted time for each question, so don't be afraid to spend that time. Practice an efficient but careful pace to get the most out of the time you have.

Test-Taking Strategies

This section contains a list of test-taking strategies that you may find helpful as you work through the test. By taking what you know and applying logical thought, you can maximize your chances of answering any question correctly!

It is very important to realize that every question is different and every person is different: no single strategy will work on every question, and no single strategy will work for every person. That's why we've included all of them here, so you can try them out and determine which ones work best for different types of questions and which ones work best for you.

Question Strategies

⊘ Read Carefully

Read the question and the answer choices carefully. Don't miss the question because you misread the terms. You have plenty of time to read each question thoroughly and make sure you understand what is being asked. Yet a happy medium must be attained, so don't waste too much time. You must read carefully and efficiently.

⊘ Contextual Clues

Look for contextual clues. If the question includes a word you are not familiar with, look at the immediate context for some indication of what the word might mean. Contextual clues can often give you all the information you need to decipher the meaning of an unfamiliar word. Even if you can't determine the meaning, you may be able to narrow down the possibilities enough to make a solid guess at the answer to the question.

⊘ Prefixes

If you're having trouble with a word in the question or answer choices, try dissecting it. Take advantage of every clue that the word might include. Prefixes can be a huge help. Usually, they allow you to determine a basic meaning. *Pre-* means before, *post-* means after, *pro-* is positive, *de-* is negative. From prefixes, you can get an idea of the general meaning of the word and try to put it into context.

⊘ Hedge Words

Watch out for critical hedge words, such as *likely, may, can, often, almost, mostly, usually, generally, rarely,* and *sometimes.* Question writers insert these hedge phrases to cover every possibility. Often an answer choice will be wrong simply because it leaves no room for exception. Be on guard for answer choices that have definitive words such as *exactly* and *always.*

⊘ Switchback Words

Stay alert for *switchbacks.* These are the words and phrases frequently used to alert you to shifts in thought. The most common switchback words are *but, although,* and *however.* Others include *nevertheless, on the other hand, even though, while, in spite of, despite,* and *regardless of.* Switchback words are important to catch because they can change the direction of the question or an answer choice.

⊘ Face Value

When in doubt, use common sense. Accept the situation in the problem at face value. Don't read too much into it. These problems will not require you to make wild assumptions. If you have to go beyond creativity and warp time or space in order to have an answer choice fit the question, then you should move on and consider the other answer choices. These are normal problems rooted in reality. The applicable relationship or explanation may not be readily apparent, but it is there for you to figure out. Use your common sense to interpret anything that isn't clear.

Answer Choice Strategies

✓ Answer Selection

The most thorough way to pick an answer choice is to identify and eliminate wrong answers until only one is left, then confirm it is the correct answer. Sometimes an answer choice may immediately seem right, but be careful. The test writers will usually put more than one reasonable answer choice on each question, so take a second to read all of them and make sure that the other choices are not equally obvious. As long as you have time left, it is better to read every answer choice than to pick the first one that looks right without checking the others.

✓ Answer Choice Families

An answer choice family consists of two (in rare cases, three) answer choices that are very similar in construction and cannot all be true at the same time. If you see two answer choices that are direct opposites or parallels, one of them is usually the correct answer. For instance, if one answer choice says that quantity *x* increases and another either says that quantity *x* decreases (opposite) or says that quantity *y* increases (parallel), then those answer choices would fall into the same family. An answer choice that doesn't match the construction of the answer choice family is more likely to be incorrect. Most questions will not have answer choice families, but when they do appear, you should be prepared to recognize them.

✓ Eliminate Answers

Eliminate answer choices as soon as you realize they are wrong, but make sure you consider all possibilities. If you are eliminating answer choices and realize that the last one you are left with is also wrong, don't panic. Start over and consider each choice again. There may be something you missed the first time that you will realize on the second pass.

✓ Avoid Fact Traps

Don't be distracted by an answer choice that is factually true but doesn't answer the question. You are looking for the choice that answers the question. Stay focused on what the question is asking for so you don't accidentally pick an answer that is true but incorrect. Always go back to the question and make sure the answer choice you've selected actually answers the question and is not merely a true statement.

✓ Extreme Statements

In general, you should avoid answers that put forth extreme actions as standard practice or proclaim controversial ideas as established fact. An answer choice that states the "process should be used in certain situations, if..." is much more likely to be correct than one that states the "process should be discontinued completely." The first is a calm rational statement and doesn't even make a definitive, uncompromising stance, using a hedge word *if* to provide wiggle room, whereas the second choice is far more extreme.

✓ Benchmark

As you read through the answer choices and you come across one that seems to answer the question well, mentally select that answer choice. This is not your final answer, but it's the one that will help you evaluate the other answer choices. The one that you selected is your benchmark or standard for judging each of the other answer choices. Every other answer choice must be compared to your benchmark. That choice is correct until proven otherwise by another answer choice beating it. If you find a better answer, then that one becomes your new benchmark. Once you've decided that no other choice answers the question as well as your benchmark, you have your final answer.

✓ PREDICT THE ANSWER

Before you even start looking at the answer choices, it is often best to try to predict the answer. When you come up with the answer on your own, it is easier to avoid distractions and traps because you will know exactly what to look for. The right answer choice is unlikely to be word-for-word what you came up with, but it should be a close match. Even if you are confident that you have the right answer, you should still take the time to read each option before moving on.

General Strategies

✓ TOUGH QUESTIONS

If you are stumped on a problem or it appears too hard or too difficult, don't waste time. Move on! Remember though, if you can quickly check for obviously incorrect answer choices, your chances of guessing correctly are greatly improved. Before you completely give up, at least try to knock out a couple of possible answers. Eliminate what you can and then guess at the remaining answer choices before moving on.

✓ CHECK YOUR WORK

Since you will probably not know every term listed and the answer to every question, it is important that you get credit for the ones that you do know. Don't miss any questions through careless mistakes. If at all possible, try to take a second to look back over your answer selection and make sure you've selected the correct answer choice and haven't made a costly careless mistake (such as marking an answer choice that you didn't mean to mark). This quick double check should more than pay for itself in caught mistakes for the time it costs.

✓ PACE YOURSELF

It's easy to be overwhelmed when you're looking at a page full of questions; your mind is confused and full of random thoughts, and the clock is ticking down faster than you would like. Calm down and maintain the pace that you have set for yourself. Especially as you get down to the last few minutes of the test, don't let the small numbers on the clock make you panic. As long as you are on track by monitoring your pace, you are guaranteed to have time for each question.

✓ DON'T RUSH

It is very easy to make errors when you are in a hurry. Maintaining a fast pace in answering questions is pointless if it makes you miss questions that you would have gotten right otherwise. Test writers like to include distracting information and wrong answers that seem right. Taking a little extra time to avoid careless mistakes can make all the difference in your test score. Find a pace that allows you to be confident in the answers that you select.

✓ KEEP MOVING

Panicking will not help you pass the test, so do your best to stay calm and keep moving. Taking deep breaths and going through the answer elimination steps you practiced can help to break through a stress barrier and keep your pace.

Final Notes

The combination of a solid foundation of content knowledge and the confidence that comes from practicing your plan for applying that knowledge is the key to maximizing your performance on test day. As your foundation of content knowledge is built up and strengthened, you'll find that the strategies included in this chapter become more and more effective in helping you quickly sift through the distractions and traps of the test to isolate the correct answer.

Now that you're preparing to move forward into the test content chapters of this book, be sure to keep your goal in mind. As you read, think about how you will be able to apply this information on the test. If you've already seen sample questions for the test and you have an idea of the question format and style, try to come up with questions of your own that you can answer based on what you're reading. This will give you valuable practice applying your knowledge in the same ways you can expect to on test day.

Good luck and good studying!

Reading Language Arts

Main Ideas and Supporting Details

Identifying Topics and Main Ideas

One of the most important skills in reading comprehension is the identification of **topics** and **main ideas**. There is a subtle difference between these two features. The topic is the subject of a text (i.e., what the text is all about). The main idea, on the other hand, is the most important point being made by the author. The topic is usually expressed in a few words at the most while the main idea often needs a full sentence to be completely defined. As an example, a short passage might be written on the topic of penguins, and the main idea could be written as *Penguins are different from other birds in many ways*. In most nonfiction writing, the topic and the main idea will be **stated directly** and often appear in a sentence at the very beginning or end of the text. When being tested on an understanding of the author's topic, you may be able to skim the passage for the general idea by reading only the first sentence of each paragraph. A body paragraph's first sentence is often—but not always—the main **topic sentence** which gives you a summary of the content in the paragraph.

However, there are cases in which the reader must figure out an **unstated** topic or main idea. In these instances, you must read every sentence of the text and try to come up with an overarching idea that is supported by each of those sentences.

Note: The main idea should not be confused with the thesis statement. While the main idea gives a brief, general summary of a text, the thesis statement provides a **specific perspective** on an issue that the author supports with evidence.

Review Video: Topics and Main Ideas
Visit mometrix.com/academy and enter code: 407801

Supporting Details

Supporting details are smaller pieces of evidence that provide backing for the main point. In order to show that a main idea is correct or valid, an author must add details that prove their point. All texts contain details, but they are only classified as supporting details when they serve to reinforce some larger point. Supporting details are most commonly found in informative and persuasive texts. In some cases, they will be clearly indicated with terms like *for example* or *for instance*, or they will be enumerated with terms like *first*, *second*, and *last*. However, you need to be prepared for texts that do not contain those indicators. As a reader, you should consider whether the author's supporting details really back up his or her main point. Details can be factual and correct, yet they may not be **relevant** to the author's point. Conversely, details can be relevant, but be ineffective because they are based on opinion or assertions that cannot be proven.

Review Video: Supporting Details
Visit mometrix.com/academy and enter code: 396297

Author's Purpose

Author's Purpose

Usually, identifying the author's **purpose** is easier than identifying his or her **position**. In most cases, the author has no interest in hiding his or her purpose. A text that is meant to entertain, for instance, should be written to please the reader. Most narratives, or stories, are written to entertain, though they may also inform or persuade. Informative texts are easy to identify, while the most difficult purpose of a text to identify is persuasion because the author has an interest in making this purpose hard to detect. When a reader discovers that the author is trying to persuade, he or she should be skeptical of the argument. For this reason, persuasive texts often try to establish an entertaining tone and hope to amuse the reader into agreement. On the other hand, an informative tone may be implemented to create an appearance of authority and objectivity.

An author's purpose is evident often in the **organization** of the text (e.g., section headings in bold font points to an informative text). However, you may not have such organization available to you in your exam. Instead, if the author makes his or her main idea clear from the beginning, then the likely purpose of the text is to **inform**. If the author begins by making a claim and provides various arguments to support that claim, then the purpose is probably to **persuade**. If the author tells a story or wants to gain the reader's attention more than to push a particular point or deliver information, then his or her purpose is most likely to **entertain**. As a reader, you must judge authors on how well they accomplish their purpose. In other words, you need to consider the type of passage (e.g., technical, persuasive, etc.) that the author has written and if the author has followed the requirements of the passage type.

Review Video: Understanding the Author's Intent
Visit mometrix.com/academy and enter code: 511819

Informational Texts

An **informational text** is written to educate and enlighten readers. Informational texts are almost always nonfiction and are rarely structured as a story. The intention of an informational text is to deliver information in the most comprehensible way. So, look for the structure of the text to be very clear. In an informational text, the thesis statement is one or two sentences that normally appears at the end of the first paragraph. The author may use some colorful language, but he or she is likely to put more emphasis on clarity and precision. Informational essays do not typically appeal to the emotions. They often contain facts and figures and rarely include the opinion of the author; however, readers should remain aware of the possibility for bias as those facts are presented. Sometimes a persuasive essay can resemble an informative essay, especially if the author maintains an even tone and presents his or her views as if they were established fact.

Review Video: Informational Text
Visit mometrix.com/academy and enter code: 924964

Persuasive Writing

In a persuasive essay, the author is attempting to change the reader's mind or **convince** him or her of something that he or she did not believe previously. There are several identifying characteristics of **persuasive writing**. One is **opinion presented as fact**. When authors attempt to persuade readers, they often present their opinions as if they were fact. Readers must be on guard for statements that sound factual but which cannot be subjected to research, observation, or experiment. Another characteristic of persuasive writing is **emotional language**. An author will often try to play on the emotions of readers by appealing to their sympathy or sense of morality. When an author uses colorful or evocative language with the intent of arousing the reader's passions, then the author may be attempting to persuade. Finally, in many cases, a persuasive text will give an **unfair explanation of opposing positions**, if these positions are mentioned at all.

Entertaining Texts

The success or failure of an author's intent to **entertain** is determined by those who read the author's work. Entertaining texts may be either fiction or nonfiction, and they may describe real or imagined people, places, and events. Entertaining texts are often narratives or poems. A text that is written to entertain is likely to contain **colorful language** that engages the imagination and the emotions. Such writing often features a great deal of figurative language, which typically enlivens the subject matter with images and analogies.

Though an entertaining text is not usually written to persuade or inform, authors may accomplish both of these tasks in their work. An entertaining text may *appeal to the reader's emotions* and cause him or her to think differently about a particular subject. In any case, entertaining texts tend to showcase the personality of the author more than other types of writing.

Descriptive Text

In a sense, almost all writing is descriptive, insofar as an author seeks to describe events, ideas, or people to the reader. Some texts, however, are primarily concerned with **description**. A descriptive text focuses on a particular subject and attempts to depict the subject in a way that will be clear to readers. Descriptive texts contain many adjectives and adverbs (i.e., words that give shades of meaning and create a more detailed mental picture for the reader). A descriptive text fails when it is unclear to the reader. A descriptive text will certainly be informative and may be persuasive and entertaining as well.

Review Video: Descriptive Texts
Visit mometrix.com/academy and enter code: 174903

Expression of Feelings

When an author intends to **express feelings**, he or she may use **expressive and bold language**. An author may write with emotion for any number of reasons. Sometimes, authors will express feelings because they are describing a personal situation of great pain or happiness. In other situations, authors will attempt to persuade the reader and will use emotion to stir up the passions. This kind of expression is easy to identify when the writer uses phrases like *I felt* and *I sense*. However, readers may find that the author will simply describe feelings without introducing them. As a reader, you must know the importance of recognizing when an author is expressing emotion and not to become overwhelmed by sympathy or passion. Readers should maintain some **detachment** so that they can still evaluate the strength of the author's argument or the quality of the writing.

Review Video: Emotional Language in Literature
Visit mometrix.com/academy and enter code: 759390

Expository Passage

An **expository** passage aims to **inform** and enlighten readers. Expository passages are nonfiction and usually center around a simple, easily defined topic. Since the goal of exposition is to teach, such a passage should be as clear as possible. Often, an expository passage contains helpful organizing words, like *first, next, for example*, and *therefore*. These words keep the reader **oriented** in the text. Although expository passages do not need to feature colorful language and artful writing, they are often more effective with these features. For a reader, the challenge of expository passages is to maintain steady attention. Expository passages are not always about subjects that will naturally interest a reader, so the writer is often more concerned with **clarity** and **comprehensibility** than with engaging the reader. By reading actively, you can ensure a good habit of focus when reading an expository passage.

Review Video: Expository Passages
Visit mometrix.com/academy and enter code: 256515

Narrative Passage

A **narrative** passage is a story that can be fiction or nonfiction. However, there are a few elements that a text must have in order to be classified as a narrative. First, the text must have a **plot** (i.e., a series of events). Narratives often proceed in a clear sequence, but this is not a requirement. If the narrative is good, then these events will be interesting to readers. Second, a narrative has **characters**. These characters could be people, animals, or even inanimate objects—so long as they participate in the plot. Third, a narrative passage often contains **figurative language** which is meant to stimulate the imagination of readers by making comparisons and observations. For instance, a *metaphor*, a common piece of figurative language, is a description of one thing in terms of another. *The moon was a frosty snowball* is an example of a metaphor. In the literal sense this is obviously untrue, but the comparison suggests a certain mood for the reader.

TECHNICAL PASSAGE

A **technical** passage is written to *describe* a complex object or process. Technical writing is common in medical and technological fields, in which complex ideas of mathematics, science, and engineering need to be explained *simply* and *clearly*. To ease comprehension, a technical passage usually proceeds in a very logical order. Technical passages often have clear headings and subheadings, which are used to keep the reader oriented in the text. Additionally, you will find that these passages divide sections up with numbers or letters. Many technical passages look more like an outline than a piece of prose. The amount of **jargon** or difficult vocabulary will vary in a technical passage depending on the intended audience. As much as possible, technical passages try to avoid language that the reader will have to research in order to understand the message, yet readers will find that jargon cannot always be avoided.

> **Review Video: Technical Passages**
> Visit mometrix.com/academy and enter code: 478923

Common Organizations of Texts

ORGANIZATION OF THE TEXT

The way a text is organized can help readers understand the author's intent and his or her conclusions. There are various ways to organize a text, and each one has a purpose and use. Usually, authors will organize information logically in a passage so the reader can follow and locate the information within the text. However, since not all passages are written with the same logical structure, you need to be familiar with several different types of passage structure.

> **Review Video: Sequence of Events in a Story**
> Visit mometrix.com/academy and enter code: 807512

CHRONOLOGICAL

When using **chronological** order, the author presents information in the order that it happened. For example, biographies are typically written in chronological order. The subject's birth and childhood are presented first, followed by their adult life, and lastly the events leading up to the person's death.

CAUSE AND EFFECT

One of the most common text structures is **cause and effect**. A **cause** is an act or event that makes something happen, and an **effect** is the thing that happens as a result of the cause. A cause-and-effect relationship is not always explicit, but there are some terms in English that signal causes, such as *since*, *because*, and *due to*. Furthermore, terms that signal effects include *consequently, therefore, this leads to*. As an example, consider the sentence *Because the sky was clear, Ron did not bring an umbrella.* The cause is the clear sky, and the effect is that Ron did not bring an umbrella. However, readers may find that sometimes the cause-and-effect relationship will not be clearly noted. For instance, the sentence *He was late and missed the meeting* does not contain any signaling words, but the sentence still contains a cause (he was late) and an effect (he missed the meeting).

> **Review Video: Cause and Effect**
> Visit mometrix.com/academy and enter code: 868099
>
> **Review Video: Rhetorical Strategy of Cause and Effect Analysis**
> Visit mometrix.com/academy and enter code: 725944

MULTIPLE EFFECTS

Be aware of the possibility for a single cause to have **multiple effects.** (e.g., *Single cause*: Because you left your homework on the table, your dog engulfed the assignment. *Multiple effects*: As a result, you receive a failing grade, your parents do not allow you to go out with your friends, you miss out on the new movie, and one of your classmates spoils it for you before you have another chance to watch it).

MULTIPLE CAUSES

Also, there is the possibility for a single effect to have **multiple causes.** (e.g., *Single effect*: Alan has a fever. *Multiple causes*: An unexpected cold front came through the area, and Alan forgot to take his multi-vitamin to avoid getting sick.) Additionally, an effect can in turn be the cause of another effect, in what is known as a cause-and-effect chain. (e.g., As a result of her disdain for procrastination, Lynn prepared for her exam. This led to her passing her test with high marks. Hence, her resume was accepted and her application was approved.)

CAUSE AND EFFECT IN PERSUASIVE ESSAYS

Persuasive essays, in which an author tries to make a convincing argument and change the minds of readers, usually include cause-and-effect relationships. However, these relationships should not always be taken at face value. Frequently, an author will assume a cause or take an effect for granted. To read a persuasive essay effectively, readers need to judge the cause-and-effect relationships that the author is presenting. For instance, imagine an author wrote the following: *The parking deck has been unprofitable because people would prefer to ride their bikes.* The relationship is clear: the cause is that people prefer to ride their bikes, and the effect is that the parking deck has been unprofitable. However, readers should consider whether this argument is conclusive. Perhaps there are other reasons for the failure of the parking deck: a down economy, excessive fees, etc. Too often, authors present causal relationships as if they are fact rather than opinion. Readers should be on the alert for these dubious claims.

PROBLEM-SOLUTION

Some nonfiction texts are organized to **present a problem** followed by a solution. For this type of text, the problem is often explained before the solution is offered. In some cases, as when the problem is well known, the solution may be introduced briefly at the beginning. Other passages may focus on the solution, and the problem will be referenced only occasionally. Some texts will outline multiple solutions to a problem, leaving readers to choose among them. If the author has an interest or an allegiance to one solution, he or she may fail to mention or describe accurately some of the other solutions. Readers should be careful of the author's agenda when reading a problem-solution text. Only by understanding the author's perspective and interests can one develop a proper judgment of the proposed solution.

COMPARE AND CONTRAST

Many texts follow the **compare-and-contrast** model in which the similarities and differences between two ideas or things are explored. Analysis of the similarities between ideas is called **comparison**. In an ideal comparison, the author places ideas or things in an equivalent structure, i.e., the author presents the ideas in the same way. If an author wants to show the similarities between cricket and baseball, then he or she may do so by summarizing the equipment and rules for each game. Be mindful of the similarities as they appear in the passage and take note of any differences that are mentioned. Often, these small differences will only reinforce the more general similarity.

Review Video: Compare and Contrast
Visit mometrix.com/academy and enter code: 798319

Thinking critically about ideas and conclusions can seem like a daunting task. One way to ease this task is to understand the basic elements of ideas and writing techniques. Looking at the ways different ideas relate to each other can be a good way for readers to begin their analysis. For instance, sometimes authors will write about two ideas that are in opposition to each other. Or, one author will provide his or her ideas on a topic, and another author may respond in opposition. The analysis of these opposing ideas is known as **contrast**. Contrast is often marred by the author's obvious partiality to one of the ideas. A discerning reader will be put off by an author who does not engage in a fair fight. In an analysis of opposing ideas, both ideas should be presented in clear and reasonable terms. If the author does prefer a side, you need to read carefully to determine the areas where the author shows or avoids this preference. In an analysis of opposing ideas, you should proceed through the passage by marking the major differences point by point with an eye that is looking for an explanation of each side's view. For instance, in an analysis of capitalism and communism, there is an importance in outlining each side's view on labor, markets, prices, personal responsibility, etc. Additionally, as you read through the passages, you should note whether the opposing views present each side in a similar manner.

SEQUENCE

Readers must be able to identify a text's **sequence**, or the order in which things happen. Often, when the sequence is very important to the author, the text is indicated with signal words like *first, then, next,* and *last.* However, a sequence can be merely implied and must be noted by the reader. Consider the sentence *He walked through the garden and gave water and fertilizer to the plants.* Clearly, the man did not walk through the garden before he collected water and fertilizer for the plants. So, the implied sequence is that he first collected water, then he collected fertilizer, next he walked through the garden, and last he gave water or fertilizer as necessary to the plants. Texts do not always proceed in an orderly sequence from first to last. Sometimes they begin at the end and start over at the beginning. As a reader, you can enhance your understanding of the passage by taking brief notes to clarify the sequence.

Review Video: Sequence
Visit mometrix.com/academy and enter code: 489027

Making and Evaluating Predictions

MAKING PREDICTIONS

When we read literature, **making predictions** about what will happen in the writing reinforces our purpose for reading and prepares us mentally. A **prediction** is a guess about what will happen next. Readers constantly make predictions based on what they have read and what they already know. We can make predictions before we begin reading and during our reading. Consider the following sentence: *Staring at the computer screen in shock, Kim blindly reached over for the brimming glass of water on the shelf to her side.* The sentence suggests that Kim is distracted, and that she is not looking at the glass that she is going to pick up. So, a reader might predict that Kim is going to knock over the glass. Of course, not every prediction will be accurate: perhaps Kim will pick the glass up cleanly. Nevertheless, the author has certainly created the expectation that the water might be spilled.

As we read on, we can test the accuracy of our predictions, revise them in light of additional reading, and confirm or refute our predictions. Predictions are always subject to revision as the reader acquires more information. A reader can make predictions by observing the title and illustrations; noting the structure, characters, and subject; drawing on existing knowledge relative to the subject; and asking "why" and "who" questions. Connecting reading to what we already know enables us to learn new information and construct meaning. For example, before third-graders read a book about Johnny Appleseed, they may start a KWL chart—a list of what they *Know*, what they *Want* to know or learn, and what they have *Learned* after reading. Activating existing background knowledge and thinking about the text before reading improves comprehension.

Review Video: Predictive Reading
Visit mometrix.com/academy and enter code: 437248

Test-taking tip: To respond to questions requiring future predictions, your answers should be based on evidence of past or present behavior and events.

Evaluating Predictions

When making predictions, readers should be able to explain how they developed their prediction. One way readers can defend their thought process is by citing textual evidence. Textual evidence to evaluate reader predictions about literature includes specific synopses of the work, paraphrases of the work or parts of it, and direct quotations from the work. These references to the text must support the prediction by indicating, clearly or unclearly, what will happen later in the story. A text may provide these indications through literary devices such as foreshadowing. Foreshadowing is anything in a text that gives the reader a hint about what is to come by emphasizing the likelihood of an event or development. Foreshadowing can occur through descriptions, exposition, and dialogue. Foreshadowing in dialogue usually occurs when a character gives a warning or expresses a strong feeling that a certain event will occur. Foreshadowing can also occur through irony. However, unlike other forms of foreshadowing, the events that seem the most likely are the opposite of what actually happens. Instances of foreshadowing and irony can be summarized, paraphrased, or quoted to defend a reader's prediction.

Review Video: Textual Evidence for Predictions
Visit mometrix.com/academy and enter code: 261070

Making Inferences and Drawing Conclusions

Inferences are logical conclusions that readers make based on their observations and previous knowledge. An inference is based on both what is found in a passage or a story and what is known from personal experience. For instance, a story may say that a character is frightened and can hear howling in the distance. Based on both what is in the text and personal knowledge, it is a logical conclusion that the character is frightened because he hears the sound of wolves. A good inference is supported by the information in a passage.

Implicit and Explicit Information

By inferring, readers construct meanings from text that are personally relevant. By combining their own schemas or concepts and their background information pertinent to the text with what they read, readers interpret it according to both what the author has conveyed and their own unique perspectives. Inferences are different from **explicit information**, which is clearly stated in a passage. Authors do not always explicitly spell out every meaning in what they write; many meanings are implicit. Through inference, readers can comprehend implied meanings in the text, and also derive personal significance from it, making the text meaningful and memorable to them. Inference is a natural process in everyday life. When readers infer, they can draw conclusions about what the author is saying, predict what may reasonably follow, amend these predictions as they continue to read, interpret the import of themes, and analyze the characters' feelings and motivations through their actions.

Example of Drawing Conclusions from Inferences

Read the excerpt and decide why Jana finally relaxed.

> Jana loved her job, but the work was very demanding. She had trouble relaxing. She called a friend, but she still thought about work. She ordered a pizza, but eating it did not help. Then, her kitten jumped on her lap and began to purr. Jana leaned back and began to hum a little tune. She felt better.

You can draw the conclusion that Jana relaxed because her kitten jumped on her lap. The kitten purred, and Jana leaned back and hummed a tune. Then she felt better. The excerpt does not explicitly say that this is the reason why she was able to relax. The text leaves the matter unclear, but the reader can infer or make a "best guess" that this is the reason she is relaxing. This is a logical conclusion based on the information in the passage. It is the best conclusion a reader can make based on the information he or she has read. Inferences are based on the information in a passage, but they are not directly stated in the passage.

Test-taking tip: While being tested on your ability to make correct inferences, you must look for **contextual clues**. An answer can be true, but not the best or most correct answer. The contextual clues will help you find the answer that is the **best answer** out of the given choices. Be careful in your reading to understand the context in which a phrase is stated. When asked for the implied meaning of a statement made in the passage, you should immediately locate the statement and read the **context** in which the statement was made. Also, look for an answer choice that has a similar phrase to the statement in question.

Review Video: Inference
Visit mometrix.com/academy and enter code: 379203

Review Video: How to Support a Conclusion
Visit mometrix.com/academy and enter code: 281653

Critical Reading Skills

Opinions, Facts, and Fallacies

Critical thinking skills are mastered through understanding various types of writing and the different purposes authors can have for writing different passages. Every author writes for a purpose. When you understand their purpose and how they accomplish their goal, you will be able to analyze their writing and determine whether or not you agree with their conclusions.

Readers must always be aware of the difference between fact and opinion. A **fact** can be subjected to analysis and proven to be true. An **opinion**, on the other hand, is the author's personal thoughts or feelings and may not be altered by research or evidence. If the author writes that the distance from New York City to Boston is about two hundred miles, then he or she is stating a fact. If the author writes that New York City is too crowded, then he or she is giving an opinion because there is no objective standard for overpopulation. Opinions are often supported by facts. For instance, an author might use a comparison between the population density of New York City and that of other major American cities as evidence of an overcrowded population. An opinion supported by facts tends to be more convincing. On the other hand, when authors support their opinions with other opinions, readers should employ critical thinking and approach the argument with skepticism.

Review Video: Distinguishing Fact and Opinion
Visit mometrix.com/academy and enter code: 870899

Reliable Sources

When you read an argumentative passage, you need to be sure that facts are presented to the reader from **reliable sources**. An opinion is what the author thinks about a given topic. An opinion is not common knowledge or proven by expert sources, instead the information is the personal beliefs and thoughts of the author. To distinguish between fact and opinion, a reader needs to consider the type of source that is presenting information, the information that backs-up a claim, and the author's motivation to have a certain point-of-view on a given topic. For example, if a panel of scientists has conducted multiple studies on the effectiveness of taking a certain vitamin, then the results are more likely to be factual than those of a company that is selling a vitamin and simply claims that taking the vitamin can produce positive effects. The company is motivated to sell their product, and the scientists are using the scientific method to prove a theory. Remember, if you find sentences that contain phrases such as "I think...", then the statement is an opinion.

Biases

In their attempts to persuade, writers often make mistakes in their thought processes and writing choices. These processes and choices are important to understand so you can make an informed decision about the author's credibility. Every author has a point of view, but authors demonstrate a **bias** when they ignore reasonable counterarguments or distort opposing viewpoints. A bias is evident whenever the author's claims are presented in a way that is unfair or inaccurate. Bias can be intentional or unintentional, but readers should be skeptical of the author's argument in either case. Remember that a biased author may still be correct. However, the author will be correct in spite of, not because of, his or her bias.

A **stereotype** is a bias applied specifically to a group of people or a place. Stereotyping is considered to be particularly abhorrent because it promotes negative, misleading generalizations about people. Readers should be very cautious of authors who use stereotypes in their writing. These faulty assumptions typically reveal the author's ignorance and lack of curiosity.

Review Video: Bias and Stereotype
Visit mometrix.com/academy and enter code: 644829

Persuasion and Rhetoric

Persuasive Techniques

To **appeal using reason**, writers present logical arguments, such as using "If... then... because" statements. To **appeal to emotions**, authors may ask readers how they would feel about something or to put themselves in another's place, present their argument as one that will make the audience feel good, or tell readers how they should feel. To **appeal to character**, **morality**, or **ethics**, authors present their points to readers as the right or most moral choices. Authors cite expert opinions to show readers that someone very knowledgeable about the subject or viewpoint agrees with the author's claims. **Testimonials**, usually via anecdotes or quotations regarding the author's subject, help build the audience's trust in an author's message through positive support from ordinary people. **Bandwagon appeals** claim that everybody else agrees with the author's argument and persuade readers to conform and agree, also. Authors **appeal to greed** by presenting their choice as cheaper, free, or more valuable for less cost. They **appeal to laziness** by presenting their views as more convenient, easy, or relaxing. Authors also anticipate potential objections and argue against them before audiences think of them, thereby depicting those objections as weak.

Authors can use **comparisons** like analogies, similes, and metaphors to persuade audiences. For example, a writer might represent excessive expenses as "hemorrhaging" money, which the author's recommended solution will stop. Authors can use negative word connotations to make some choices unappealing to readers, and positive word connotations to make others more appealing. Using **humor** can relax readers and garner their agreement. However, writers must take care: ridiculing opponents can be a successful strategy for appealing to readers who already agree with the author, but can backfire by angering other readers. **Rhetorical questions** need no answer, but create effect that can force agreement, such as asking the question, "Wouldn't you rather be paid more than less?" **Generalizations** persuade readers by being impossible to disagree with. Writers can easily make generalizations that appear to support their viewpoints, like saying, "We all want peace, not war" regarding more specific political arguments. **Transfer** and **association** persuade by example: if advertisements show attractive actors enjoying their products, audiences imagine they will experience the same. **Repetition** can also sometimes effectively persuade audiences.

Review Video: Using Rhetorical Strategies for Persuasion
Visit mometrix.com/academy and enter code: 302658

Classical Author Appeals

In his *On Rhetoric,* ancient Greek philosopher Aristotle defined three basic types of appeal used in writing, which he called *pathos*, *ethos*, and *logos*. ***Pathos*** means suffering or experience and refers to appeals to the emotions (the English word *pathetic* comes from this root). Writing that is meant to entertain audiences, by making them either happy, as with comedy, or sad, as with tragedy, uses *pathos*. Aristotle's *Poetics* states that evoking the emotions of terror and pity is one of the criteria for writing tragedy. ***Ethos*** means character and connotes ideology (the English word *ethics* comes from this root). Writing that appeals to credibility, based on academic, professional, or personal merit, uses *ethos*. ***Logos*** means "I say" and refers to a plea, opinion, expectation, word or speech, account, opinion, or reason (the English word *logic* comes from this root.)

Aristotle used it to mean persuasion that appeals to the audience through reasoning and logic to influence their opinions.

Rhetorical Devices

- An **anecdote** is a brief story authors may relate to their argument, which can illustrate their points in a more real and relatable way.
- **Aphorisms** concisely state common beliefs and may rhyme. For example, Benjamin Franklin's "Early to bed and early to rise / Makes a man healthy, wealthy, and wise" is an aphorism.
- **Allusions** refer to literary or historical figures to impart symbolism to a thing or person and to create reader resonance. In John Steinbeck's *Of Mice and Men,* protagonist George's last name is Milton. This alludes to John Milton, who wrote *Paradise Lost*, and symbolizes George's eventual loss of his dream.
- **Satire** exaggerates, ridicules, or pokes fun at human flaws or ideas, as in the works of Jonathan Swift and Mark Twain.
- A **parody** is a form of satire that imitates another work to ridicule its topic or style.
- A **paradox** is a statement that is true despite appearing contradictory.
- **Hyperbole** is overstatement using exaggerated language.
- An **oxymoron** combines seeming contradictions, such as "deafening silence."
- **Analogies** compare two things that share common elements.
- **Similes** (stated comparisons using the words *like* or *as*) and **metaphors** (stated comparisons that do not use *like* or *as*) are considered forms of analogy.
- When using logic to reason with audiences, **syllogism** refers either to deductive reasoning or a deceptive, very sophisticated, or subtle argument.
- **Deductive reasoning** moves from general to specific, **inductive reasoning** from specific to general.
- **Diction** is author word choice that establishes tone and effect.
- **Understatement** achieves effects like contrast or irony by downplaying or describing something more subtly than warranted.
- **Chiasmus** uses parallel clauses, the second reversing the order of the first. Examples include T. S. Eliot's "Has the Church failed mankind, or has mankind failed the Church?" and John F. Kennedy's "Ask not what your country can do for you; ask what you can do for your country."
- **Anaphora** regularly repeats a word or phrase at the beginnings of consecutive clauses or phrases to add emphasis to an idea. A classic example of anaphora was Winston Churchill's emphasis of determination: "[W]e shall fight on the beaches, we shall fight on the landing grounds, we shall fight in the fields and in the streets, we shall fight in the hills; we shall never surrender..."

Reading Comprehension and Connecting with Texts

Comparing Two Stories

When presented with two different stories, there will be **similarities** and **differences** between the two. A reader needs to make a list, or other graphic organizer, of the points presented in each story. Once the reader has written down the main point and supporting points for each story, the two sets of ideas can be compared. The reader can then present each idea and show how it is the same or different in the other story. This is called **comparing and contrasting ideas**.

The reader can compare ideas by stating, for example: "In Story 1, the author believes that humankind will one day land on Mars, whereas in Story 2, the author believes that Mars is too far away for humans to ever step foot on." Note that the two viewpoints are different in each story that the reader is comparing. A reader may state that: "Both stories discussed the likelihood of humankind landing on Mars." This statement shows how the viewpoint presented in both stories is based on the same topic, rather than how each viewpoint is different. The reader will complete a comparison of two stories with a conclusion.

Review Video: How to Compare and Contrast
Visit mometrix.com/academy and enter code: 833765

Outlining a Passage

As an aid to drawing conclusions, **outlining** the information contained in the passage should be a familiar skill to readers. An effective outline will reveal the structure of the passage and will lead to solid conclusions. An effective outline will have a title that refers to the basic subject of the text, though the title does not need to restate the main idea. In most outlines, the main idea will be the first major section. Each major idea in the passage will be established as the head of a category. For instance, the most common outline format calls for the main ideas of the passage to be indicated with Roman numerals. In an effective outline of this kind, each of the main ideas will be represented by a Roman numeral and none of the Roman numerals will designate minor details or secondary ideas. Moreover, all supporting ideas and details should be placed in the appropriate place on the outline. An outline does not need to include every detail listed in the text, but it should feature all of those that are central to the argument or message. Each of these details should be listed under the corresponding main idea.

Review Video: Outlining as an Aid to Drawing Conclusions
Visit mometrix.com/academy and enter code: 584445

USING GRAPHIC ORGANIZERS

Ideas from a text can also be organized using **graphic organizers**. A graphic organizer is a way to simplify information and take key points from the text. A graphic organizer such as a timeline may have an event listed for a corresponding date on the timeline, while an outline may have an event listed under a key point that occurs in the text. Each reader needs to create the type of graphic organizer that works the best for him or her in terms of being able to recall information from a story. Examples include a spider-map, which takes a main idea from the story and places it in a bubble with supporting points branching off the main idea. An outline is useful for diagramming the main and supporting points of the entire story, and a Venn diagram compares and contrasts characteristics of two or more ideas.

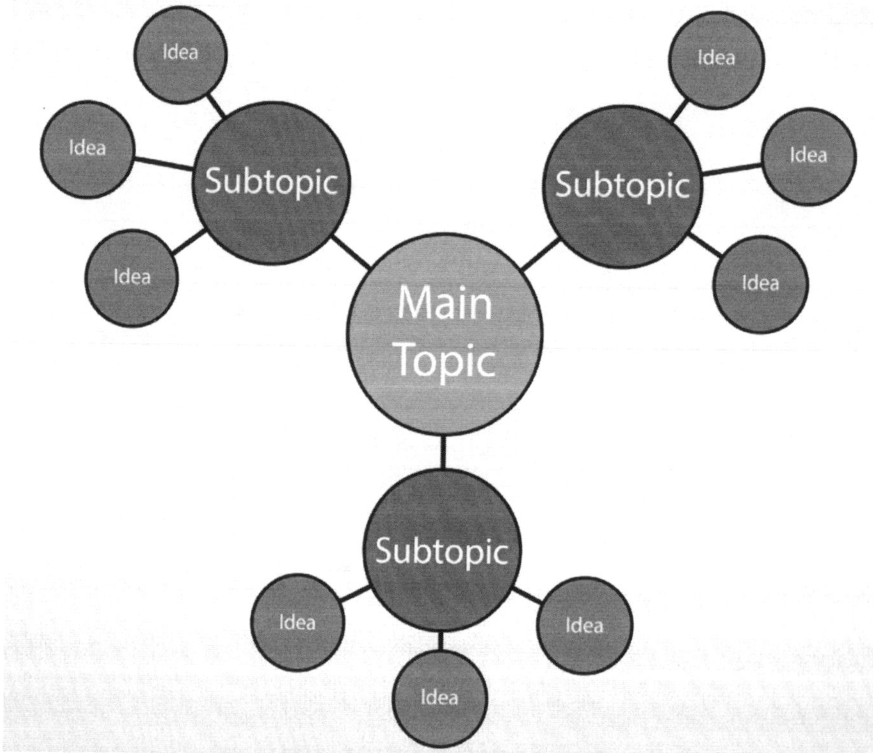

Review Video: Graphic Organizers
Visit mometrix.com/academy and enter code: 665513

MAKING LOGICAL CONCLUSIONS ABOUT A PASSAGE

A reader should always be drawing conclusions from the text. Sometimes conclusions are **implied** from written information, and other times the information is **stated directly** within the passage. One should always aim to draw conclusions from information stated within a passage, rather than to draw them from mere implications. At times an author may provide some information and then describe a counterargument. Readers should be alert for direct statements that are subsequently rejected or weakened by the author. Furthermore, you should always read through the entire passage before drawing conclusions. Many readers are trained to expect the author's conclusions at either the beginning or the end of the passage, but many texts do not adhere to this format.

Drawing conclusions from information implied within a passage requires confidence on the part of the reader. **Implications** are things that the author does not state directly, but readers can assume based on what the author does say. Consider the following passage: *I stepped outside and opened my umbrella. By the time I got to work, the cuffs of my pants were soaked.* The author never states that it is raining, but this fact is clearly implied. Conclusions based on implication must be well supported by the text. In order to draw a solid conclusion, readers should have **multiple pieces of evidence**. If readers have only one piece, they must be assured that there is no other possible explanation than their conclusion. A good reader will be able to draw many conclusions from information implied by the text, which will be a great help on the exam.

Drawing Conclusions

A common type of inference that a reader has to make is **drawing a conclusion**. The reader makes this conclusion based on the information provided within a text. Certain facts are included to help a reader come to a specific conclusion. For example, a story may open with a man trudging through the snow on a cold winter day, dragging a sled behind him. The reader can logically **infer** from the setting of the story that the man is wearing heavy winter clothes in order to stay warm. Information is implied based on the setting of a story, which is why **setting** is an important element of the text. If the same man in the example was trudging down a beach on a hot summer day, dragging a surf board behind him, the reader would assume that the man is not wearing heavy clothes. The reader makes inferences based on their own experiences and the information presented to them in the story.

Test-taking tip: When asked to identify a conclusion that may be drawn, look for critical "hedge" phrases, such as *likely*, *may*, *can*, and *will often*, among many others. When you are being tested on this knowledge, remember the question that writers insert into these hedge phrases to cover every possibility. Often an answer will be wrong simply because there is no room for exception. Extreme positive or negative answers (such as always or never) are usually not correct. When answering these questions, the reader **should not** use any outside knowledge that is not gathered directly or reasonably inferred from the passage. Correct answers can be derived straight from the passage.

Example

Read the following sentence from *Little Women* by Louisa May Alcott and draw a conclusion based upon the information presented:

> *You know the reason Mother proposed not having any presents this Christmas was because it is going to be a hard winter for everyone; and she thinks we ought not to spend money for pleasure, when our men are suffering so in the army.*

Based on the information in the sentence, the reader can conclude, or **infer**, that the men are away at war while the women are still at home. The pronoun *our* gives a clue to the reader that the character is speaking about men she knows. In addition, the reader can assume that the character is speaking to a brother or sister, since the term "Mother" is used by the character while speaking to another person. The reader can also come to the conclusion that the characters celebrate Christmas, since it is mentioned in the **context** of the sentence. In the sentence, the mother is presented as an unselfish character who is opinionated and thinks about the wellbeing of other people.

Summarizing

A helpful tool is the ability to **summarize** the information that you have read in a paragraph or passage format. This process is similar to creating an effective outline. First, a summary should accurately define the main idea of the passage, though the summary does not need to explain this main idea in exhaustive detail. The summary should continue by laying out the most important supporting details or arguments from the passage. All of the significant supporting details should be included, and none of the details included should be irrelevant or insignificant. Also, the summary should accurately report all of these details. Too often, the desire for brevity in a summary leads to the sacrifice of clarity or accuracy. Summaries are often difficult to read because they omit all of the graceful language, digressions, and asides that distinguish great writing. However, an effective summary should communicate the same overall message as the original text.

Review Video: Summarizing Text
Visit mometrix.com/academy and enter code: 172903

Paraphrasing

Paraphrasing is another method that the reader can use to aid in comprehension. When paraphrasing, one puts what they have read into their own words by rephrasing what the author has written, or one "translates" all of what the author shared into their own words by including as many details as they can.

Evaluating a Passage

It is important to understand the logical conclusion of the ideas presented in an informational text. **Identifying a logical conclusion** can help you determine whether you agree with the writer or not. Coming to this conclusion is much like making an inference: the approach requires you to combine the information given by the text with what you already know and make a logical conclusion. If the author intended for the reader to draw a certain conclusion, then you can expect the author's argumentation and detail to be leading in that direction.

One way to approach the task of drawing conclusions is to make brief **notes** of all the points made by the author. When the notes are arranged on paper, they may clarify the logical conclusion. Another way to approach conclusions is to consider whether the reasoning of the author raises any pertinent questions. Sometimes you will be able to draw several conclusions from a passage. On occasion these will be conclusions that were never imagined by the author. Therefore, be aware that these conclusions must be **supported directly by the text**.

Evaluation of Summaries

A summary of a literary passage is a condensation in the reader's own words of the passage's main points. Several guidelines can be used in evaluating a summary. The summary should be complete yet concise. It should be accurate, balanced, fair, neutral, and objective, excluding the reader's own opinions or reactions. It should reflect in similar proportion how much each point summarized was covered in the original passage. Summary writers should include tags of attribution, like "Macaulay argues that" to reference the original author whose ideas are represented in the summary. Summary writers should not overuse quotations; they should only quote central concepts or phrases they cannot precisely convey in words other than those of the original author. Another aspect of evaluating a summary is considering whether it can stand alone as a coherent, unified composition. In addition, evaluation of a summary should include whether its writer has cited the original source of the passage they have summarized so that readers can find it.

Making Connections to Enhance Comprehension

Reading involves thinking. For good comprehension, readers make **text-to-self**, **text-to-text**, and **text-to-world connections**. Making connections helps readers understand text better and predict what might occur next based on what they already know, such as how characters in the story feel or what happened in another text. Text-to-self connections with the reader's life and experiences make literature more personally relevant and meaningful to readers. Readers can make connections before, during, and after reading—including whenever the text reminds them of something similar they have encountered in life or other texts. The genre, setting, characters, plot elements, literary structure and devices, and themes an author uses allow a reader to make connections to other works of literature or to people and events in their own lives. Venn diagrams and other graphic organizers help visualize connections. Readers can also make double-entry notes: key content, ideas, events, words, and quotations on one side, and the connections with these on the other.

Comparing Two Texts

Synthesis of Multiple Texts

Synthesizing, i.e., understanding and integrating, information from multiple texts can at times be among the most challenging skills for some students to succeed with on tests and in school, and yet it is also among the most important. Students who read at the highest cognitive levels can select related material from different text sources and construct coherent arguments that account for these varied information sources. Synthesizing ideas and information from multiple texts actually combines other reading skills that students should have mastered previously in reading one text at a time, and applies them in the context of reading more than one text. For example, students are required to read texts closely, including identifying explicit and implicit meanings; use critical thinking and reading; draw inferences; assess author reasoning; analyze supporting evidence; and formulate opinions they can justify, based on more passages than one. When two paired texts represent opposing sides of the same argument, students can find analyzing them easier; but this is not always the case.

Similarities in Texts

When students are called upon to compare things two texts share in common, the most obvious commonality might be the same subject matter or specific topic. However, two texts need not be about the same thing to compare them. Some other features texts can share include structural characteristics. For example, they may both be written using a sequential format, such as narrating events or giving instructions in chronological order; listing and/or discussing subtopics by order of importance; or describing a place spatially in sequence from each point to the next. They may both use a comparison-contrast structure, identifying similarities and differences between, among, or within topics. They might both organize information by identifying cause-and-effect relationships. Texts can be similar in type, e.g., description, narration, persuasion, or exposition. They can be similar in using technical vocabulary or using formal or informal language. They may share similar tones and/or styles, e.g., humorous, satirical, serious, etc. They can share similar purposes, e.g., to alarm audiences, incite them to action, reassure them, inspire them, provoke strong emotional responses, etc.

Contrasts in Texts

When analyzing paired or multiple texts, students might observe differences in tone; for example, one text might take a serious approach while another uses a humorous one. Even within approaches or treatments, style can differ: one text may be humorous in a witty, sophisticated, clever way while another may exercise broad, "lowbrow" humor; another may employ mordant sarcasm; another may use satire, couching outrageous suggestions in a "deadpan" logical voice to lampoon social attitudes and behaviors as Jonathan Swift did in *A Modest Proposal.* Serious writing can range from darkly pessimistic to alarmist to objective and unemotional. Texts might have similar information, yet organize it using different structures. One text may support points or ideas using logical arguments, while another may seek to persuade its audience by appealing to their emotions. A very obvious difference in text is genre: for example, the same mythological or traditional stories have been told as oral folk tales, written dramas, written novels, etc.; and/or set in different times and places (e.g., Shakespeare's *Romeo and Juliet* vs. Laurents, Bernstein, and Sondheim's *West Side Story*).

Reading Informational Texts

Language Use

Literal and Figurative Language

As in fictional literature, informational text also uses both **literal language**, which means just what it says, and **figurative language**, which imparts more than literal meaning. For example, an informational text author might use a simile or direct comparison, such as writing that a racehorse "ran like the wind." Informational text authors also use metaphors or implied comparisons, such as "the cloud of the Great Depression." Imagery may also appear in informational texts to increase the reader's understanding of ideas and concepts discussed in the text.

Explicit and Implicit Information

When informational text states something explicitly, the reader is told by the author exactly what is meant, which can include the author's interpretation or perspective of events. For example, a professor writes, "I have seen students go into an absolute panic just because they weren't able to complete the exam in the time they were allotted." This explicitly tells the reader that the students were afraid, and by using the words "just because," the writer indicates their fear was exaggerated out of proportion relative to what happened.

However, another professor writes, "I have had students come to me, their faces drained of all color, saying 'We weren't able to finish the exam.'" This is an example of implicit meaning: the second writer did not state explicitly that the students were panicked. Instead, he wrote a description of their faces being "drained of all color." From this description, the reader can infer that the students were so frightened that their faces paled.

Review Video: Explicit and Implicit Information
Visit mometrix.com/academy and enter code: 735771

Making Inferences About Informational Text

With informational text, reader comprehension depends not only on recalling important statements and details, but also on reader inferences based on examples and details. Readers add information from the text to what they already know to draw inferences about the text. These inferences help the readers to fill in the information that the text does not explicitly state, enabling them to understand the text better. When reading a nonfictional autobiography or biography, for example, the most appropriate inferences might concern the events in the book, the actions of the subject of the autobiography or biography, and the message the author means to convey. When reading a nonfictional expository (informational) text, the reader would best draw inferences about problems and their solutions, and causes and their effects. When reading a nonfictional persuasive text, the reader will want to infer ideas supporting the author's message and intent.

Structures or Organizational Patterns in Informational Texts

Informational text can be **descriptive**, appealing to the five senses and answering the questions what, who, when, where, and why. Another method of structuring informational text is sequence and order. **Chronological** texts relate events in the sequence that they occurred, from start to finish, while how-to texts organize information into a series of instructions in the sequence in which the steps should be followed. **Comparison-contrast** structures of informational text describe various ideas to their readers by pointing out how things or ideas are similar and how they are different. **Cause and effect** structures of informational text describe events that occurred and identify the causes or reasons that those events occurred. **Problem and solution** structures of informational texts introduce and describe problems and offer one or more solutions for each problem described.

Determining an Informational Author's Purpose

Informational authors' purposes are why they write texts. Readers must determine authors' motivations and goals. Readers gain greater insight into a text by considering the author's motivation. This develops critical reading skills. Readers perceive writing as a person's voice, not simply printed words. Uncovering author motivations and purposes empowers readers to know what to expect from the text, read for relevant details, evaluate authors and their work critically, and respond effectively to the motivations and persuasions of the text. The main idea of a text is what the reader is supposed to understand from reading it; the purpose of the text is why the author has written it and what the author wants readers to do with its information. Authors state some purposes clearly, while other purposes may be unstated but equally significant. When stated purposes contradict other parts of a text, the author may have a hidden agenda. Readers can better evaluate a text's effectiveness, whether they agree or disagree with it, and why they agree or disagree through identifying unstated author purposes.

Identifying Author's Point of View or Purpose

In some informational texts, readers find it easy to identify the author's point of view and purpose, such as when the author explicitly states his or her position and reason for writing. But other texts are more difficult, either because of the content or because the authors give neutral or balanced viewpoints. This is particularly true in scientific texts, in which authors may state the purpose of their research in the report, but never state their point of view except by interpreting evidence or data.

To analyze text and identify point of view or purpose, readers should ask themselves the following four questions:

1. With what main point or idea does this author want to persuade readers to agree?
2. How does this author's word choice affect the way that readers consider this subject?
3. How do this author's choices of examples and facts affect the way that readers consider this subject?
4. What is it that this author wants to accomplish by writing this text?

Review Video: Understanding the Author's Intent
Visit mometrix.com/academy and enter code: 511819

Review Video: Author's Position
Visit mometrix.com/academy and enter code: 827954

Evaluating Arguments Made by Informational Text Writers

When evaluating an informational text, the first step is to identify the argument's conclusion. Then identify the author's premises that support the conclusion. Try to paraphrase premises for clarification and make the conclusion and premises fit. List all premises first, sequentially numbered, then finish with the conclusion. Identify any premises or assumptions not stated by the author but required for the stated premises to support the conclusion. Read word assumptions sympathetically, as the author might. Evaluate whether premises reasonably support the conclusion. For inductive reasoning, the reader should ask if the premises are true, if they support the conclusion, and if so, how strongly. For deductive reasoning, the reader should ask if the argument is valid or invalid. If all premises are true, then the argument is valid unless the conclusion can be false. If it can, then the argument is invalid. An invalid argument can be made valid through alterations such as the addition of needed premises.

Use of Rhetoric in Informational Texts

There are many ways authors can support their claims, arguments, beliefs, ideas, and reasons for writing in informational texts. For example, authors can appeal to readers' sense of **logic** by communicating their reasoning through a carefully sequenced series of logical steps to help "prove" the points made. Authors can appeal to readers' **emotions** by using descriptions and words that evoke feelings of sympathy, sadness, anger, righteous indignation, hope, happiness, or any other emotion to reinforce what they express and share with their audience. Authors may appeal to the **moral** or **ethical values** of readers by using words and descriptions that can convince readers that something is right or wrong. By relating personal anecdotes, authors can supply readers with more accessible, realistic examples of points they make, as well as appealing to their emotions. They can provide supporting evidence by reporting case studies. They can also illustrate their points by making analogies to which readers can better relate.

Organizational Features in Texts

Text Features in Informational Texts

- The **title of a text** gives readers some idea of its content.
- The **table of contents** is a list near the beginning of a text, showing the book's sections and chapters and their coinciding page numbers. This gives readers an overview of the whole text and helps them find specific chapters easily.
- An **appendix**, at the back of the book or document, includes important information that is not present in the main text.
- Also at the back, an **index** lists the book's important topics alphabetically with their page numbers to help readers find them easily.

- **Glossaries**, usually found at the backs of books, list technical terms alphabetically with their definitions to aid vocabulary learning and comprehension. Boldface print is used to emphasize certain words, often identifying words included in the text's glossary where readers can look up their definitions.
- **Headings** separate sections of text and show the topic of each.
- **Subheadings** divide subject headings into smaller, more specific categories to help readers organize information.
- **Footnotes**, at the bottom of the page, give readers more information, such as citations or links.
- **Bullet points** list items separately, making facts and ideas easier to see and understand.
- A **sidebar** is a box of information to one side of the main text giving additional information, often on a more focused or in-depth example of a topic.

VISUAL FEATURES IN TEXTS

- **Illustrations** and **photographs** are pictures that visually emphasize important points in text.
- The **captions** below the illustrations explain what those images show.
- **Charts** and **tables** are visual forms of information that make something easier to understand quickly.
- **Diagrams** are drawings that show relationships or explain a process.
- **Graphs** visually show the relationships among multiple sets of information plotted along vertical and horizontal axes.
- **Maps** show geographical information visually to help readers understand the relative locations of places covered in the text.
- **Timelines** are visual graphics that show historical events in chronological order to help readers see their sequence.

Visual Information in Informational Texts

CHARTS, GRAPHS, AND VISUALS

TABLES

Tables are presented in a standard format so they will be easy to read and understand. A title is at the top, a short phrase indicating the information the table or graph intends to convey. The title of a table could be something like "Median Income for Various Education Levels" or "Price of Milk Compared to Demand." A table is composed of information laid out in vertical columns and horizontal rows. Typically, each column will have a label. If "Median Income for Various Education Levels" was placed in a table format, the two columns could be labeled "Education Level" and "Median Annual Salary." Each location on the table is called a cell, which holds a piece of information. Cells are defined by their column and row (e.g., second column, fifth row).

Median Annual Salary for Various Education Levels

Education Level	Median Annual Salary
Associate degree	$52,260
Bachelor's degree	$74,464
Master's degree	$86,372
Professional degree	$108,160
Doctoral degree	$108,316

GRAPHS

Like a table, a graph typically has a title at the top. This title may simply state the identities of the two axes: e.g., "Income vs. Education." However, the title may also be something more descriptive, like "A comparison of average income with level of education." In any case, bar and line graphs are laid out along two perpendicular lines, or axes. The vertical axis is called the *y*-axis, and the horizontal axis is called the *x*-axis. It is typical for the *x*-axis to be the independent variable and the *y*-axis to be the dependent variable. The independent variable is the one manipulated by the researcher or creator of the graph. In the above example, the independent variable would be "education level," since the maker of the graph will define these values (associate degree, bachelor's degree, master's degree, etc.). The dependent value is not controlled by the researcher.

When selecting a graph format, it is important to consider the intention and the structure of the presentation. A bar graph is appropriate for displaying the relations between a series of distinct quantities that are on the same scale. For instance, if one wanted to display the amount of money spent on groceries during the months of a year, a bar graph would be appropriate. The vertical axis would represent values of money, and the horizontal axis would identify each month. A line graph also requires data expressed in common units, but it is better for demonstrating the general trend in that data. If the grocery expenses were plotted on a line graph instead of a bar graph, there would be more emphasis on whether the amount of money spent rose or fell over the course of the year. Whereas a bar graph is good for showing the relationships between the different values plotted, the line graph is good for showing whether the values tended to increase, decrease, or remain stable.

PIE CHART

A pie chart, also known as a circle graph, is useful for depicting how a single unit or category is divided. The standard pie chart is a circle with designated wedges. Each wedge is **proportional** in size to a part of the whole. For instance, consider Shawna, a student at City College, who uses a pie chart to represent her budget. If she spends half of her money on rent, then the pie chart will represent that amount with a line through the center of the pie. If she spends a quarter of her money on food, there will be a line extending from the edge of the circle to the center at a right angle to the line depicting rent. This illustration would make it clear that the student spends twice the amount of money on rent as she does on food.

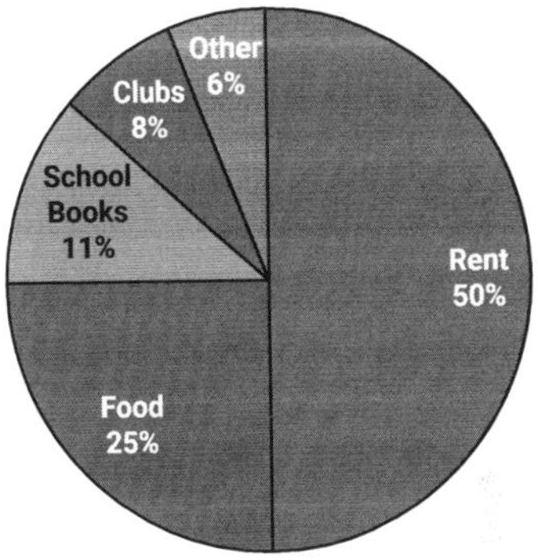

A pie chart is effective at showing how a single entity is divided into parts. They are not effective at demonstrating the relationships between parts of different wholes. For example, an unhelpful use of a pie chart would be to compare the respective amounts of state and federal spending devoted to infrastructure since these values are only meaningful in the context of the entire budget.

BAR GRAPH

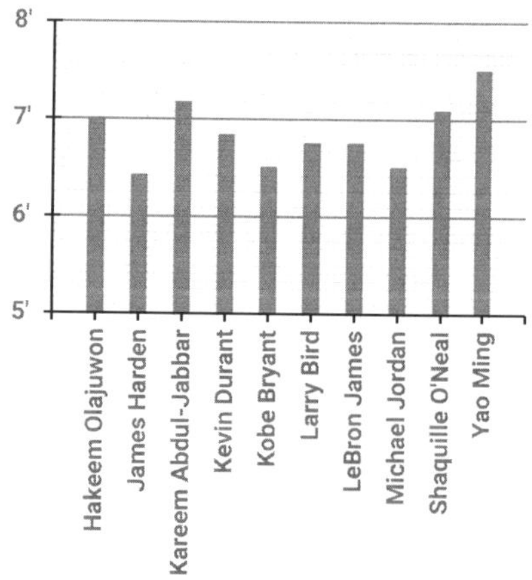

The bar graph is one of the most common visual representations of information. **Bar graphs** are used to illustrate sets of numerical **data**. The graph has a vertical axis (along which numbers are listed) and a horizontal axis (along which categories, words, or some other indicators are placed). One example of a bar graph is a depiction of the respective heights of famous basketball players: the vertical axis would contain numbers ranging from five to eight feet, and the horizontal axis would contain the names of the players. The length of the bar above the player's name would illustrate his height, and the top of the bar would stop perpendicular to the height listed along the left side. In this representation, one would see that Yao Ming is taller than Michael Jordan because Yao's bar would be higher.

LINE GRAPH

A line graph is a type of graph that is typically used for measuring trends over time. The graph is set up along a vertical and a horizontal **axis**. The variables being measured are listed along the left side and the bottom side of the axes. Points are then plotted along the graph as they correspond with their values for each variable. For instance, consider a line graph measuring a person's income for each month of the year. If the person earned $1500 in January, there should be a point directly above January (perpendicular to the horizontal axis) and directly to the right of $1500 (perpendicular to the vertical axis). Once all of the lines are plotted, they are connected with a line from left to right. This line provides a nice visual illustration of the general **trends** of the data, if they exist. For instance, using the earlier example, if the line sloped up, then one would see that the person's income had increased over the course of the year.

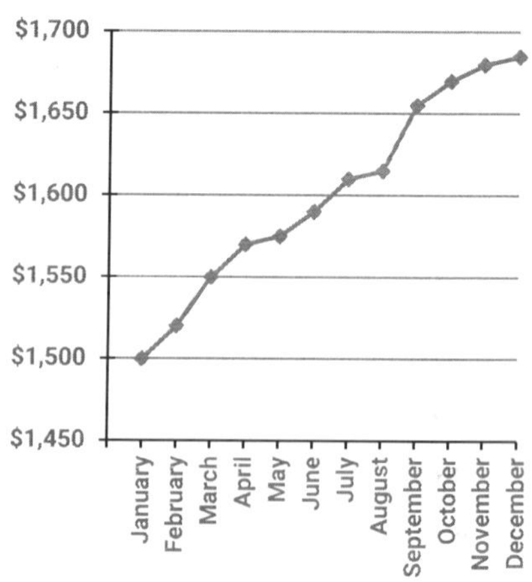

PICTOGRAPHS

A **pictograph** is a graph, generally in the horizontal orientation, that uses pictures or symbols to represent the data. Each pictograph must have a key that defines the picture or symbol and gives the quantity each picture or symbol represents. Pictures or symbols on a pictograph are not always shown as whole elements. In this case, the fraction of the picture or symbol shown represents the same fraction of the quantity a whole picture or symbol stands for.

Review Video: Pictographs
Visit mometrix.com/academy and enter code: 147860

Genres in Fiction

Common Genres in Prose Fiction

- The **mystery** genre includes stories with plots that follow a protagonist as they work to solve an unexplained situation, such as a murder, disappearance, or robbery. Protagonists of mysteries may be hired professionals or amateurs who solve the mystery despite their lack of experience and resources. Mysteries allow the reader to solve the case along with the protagonist, and often grant the reader an advantageous perspective, creating dramatic irony. The *Sherlock Holmes* novels by Sir Arthur Conan Doyle are examples of mystery novels.
- **Science fiction** is a genre that is based on the manipulation and exaggeration of real scientific discoveries and processes. These works are speculative and frequently depict a world where scientific discoveries and society have progressed beyond the point reached at the time of the work's creation. Works of science fiction often take place in a distant location or time, allowing for the dramatic advancements and conveniences they often depict. *Dune*, written by Frank Herbert, is an example of a science-fiction novel.
- The **fantasy** genre includes stories that feature imaginary creatures and supernatural abilities, but often take place in settings that resemble real places and cultures in history. Fantasy novels usually follow a gifted protagonist from humble beginnings as they embark on a quest, journey, or adventure and encounter mystical beings and personally challenging obstacles. Common themes in the fantasy genre include personal growth, good versus evil, and the value of the journey. J.R.R. Tolkien's *The Lord of the Rings* trilogy belongs to the fantasy genre.
- **Realistic fiction** describes fictional narratives that include events and characters that do not exist, but could appear in reality. Within the narrative, these characters and events may be depicted in real places. For example, Pip, the protagonist of Charles Dickens's *Great Expectations*, was not a real person, but the novel shows him living in London, England for much of his young adulthood. Realistic fiction contains no far-fetched or impossible elements and presents situations that can or do occur in real life. A contemporary example of realistic fiction is *Wonder* by R.J. Palacio.
- **Historical fiction** includes works that take place in the past and model their setting after real historical cultures, societies, and time periods. These works may include real historical figures and events, but they also may not. Works of historical fiction must be fully informed by the period and location they are set in, meaning both the major and minor details of the work must be historically compatible with the work's setting. Examples of historical fiction include Kathryn Stockett's *The Help* and Markus Zusak's *The Book Thief*.
- The phrase **literary nonfiction** describes nonfiction narratives that present true facts and events in a way that entertains readers and displays creativity. Literary nonfiction, also called creative nonfiction, may resemble fiction in its style and flow, but the truth of the events it describes sets it apart from fictional literature. Different types of books may be considered literary nonfiction, such as biographies, if they appear to employ creativity in their writing. An example of literary nonfiction is *The Immortal Life of Henrietta Lacks* by Rebecca Skloot.

Realism and Satire

Realism

Realism is a literary form with the goal of representing reality as faithfully as possible. Its genesis in Western literature was a reaction against the sentimentality and extreme emotionalism of the works written during the Romantic literary movement, which championed feelings and emotional expression. Realists focused in great detail on immediacy of time and place, on specific actions of their characters, and the justifiable consequences of those actions. Some techniques of **realism** include writing in vernacular (conversational language), using specific dialects, and placing an emphasis on character rather than plot. Realistic literature also often addresses ethical issues. Historically, realistic works have often concentrated on the middle classes of the authors' societies. Realists eschew treatments that are too dramatic or sensationalistic as exaggerations of the reality that they strive to portray as closely as they are able. Influenced by his own bleak past, Fyodor Dostoevsky wrote several novels, such as *Crime and Punishment* (1866) that shunned romantic ideals and sought to portray a stark reality. Henry James was a prominent writer of realism in novels such as *Daisy Miller* (1879). Samuel Clemens (Mark Twain) skillfully represented the language and culture of lower-class Mississippi in his novel *The Adventures of Huckleberry Finn* (1885).

Satire

Satire uses sarcasm, irony, and humor as social criticism to lampoon human folly. Unlike realism, which intends to depict reality as it exists without exaggeration, **satire** often involves creating situations or ideas that deliberately exaggerate reality to appear ridiculous to illuminate flawed behaviors. Ancient Roman satirists included Horace and Juvenal. Alexander Pope's poem "The Rape of the Lock" satirized the values of fashionable members of the 18th-century upper-middle class, which Pope found shallow and trivial. The theft of a lock of hair from a young woman is blown out of proportion: the poem's characters regard it as seriously as they would a rape. Irishman Jonathan Swift satirized British society, politics, and religion in works like "A Modest Proposal" and *Gulliver's Travels.* In "A Modest Proposal," Swift used essay form and mock-serious tone, satirically "proposing" cannibalism of babies and children as a solution to poverty and overpopulation. He satirized petty political disputes in *Gulliver's Travels.*

Types of Stories

Other Common Types of Prose

- A **narrative** is any composition that tells a story. Narratives have characters, settings, and a structure. Narratives may be fiction or nonfiction stories and may follow a linear or nonlinear structure. The purpose of a narrative is generally to entertain, but nonfiction narratives can be informative, as well. Narratives also appear in a variety of structures and formats.
- **Biographies** are books written about another person's life. Biographies can be valuable historical resources. Though they provide a narrow view of the relevant time period and culture, their specificity can also provide a unique context for that period or culture. Biographies, especially those whose subject was a well-known and influential figure, can provide a more complete picture of the figure's life or contributions. Biographies can also serve as a source of inspiration or communicate a moral because of their focus on one person over an extended period of time.
- **Myths** that explain how the world works, its creation, and human behavior exist in most ancient cultures and continue to influence modern cultures. Myths are stories that are part of a certain **mythology**, such as Norse mythology. Myths are so influential that they have even inspired numerous pieces of modern literature and media in popular culture. While popular culture most clearly references myths from the Ancient Greek and Roman cultures, literature has been influenced by mythologies from around the entire world. Since myths are so prevalent in ancient literature, it makes sense that universal themes and morals often appear in mythologies from different cultures. The similarities and parallels in different mythologies (e.g., Greek myths about Zeus are very similar to Roman myths about Jupiter) suggest connections between cultures.

- **Folktales** are stories that have withstood time and are usually popular in a particular region or culture. Folktales often depict the clever success of a common person, though the story may, alternatively, end poorly for the protagonist. A collection of folktales relevant to a particular region or culture is referred to as that culture's **folklore**. There are three common types of folktales: fables, fairy tales, and legends.
    - **Fables** are short, didactic stories that typically feature imaginary creatures or talking animals. The famous story "The Tortoise and the Hare" is a fable. Fables are still told and used today because of their universally understandable morals and characters, which also make them suitable for children's literature and media.
    - **Fairy tales** are stories that involve fictional creatures or realistic characters with fantastical traits and abilities. Fairy tales often end happily and depict the victory of good over evil. The plots and characters in fairy tales are often far-fetched and whimsical.
    - **Legends** are stories that typically focus on one character and highlight their victory over a particular enemy or obstacle. Legends often feature some facts or are inspired by true events, but are generally considered both unproven and unprovable. Heroes are often the protagonists of legends, and they generally save or protect others as they conquer enemies and obstacles.
- A **short story** is a fictional narrative that is shorter than a novel. However, there is not a definite page or word count that defines the short story category. Short stories tend to focus on one or few elements of a story in order to efficiently tell the story. Though they are often brief, short stories may still contain a moral or impact their readers.

Review Video: Myths, Fables, Legends, and Fairy Tales
Visit mometrix.com/academy and enter code: 347199

Poetry

Poetry Terminology

Unlike prose, which traditionally (except in forms like stream of consciousness) consists of complete sentences connected into paragraphs, poetry is written in **verses**. These may form complete sentences, clauses, or phrases. Poetry may be written with or without rhyme. It can be metered, following a particular rhythmic pattern such as iambic, dactylic, spondaic, trochaic, or **anapestic**, or may be without regular meter. The terms **iamb** and **trochee**, among others, identify stressed and unstressed syllables in each verse. Meter is also described by the number of beats or stressed syllables per verse: **dimeter** (2), **trimeter** (3), **tetrameter** (4), **pentameter** (5), and so forth. Using the symbol ᴗ to denote unstressed and / to denote stressed syllables, **iambic** = ᴗ/; **trochaic** = /ᴗ; **spondaic** =//; **dactylic** =/ᴗᴗ; **anapestic** =ᴗᴗ/. **Rhyme schemes** identify which lines rhyme, such as ABAB, ABCA, AABA, and so on. Poetry with neither rhyme nor meter is called **free verse**. Poems may be in free verse, metered but unrhymed, rhymed but without meter, or using both rhyme and meter. In English, the most common meter is iambic pentameter. Unrhymed iambic pentameter is called **blank verse**.

Review Video: Different Types of Rhyme
Visit mometrix.com/academy and enter code: 999342

Review Video: Evocative Words and Rhythm
Visit mometrix.com/academy and enter code: 894610

Major Forms of Poetry

From man's earliest days, he expressed himself with poetry. A large percentage of the surviving literature from ancient times is in **epic poetry**, utilized by Homer and other Greco-Roman poets. Epic poems typically recount heroic deeds and adventures, using stylized language and combining dramatic and lyrical conventions. **Epistolary poems**, poems that are written and read as letters, also developed in ancient times. In the fourteenth and fifteenth centuries, the **ballad** became a popular convention. Ballads often follow a rhyme scheme and meter and focus on subjects such as love, death, and religion. Many ballads tell stories, and several modern ballads are put to music. From these early conventions, numerous other poetic forms developed, such as **elegies**, **odes**, and **pastoral poems**. Elegies are mourning poems written in three parts: lament, praise of the deceased, and solace for loss. Odes evolved from songs to the typical poem of the Romantic time period, expressing strong feelings and contemplative thoughts. Pastoral poems idealize nature and country living. Poetry can also be used to make short, pithy statements. **Epigrams** (memorable rhymes with one or two lines) and **limericks** (two lines of iambic dimeter followed by two lines of iambic dimeter and another of iambic trimeter) are known for humor and wit.

Haiku

Haiku was originally a Japanese poetry form. In the 13th century, haiku was the opening phrase of renga, a 100-stanza oral poem. By the 16th century, haiku diverged into a separate short poem. When Western writers discovered haiku, the form became popular in English, as well as other languages. A haiku has 17 syllables, traditionally distributed across three lines as 5/7/5, with a pause after the first or second line. Haiku are syllabic and unrhymed. Haiku philosophy and technique are that brevity's compression forces writers to express images concisely, depict a moment in time, and evoke illumination and enlightenment. An example is 17th-century haiku master Matsuo Basho's classic: "An old silent pond... / A frog jumps into the pond, / splash! Silence again." Modern American poet Ezra Pound revealed the influence of haiku in his two-line poem "In a Station of the Metro." In this poem, line 1 has 12 syllables (combining the syllable count of the first two lines of a haiku) and line 2 has 7, but it still preserves haiku's philosophy and imagistic technique: "The apparition of these faces in the crowd; / Petals on a wet, black bough."

Sonnets

The sonnet traditionally has 14 lines of iambic pentameter, tightly organized around a theme. The Petrarchan sonnet, named for 14th-century Italian poet Petrarch, has an eight-line stanza, the octave, and a six-line stanza, the sestet. There is a change or turn, known as the volta, between the eighth and ninth verses, setting up the sestet's answer or summary. The rhyme scheme is ABBA/ABBA/CDECDE or CDCDCD. The English or Shakespearean sonnet has three quatrains and one couplet, with the rhyme scheme ABAB/CDCD/EFEF/GG. This format better suits English, which has fewer rhymes than Italian. The final couplet often contrasts sharply with the preceding quatrains, as in Shakespeare's sonnets—for example, Sonnet 130, "My mistress' eyes are nothing like the sun...And yet, by heaven, I think my love as rare / As any she belied with false compare." Variations on the sonnet form include Edmund Spenser's Spenserian sonnet in the 16th century, John Milton's Miltonic sonnet in the 17th century, and sonnet sequences. Sonnet sequences are seen in works such as John Donne's *La Corona* and Elizabeth Barrett Browning's *Sonnets from the Portuguese.*

Review Video: Structural Elements of Poetry
Visit mometrix.com/academy and enter code: 265216

Plot and Story Structure

Plot and Story Structure

The **plot** includes the events that happen in a story and the order in which they are told to the reader. There are several types of plot structures, as stories can be told in many ways. The most common plot structure is the chronological plot, which presents the events to the reader in the same order they occur for the characters in the story. Chronological plots usually have five main parts, the **exposition**, **rising action**, the **climax**, **falling action**, and the **resolution**. This type of plot structure guides the reader through the story's events as the characters experience them and is the easiest structure to understand and identify. While this is the most common plot structure, many stories are nonlinear, which means the plot does not sequence events in the same order the characters experience them. Such stories might include elements like flashbacks that cause the story to be nonlinear.

Review Video: How to Make a Story Map
Visit mometrix.com/academy and enter code: 261719

Exposition

The **exposition** is at the beginning of the story and generally takes place before the rising action begins. The purpose of the exposition is to give the reader context for the story, which the author may do by introducing one or more characters, describing the setting or world, or explaining the events leading up to the point where the story begins. The exposition may still include events that contribute to the plot, but the **rising action** and main conflict of the story are not part of the exposition. Some narratives skip the exposition and begin the story with the beginning of the rising action, which causes the reader to learn the context as the story intensifies.

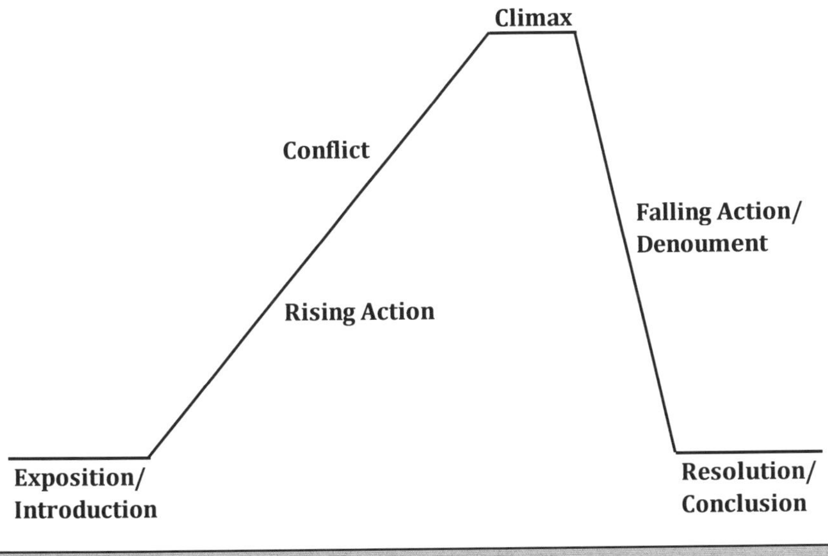

Review Video: Plot Line
Visit mometrix.com/academy and enter code: 944011

Conflict

A **conflict** is a problem to be solved. Literary plots typically include one conflict or more. Characters' attempts to resolve conflicts drive the narrative's forward movement. **Conflict resolution** is often the protagonist's primary occupation. Physical conflicts like exploring, wars, and escapes tend to make plots most suspenseful and exciting. Emotional, mental, or moral conflicts tend to make stories more personally gratifying or rewarding for many audiences. Conflicts can be external or internal. A major type of internal conflict is some inner personal battle, or **man versus self**. Major types of external conflicts include **man versus nature**, **man**

versus man, and **man versus society**. Readers can identify conflicts in literary plots by identifying the protagonist and antagonist and asking why they conflict, what events develop the conflict, where the climax occurs, and how they identify with the characters.

Read the following paragraph and discuss the type of conflict present:

> Timothy was shocked out of sleep by the appearance of a bear just outside his tent. After panicking for a moment, he remembered some advice he had read in preparation for this trip: he should make noise so the bear would not be startled. As Timothy started to hum and sing, the bear wandered away.

There are three main types of conflict in literature: **man versus man**, **man versus nature**, and **man versus self**. This paragraph is an example of man versus nature. Timothy is in conflict with the bear. Even though no physical conflict like an attack exists, Timothy is pitted against the bear. Timothy uses his knowledge to "defeat" the bear and keep himself safe. The solution to the conflict is that Timothy makes noise, the bear wanders away, and Timothy is safe.

Review Video: Conflict
Visit mometrix.com/academy and enter code: 559550

Review Video: Determining Relationships in a Story
Visit mometrix.com/academy and enter code: 929925

Rising Action

The **rising action** is the part of the story where conflict **intensifies**. The rising action begins with an event that prompts the main conflict of the story. This may also be called the **inciting incident**. The main conflict generally occurs between the protagonist and an antagonist, but this is not the only type of conflict that may occur in a narrative. After this event, the protagonist works to resolve the main conflict by preparing for an altercation, pursuing a goal, fleeing an antagonist, or doing some other action that will end the conflict. The rising action is composed of several additional events that increase the story's tension. Most often, other developments will occur alongside the growth of the main conflict, such as character development or the development of minor conflicts. The rising action ends with the **climax**, which is the point of highest tension in the story.

Climax

The **climax** is the event in the narrative that marks the height of the story's conflict or tension. The event that takes place at the story's climax will end the rising action and bring about the results of the main conflict. If the conflict was between a good protagonist and an evil antagonist, the climax may be a final battle between the two characters. If the conflict is an adventurer looking for heavily guarded treasure, the climax may be the adventurer's encounter with the final obstacle that protects the treasure. The climax may be made of multiple scenes, but can usually be summarized as one event. Once the conflict and climax are complete, the **falling action** begins.

Falling Action

The **falling action** shows what happens in the story between the climax and the resolution. The falling action often composes a much smaller portion of the story than the rising action does. While the climax includes the end of the main conflict, the falling action may show the results of any minor conflicts in the story. For example, if the protagonist encountered a troll on the way to find some treasure, and the troll demanded the protagonist share the treasure after retrieving it, the falling action would include the protagonist returning to share the treasure with the troll. Similarly, any unexplained major events are usually made clear during the falling action. Once all significant elements of the story are resolved or addressed, the story's resolution will occur. The **resolution** is the end of the story, which shows the final result of the plot's events and shows what life is like for the main characters once they are no longer experiencing the story's conflicts.

Resolution

The way the conflict is **resolved** depends on the type of conflict. The plot of any book starts with the lead up to the conflict, then the conflict itself, and finally the solution, or **resolution**, to the conflict. In **man versus man** conflicts, the conflict is often resolved by two parties coming to some sort of agreement or by one party triumphing over the other party. In **man versus nature** conflicts, the conflict is often resolved by man coming to some realization about some aspect of nature. In **man versus self** conflicts, the conflict is often resolved by the character growing or coming to an understanding about part of himself.

Theme

A **theme** is a central idea demonstrated by a passage. Often, a theme is a lesson or moral contained in the text, but it does not have to be. It also is a unifying idea that is used throughout the text; it can take the form of a common setting, idea, symbol, design, or recurring event. A passage can have two or more themes that convey its overall idea. The theme or themes of a passage are often based on **universal themes**. They can frequently be expressed using well-known sayings about life, society, or human nature, such as "Hard work pays off" or "Good triumphs over evil." Themes are not usually stated **explicitly**. The reader must figure them out by carefully reading the passage. Themes are created through descriptive language or events in the plot. The events of a story help shape the themes of a passage.

Example

Explain why "if you care about something, you need to take care of it" accurately describes the theme of the following excerpt.

> Luca collected baseball cards, but he wasn't very careful with them. He left them around the house. His dog liked to chew. One day, Luca and his friend Bart were looking at his collection. Then they went outside. When Luca got home, he saw his dog chewing on his cards. They were ruined.

This excerpt tells the story of a boy who is careless with his baseball cards and leaves them lying around. His dog ends up chewing them and ruining them. The lesson is that if you care about something, you need to take care of it. This is the theme, or point, of the story. Some stories have more than one theme, but this is not really true of this excerpt. The reader needs to figure out the theme based on what happens in the story. Sometimes, as in the case of fables, the theme is stated directly in the text. However, this is not usually the case.

Review Video: Themes in Literature
Visit mometrix.com/academy and enter code: 732074

Narrator's Point of View

Point of View

Another element that impacts a text is the author's point of view. The **point of view** of a text is the perspective from which a passage is told. An author will always have a point of view about a story before he or she draws up a plot line. The author will know what events they want to take place, how they want the characters to interact, and how they want the story to resolve. An author will also have an opinion on the topic or series of events which is presented in the story that is based on their prior experience and beliefs.

The two main points of view that authors use, especially in a work of fiction, are first person and third person. If the narrator of the story is also the main character, or *protagonist*, the text is written in first-person point of view. In first person, the author writes from the perspective of *I*. Third-person point of view is probably the most common that authors use in their passages. Using third person, authors refer to each character by using *he* or *she.* In third-person omniscient, the narrator is not a character in the story and tells the story of all of the characters at the same time.

Review Video: Point of View
Visit mometrix.com/academy and enter code: 383336

First-Person Narration

First-person narratives let narrators express inner feelings and thoughts, especially when the narrator is the protagonist as Lemuel Gulliver is in Jonathan Swift's *Gulliver's Travels.* The narrator may be a close friend of the protagonist, like Dr. Watson in Sir Arthur Conan Doyle's *Sherlock Holmes.* Or, the narrator can be less involved with the main characters and plot, like Nick Carraway in F. Scott Fitzgerald's *The Great Gatsby.* When a narrator reports others' narratives, she or he is a "**frame narrator**," like the nameless narrator of Joseph Conrad's *Heart of Darkness* or Mr. Lockwood in Emily Brontë's *Wuthering Heights.* **First-person plural** is unusual but can be effective. Isaac Asimov's *I, Robot*, William Faulkner's *A Rose for Emily*, Maxim Gorky's *Twenty-Six Men and a Girl*, and Jeffrey Eugenides' *The Virgin Suicides* all use first-person plural narration. Author Kurt Vonnegut is the first-person narrator in his semi-autobiographical novel *Timequake.* Also unusual, but effective, is a **first-person omniscient** (rather than the more common third-person omniscient) narrator, like Death in Markus Zusak's *The Book Thief* and the ghost in Alice Sebold's *The Lovely Bones.*

Second-Person Narration

While **second-person** address is very commonplace in popular song lyrics, it is the least used form of narrative voice in literary works. Popular serial books of the 1980s like *Fighting Fantasy* or *Choose Your Own Adventure* employed second-person narratives. In some cases, a narrative combines both second-person and first-person voices, using the pronouns *you* and *I*. This can draw readers into the story, and it can also enable the authors to compare directly "your" and "my" feelings, thoughts, and actions. When the narrator is also a character in the story, as in Edgar Allan Poe's short story "The Tell-Tale Heart" or Jay McInerney's novel *Bright Lights, Big City*, the narrative is better defined as first-person despite it also addressing "you."

Third-Person Narration

Narration in the third person is the most prevalent type, as it allows authors the most flexibility. It is so common that readers simply assume without needing to be informed that the narrator is not a character in the story, or involved in its events. **Third-person singular** is used more frequently than **third-person plural**, though some authors have also effectively used plural. However, both singular and plural are most often included in stories according to which characters are being described. The third-person narrator may be either objective or subjective, and either omniscient or limited. **Objective third-person** narration does not include what the characters described are thinking or feeling, while **subjective third-person** narration does. The **third-person omniscient** narrator knows everything about all characters, including their thoughts and emotions, and all related places, times, and events. However, the **third-person limited** narrator may know everything about a particular character, but is limited to that character. In other words, the narrator cannot speak about anything that character does not know.

Alternating-Person Narration

Although authors more commonly write stories from one point of view, there are also instances wherein they alternate the narrative voice within the same book. For example, they may sometimes use an omniscient third-person narrator and a more intimate first-person narrator at other times. In J. K. Rowling's series of *Harry Potter* novels, she often writes in a third-person limited narrative, but sometimes changes to narration by characters other than the protagonist. George R. R. Martin's series *A Song of Ice and Fire* changes the point of view to coincide with divisions between chapters. The same technique is used by Erin Hunter (a pseudonym for several authors of the *Warriors, Seekers,* and *Survivors* book series). Authors using first-person narrative sometimes switch to third-person to describe significant action scenes, especially those where the narrator was absent or uninvolved, as Barbara Kingsolver does in her novel *The Poisonwood Bible.*

Review Video: The Narrator of a Story
Visit mometrix.com/academy and enter code: 742528

Setting, Mood, and Tone

Setting and Time Frame

A literary text has both a setting and time frame. A **setting** is the place in which the story as a whole is set. The **time frame** is the period in which the story is set. This may refer to the historical period the story takes place in or if the story takes place over a single day. Both setting and time frame are relevant to a text's meaning because they help the reader place the story in time and space. An author uses setting and time frame to anchor a text, create a mood, and enhance its meaning. This helps a reader understand why a character acts the way he does, or why certain events in the story are important. The setting impacts the **plot** and character **motivations**, while the time frame helps place the story in **chronological context**.

Example

Read the following excerpt from The Adventures of Huckleberry Finn by Mark Twain and analyze the relevance of setting to the text's meaning:

> We said there warn't no home like a raft, after all. Other places do seem so cramped up and smothery, but a raft don't. You feel mighty free and easy and comfortable on a raft.

This excerpt from *The Adventures of Huckleberry Finn* by Mark Twain reveals information about the **setting** of the book. By understanding that the main character, Huckleberry Finn, lives on a raft, the reader can place the story on a river, in this case, the Mississippi River in the South before the Civil War. The information about the setting also gives the reader clues about the **character** of Huck Finn: he clearly values independence and freedom, and he likes the outdoors. The information about the setting in the quote helps the reader to better understand the rest of the text.

Syntax and Word Choice

Authors use words and **syntax**, or sentence structure, to make their texts unique, convey their own writing style, and sometimes to make a point or emphasis. They know that word choice and syntax contribute to the reader's understanding of the text as well as to the tone and mood of a text.

Review Video: Syntax
Visit mometrix.com/academy and enter code: 242280

Mood and Tone

Mood is a story's atmosphere, or the feelings the reader gets from reading it. The way authors set the mood in writing is comparable to the way filmmakers use music to set the mood in movies. Instead of music, though, writers judiciously select descriptive words to evoke certain **moods**. The mood of a work may convey joy, anger, bitterness, hope, gloom, fear, apprehension, or any other emotion the author wants the reader to feel. In addition to vocabulary choices, authors also use figurative expressions, particular sentence structures, and choices of diction that project and reinforce the moods they want to create. Whereas mood is the reader's emotions evoked by reading what is written, **tone** is the emotions and attitudes of the writer that she or he expresses in the writing. Authors use the same literary techniques to establish tone as they do to establish mood. An author may use a humorous tone, an angry or sad tone, a sentimental or unsentimental tone, or something else entirely.

MOOD AND TONE IN THE GREAT GATSBY

To understand the difference between mood and tone, look at this excerpt from F. Scott Fitzgerald's *The Great Gatsby*. In this passage, Nick Caraway, the novel's narrator, is describing his affordable house, which sits in a neighborhood full of expensive mansions.

> "I lived at West Egg, the—well the less fashionable of the two, though this is a most superficial tag to express the bizarre and not a little sinister contrast between them. My house was at the very tip of the egg, only fifty yard from the Sound, and squeezed between two huge places that rented for twelve or fifteen thousand a season ... My own house was an eyesore, but it was a small eyesore, and it had been overlooked, so I had a view of the water, a partial view of my neighbor's lawn, and the consoling proximity of millionaires—all for eighty dollars a month."

In this description, the mood created for the reader does not match the tone created through the narrator. The mood in this passage is one of dissatisfaction and inferiority. Nick compares his home to his neighbors', saying he lives in the "less fashionable" neighborhood and that his house is "overlooked," an "eyesore," and "squeezed between two huge" mansions. He also adds that his placement allows him the "consoling proximity of millionaires." A literal reading of these details leads the reader to have negative feelings toward Nick's house and his economic inferiority to his neighbors, creating the mood.

However, Fitzgerald also conveys an opposing attitude, or tone, through Nick's description. Nick calls the distinction between the neighborhoods "superficial," showing a suspicion of the value suggested by the neighborhoods' titles, properties, and residents. Nick also undermines his critique of his own home by calling it "a small eyesore" and claiming it has "been overlooked." However, he follows these statements with a description of his surroundings, claiming that he has "a view of the water" and can see some of his wealthy neighbor's property from his home, and a comparison between the properties' rent. While the mental image created for the reader depicts a small house shoved between looming mansions, the tone suggests that Nick enjoys these qualities about his home, or at least finds it charming. He acknowledges its shortcomings, but includes the benefits of his home's unassuming appearance.

Review Video: Style, Tone, and Mood
Visit mometrix.com/academy and enter code: 416961

HISTORICAL AND SOCIAL CONTEXT

Fiction that is heavily influenced by a historical or social context cannot be comprehended as the author intended if the reader does not keep this context in mind. Many important elements of the text will be influenced by any context, including symbols, allusions, settings, and plot events. These contexts, as well as the identity of the work's author, can help to inform the reader about the author's concerns and intended meanings. For example, George Orwell published his novel *1984* in the year 1949, soon after the end of World War II. At that time, following the defeat of the Nazis, the Cold War began between the Western Allied nations and the Eastern Soviet Communists. People were therefore concerned about the conflict between the freedoms afforded by Western democracies versus the oppression represented by Communism. Orwell had also previously fought in the Spanish Civil War against a Spanish regime that he and his fellows viewed as oppressive. From this information, readers can infer that Orwell was concerned about oppression by totalitarian governments. This informs *1984*'s story of Winston Smith's rebellion against the oppressive "Big Brother" government, of the fictional dictatorial state of Oceania, and his capture, torture, and ultimate conversion by that government. Some literary theories also seek to use historical and social contexts to reveal deeper meanings and implications in a text.

Character Development and Dialogue

Character Development

When depicting characters or figures in a written text, authors generally use actions, dialogue, and descriptions as characterization techniques. Characterization can occur in both fiction and nonfiction and is used to show a character or figure's personality, demeanor, and thoughts. This helps create a more engaging experience for the reader by providing a more concrete picture of a character or figure's tendencies and features. Characterizations also gives authors the opportunity to integrate elements such as dialects, activities, attire, and attitudes into their writing.

To understand the meaning of a story, it is vital to understand the characters as the author describes them. We can look for contradictions in what a character thinks, says, and does. We can notice whether the author's observations about a character differ from what other characters in the story say about that character. A character may be dynamic, meaning they change significantly during the story, or static, meaning they remain the same from beginning to end. Characters may be two-dimensional, not fully developed, or may be well developed with characteristics that stand out vividly. Characters may also symbolize universal properties. Additionally, readers can compare and contrast characters to analyze how each one developed.

A well-known example of character development can be found in Charles Dickens's *Great Expectations*. The novel's main character, Pip, is introduced as a young boy, and he is depicted as innocent, kind, and humble. However, as Pip grows up and is confronted with the social hierarchy of Victorian England, he becomes arrogant and rejects his loved ones in pursuit of his own social advancement. Once he achieves his social goals, he realizes the merits of his former lifestyle, and lives with the wisdom he gained in both environments and life stages. Dickens shows Pip's ever-changing character through his interactions with others and his inner thoughts, which evolve as his personal values and personality shift.

Dialogue

Effectively written dialogue serves at least one, but usually several, purposes. It advances the story and moves the plot, develops the characters, sheds light on the work's theme or meaning, and can, often subtly, account for the passage of time not otherwise indicated. It can alter the direction that the plot is taking, typically by introducing some new conflict or changing existing ones. **Dialogue** can establish a work's narrative voice and the characters' voices and set the tone of the story or of particular characters. When fictional characters display enlightenment or realization, dialogue can give readers an understanding of what those characters have discovered and how. Dialogue can illuminate the motivations and wishes of the story's characters. By using consistent thoughts and syntax, dialogue can support character development. Skillfully created, it can also represent real-life speech rhythms in written form. Via conflicts and ensuing action, dialogue also provides drama.

Dialogue in Fiction

In fictional works, effectively written dialogue does more than just break up or interrupt sections of narrative. While **dialogue** may supply exposition for readers, it must nonetheless be believable. Dialogue should be dynamic, not static, and it should not resemble regular prose. Authors should not use dialogue to write clever similes or metaphors, or to inject their own opinions. Nor should they use dialogue at all when narrative would be better. Most importantly, dialogue should not slow the plot movement. Dialogue must seem natural, which means careful construction of phrases rather than actually duplicating natural speech, which does not necessarily translate well to the written word. Finally, all dialogue must be pertinent to the story, rather than just added conversation.

Figurative Language

Literal and Figurative Meaning

When language is used **literally**, the words mean exactly what they say and nothing more. When language is used **figuratively**, the words mean something beyond their literal meaning. For example, "The weeping willow tree has long, trailing branches and leaves" is a literal description. But "The weeping willow tree looks as if it is bending over and crying" is a figurative description—specifically, a **simile** or stated comparison. Another figurative language form is **metaphor**, or an implied comparison. A good example is the metaphor of a city, state, or city-state as a ship, and its governance as sailing that ship. Ancient Greek lyrical poet Alcaeus is credited with first using this metaphor, and ancient Greek tragedian Aeschylus then used it in *Seven Against Thebes*, and then Plato used it in the *Republic*.

Figures of Speech

A **figure of speech** is a verbal expression whose meaning is figurative rather than literal. For example, the phrase "butterflies in the stomach" does not refer to actual butterflies in a person's stomach. It is a metaphor representing the fluttery feelings experienced when a person is nervous or excited—or when one "falls in love," which does not mean physically falling. "Hitting a sales target" does not mean physically hitting a target with arrows as in archery; it is a metaphor for meeting a sales quota. "Climbing the ladder of success" metaphorically likens advancing in one's career to ascending ladder rungs. Similes, such as "light as a feather" (meaning very light, not a feather's actual weight), and hyperbole, like "I'm starving/freezing/roasting," are also figures of speech. Figures of speech are often used and crafted for emphasis, freshness of expression, or clarity.

Review Video: Figures of Speech
Visit mometrix.com/academy and enter code: 111295

Figurative Language

Figurative language extends past the literal meanings of words. It offers readers new insight into the people, things, events, and subjects covered in a work of literature. Figurative language also enables readers to feel they are sharing the authors' experiences. It can stimulate the reader's senses, make comparisons that readers find intriguing or even startling, and enable readers to view the world in different ways. When looking for figurative language, it is important to consider the context of the sentence or situation. Phrases that appear out of place or make little sense when read literally are likely instances of figurative language. Once figurative language has been recognized, context is also important to determining the type of figurative language being used and its function. For example, when a comparison is being made, a metaphor or simile is likely being used. This means the comparison may emphasize or create irony through the things being compared. Seven specific types of figurative language include: alliteration, onomatopoeia, personification, imagery, similes, metaphors, and hyperbole.

Review Video: Figurative Language
Visit mometrix.com/academy and enter code: 584902

Alliteration and Onomatopoeia

Alliteration describes a series of words beginning with the same sounds. **Onomatopoeia** uses words imitating the sounds of things they name or describe. For example, in his poem "Come Down, O Maid," Alfred Tennyson writes of "The moan of doves in immemorial elms, / And murmuring of innumerable bees." The word "moan" sounds like some sounds doves make, "murmuring" represents the sounds of bees buzzing.

Onomatopoeia also includes words that are simply meant to represent sounds, such as "meow," "kaboom," and "whoosh."

Review Video: Alliteration in Everyday Expressions
Visit mometrix.com/academy and enter code: 462837

PERSONIFICATION

Another type of figurative language is **personification**. This is describing a non-human thing, like an animal or an object, as if it were human. The general intent of personification is to describe things in a manner that will be comprehensible to readers. When an author states that a tree *groans* in the wind, he or she does not mean that the tree is emitting a low, pained sound from a mouth. Instead, the author means that the tree is making a noise similar to a human groan. Of course, this personification establishes a tone of sadness or suffering. A different tone would be established if the author said that the tree was *swaying* or *dancing*. Alfred Tennyson's poem "The Eagle" uses all of these types of figurative language: "He clasps the crag with crooked hands." Tennyson used alliteration, repeating /k/ and /kr/ sounds. These hard-sounding consonants reinforce the imagery, giving visual and tactile impressions of the eagle.

Review Video: Personification
Visit mometrix.com/academy and enter code: 260066

SIMILES AND METAPHORS

Similes are stated comparisons using "like" or "as." Similes can be used to stimulate readers' imaginations and appeal to their senses. Because a simile includes *like* or *as,* the device creates more space between the description and the thing being described than a metaphor does. If an author says that *a house was like a shoebox*, then the tone is different than the author saying that the house *was* a shoebox. Authors will choose between a metaphor and a simile depending on their intended tone.

Similes also help compare fictional characters to well-known objects or experiences, so the reader can better relate to them. William Wordsworth's poem about "Daffodils" begins, "I wandered lonely as a cloud." This simile compares his loneliness to that of a cloud. It is also personification, giving a cloud the human quality loneliness. In his novel *Lord Jim* (1900), Joseph Conrad writes in Chapter 33, "I would have given anything for the power to soothe her frail soul, tormenting itself in its invincible ignorance like a small bird beating about the cruel wires of a cage." Conrad uses the word "like" to compare the girl's soul to a small bird. His description of the bird beating at the cage shows the similar helplessness of the girl's soul to gain freedom.

Review Video: Similes
Visit mometrix.com/academy and enter code: 642949

A **metaphor** is a type of figurative language in which the writer equates something with another thing that is not particularly similar, instead of using *like* or *as*. For instance, *the bird was an arrow arcing through the sky*. In this sentence, the arrow is serving as a metaphor for the bird. The point of a metaphor is to encourage the reader to consider the item being described in a *different way*. Let's continue with this metaphor for a flying bird. You are asked to envision the bird's flight as being similar to the arc of an arrow. So, you imagine the flight to be swift and bending. Metaphors are a way for the author to describe an item *without being direct and obvious*. This literary device is a lyrical and suggestive way of providing information. Note that the reference for a metaphor will not always be mentioned explicitly by the author. Consider the following description of a forest in winter: *Swaying skeletons reached for the sky and groaned as the wind blew through them.* In this example, the author is using *skeletons* as a metaphor for leafless trees. This metaphor creates a spooky tone while inspiring the reader's imagination.

LITERARY EXAMPLES OF METAPHOR

A **metaphor** is an implied comparison, i.e., it compares something to something else without using "like", "as", or other comparative words. For example, in "The Tyger" (1794), William Blake writes, "Tyger Tyger, burning bright, / In the forests of the night." Blake compares the tiger to a flame not by saying it is like a fire, but by simply describing it as "burning." Henry Wadsworth Longfellow's poem "O Ship of State" (1850) uses an extended metaphor by referring consistently throughout the entire poem to the state, union, or republic as a seagoing vessel, referring to its keel, mast, sail, rope, anchors, and to its braving waves, rocks, gale, tempest, and "false lights on the shore." Within the extended metaphor, Longfellow uses a specific metaphor: "the anchors of thy hope!"

TED HUGHES' ANIMAL METAPHORS

Ted Hughes frequently used animal metaphors in his poetry. In "The Thought Fox," a model of concise, structured beauty, Hughes characterizes the poet's creative process with succinct, striking imagery of an idea entering his head like a wild fox. Repeating "loneliness" in the first two stanzas emphasizes the poet's lonely work: "Something else is alive / Beside the clock's loneliness." He treats an idea's arrival as separate from himself. Three stanzas detail in vivid images a fox's approach from the outside winter forest at starless midnight—its nose, "Cold, delicately" touching twigs and leaves; "neat" paw prints in snow; "bold" body; brilliant green eyes; and self-contained, focused progress—"Till, with a sudden sharp hot stink of fox," he metaphorically depicts poetic inspiration as the fox's physical entry into "the dark hole of the head." Hughes ends by summarizing his vision of a poet as an interior, passive idea recipient, with the outside world unchanged: "The window is starless still; the clock ticks, / The page is printed."

Review Video: Metaphors in Writing
Visit mometrix.com/academy and enter code: 133295

METONYMY

Metonymy is naming one thing with words or phrases of a closely related thing. This is similar to metaphor. However, the comparison has a close connection, unlike metaphor. An example of metonymy is to call the news media *the press*. Of course, *the press* is the machine that prints newspapers. Metonymy is a way of naming something without using the same name constantly.

SYNECDOCHE

Synecdoche points to the whole by naming one of the parts. An example of synecdoche would be calling a construction worker a *hard hat*. Like metonymy, synecdoche is an easy way of naming something without having to overuse a name. The device allows writers to highlight pieces of the thing being described. For example, referring to businessmen as *suits* suggests professionalism and unity.

Review Video: Metonymy and Synecdoche
Visit mometrix.com/academy and enter code: 900306

HYPERBOLE

Hyperbole is excessive exaggeration used for humor or emphasis rather than for literal meaning. For example, in *To Kill a Mockingbird*, Harper Lee wrote, "People moved slowly then. There was no hurry, for there was nowhere to go, nothing to buy and no money to buy it with, nothing to see outside the boundaries of Maycomb County." This was not literally true; Lee exaggerates the scarcity of these things for emphasis. In "Old Times on the Mississippi," Mark Twain wrote, "I... could have hung my hat on my eyes, they stuck out so far." This is not literal, but makes his description vivid and funny. In his poem "As I Walked Out One Evening", W. H. Auden wrote, "I'll love you, dear, I'll love you / Till China and Africa meet, / And the river jumps over the mountain / And the salmon sing in the street." He used things not literally possible to emphasize the duration of his love.

UNDERSTATEMENT

Understatement is the opposite of hyperbole. This device discounts or downplays something. Think about someone who climbs Mount Everest. Then, they say that the journey was *a little stroll*. As with other types of figurative language, understatement has a range of uses. The device may show self-defeat or modesty as in the Mount Everest example. However, some may think of understatement as false modesty (i.e., an attempt to bring attention to you or a situation). For example, a woman is praised on her diamond engagement ring. The woman says, *Oh, this little thing?* Her understatement might be heard as stuck-up or unfeeling.

Review Video: Hyperbole and Understatement
Visit mometrix.com/academy and enter code: 308470

Literary Devices

LITERARY IRONY

In literature, irony demonstrates the opposite of what is said or done. The three types of irony are **verbal irony**, **situational irony**, and **dramatic irony**. Verbal irony uses words opposite to the meaning. Sarcasm may use verbal irony. One common example is describing something that is confusing as "clear as mud." For example, in his 1986 movie *Hannah and Her Sisters*, author, director, and actor Woody Allen says to his character's date, "I had a great evening; it was like the Nuremburg Trials." Notice these employ similes. In situational irony, what happens contrasts with what was expected. O. Henry's short story *The Gift of the Magi* uses situational irony: a husband and wife each sacrifice their most prized possession to buy each other a Christmas present. The irony is that she sells her long hair to buy him a watch fob, while he sells his heirloom pocket-watch to buy her the jeweled combs for her hair she had long wanted; in the end, neither of them can use their gifts. In dramatic irony, narrative informs audiences of more than its characters know. For example, in *Romeo and Juliet*, the audience is made aware that Juliet is only asleep, while Romeo believes her to be dead, which then leads to Romeo's death.

Review Video: Irony
Visit mometrix.com/academy and enter code: 374204

IDIOMS

Idioms create comparisons, and often take the form of similes or metaphors. Idioms are always phrases and are understood to have a meaning that is different from its individual words' literal meaning. For example, "break a leg" is a common idiom that is used to wish someone luck or tell them to perform well. Literally, the phrase "break a leg" means to injure a person's leg, but the phrase takes on a different meaning when used as an idiom. Another example is "call it a day," which means to temporarily stop working on a task, or find a stopping point, rather than literally referring to something as "a day." Many idioms are associated with a region or group. For example, an idiom commonly used in the American South is "'til the cows come home." This phrase is often used to indicate that something will take or may last for a very long time, but not that it will literally last until the cows return to where they reside.

ALLUSION

An allusion is an uncited but recognizable reference to something else. Authors use language to make allusions to places, events, artwork, and other books in order to make their own text richer. For example, an author may allude to a very important text in order to make his own text seem more important. Martin Luther King, Jr. started his "I Have a Dream" speech by saying "Five score years ago…" This is a clear allusion to President Abraham Lincoln's "Gettysburg Address" and served to remind people of the significance of the event. An author may allude to a place to ground his text or make a cultural reference to make readers feel included. There are many reasons that authors make allusions.

Review Video: Allusions
Visit mometrix.com/academy and enter code: 294065

Comic Relief

Comic relief is the use of comedy by an author to break up a dramatic or tragic scene and infuse it with a bit of **lightheartedness**. In William Shakespeare's *Hamlet*, two gravediggers digging the grave for Ophelia share a joke while they work. The death and burial of Ophelia are tragic moments that directly follow each other. Shakespeare uses an instance of comedy to break up the tragedy and give his audience a bit of a break from the tragic drama. Authors sometimes use comic relief so that their work will be less depressing; other times they use it to create irony or contrast between the darkness of the situation and the lightness of the joke. Often, authors will use comedy to parallel what is happening in the tragic scenes.

Review Video: Comic Relief
Visit mometrix.com/academy and enter code: 779604

Foreshadowing

Foreshadowing is a device authors use to give readers **hints** about events that will take place later in a story. Foreshadowing most often takes place through a character's dialogue or actions. Sometimes the character will know what is going to happen and will purposefully allude to future events. For example, consider a protagonist who is about to embark on a journey through the woods. Just before the protagonist begins the trip, another character says, "Be careful, you never know what could be out in those woods!" This alerts the reader that the woods may be dangerous and prompts the reader to expect something to attack the protagonist in the woods. This is an example of foreshadowing through warning. Alternatively, a character may unknowingly foreshadow later events. For example, consider a story where a brother and sister run through their house and knock over a vase and break it. The brother says, "Don't worry, we'll clean it up! Mom will never know!" However, the reader knows that their mother will most likely find out what they have done, so the reader expects the siblings to later get in trouble for running, breaking the vase, and hiding it from their mother.

Symbolism

Symbolism describes an author's use of a **symbol**, an element of the story that **represents** something else. Symbols can impact stories in many ways, including deepening the meaning of a story or its elements, comparing a story to another work, or foreshadowing later events in a story. Symbols can be objects, characters, colors, numbers, or anything else the author establishes as a symbol. Symbols can be clearly established through direct comparison or repetition, but they can also be established subtly or gradually over a large portion of the story. Another form of symbolism is **allusion**, which is when something in a story is used to prompt the reader to think about another work. Many well-known works use **Biblical allusions**, which are allusions to events or details in the Bible that inform a work or an element within it.

Examples of Themes and Plots in Literature

Themes in Literature

When we read parables, their themes are the lessons they aim to teach. When we read fables, the moral of each story is its theme. When we read fictional works, the authors' perspectives regarding life and human behavior are their themes. Unlike in parables and fables, themes in literary fiction are usually not meant to preach or teach the readers a lesson. Hence, themes in fiction are not as explicit as they are in parables or fables. Instead, they are implicit, and the reader only infers them. By analyzing the fictional characters through thinking about their actions and behavior, understanding the setting of the story, and reflecting on how its plot develops, the reader comes to infer the main theme of the work. When writers succeed, they communicate with their readers such that common ground is established between author and audience. While a reader's individual experience may differ in its details from the author's written story, both may share universal underlying truths which allow author and audience to connect.

DETERMINING THEME

In well-crafted literature, theme, structure, and plot are interdependent and inextricable: each element informs and reflects the others. The structure of a work is how it is organized. The theme is the central idea or meaning found in it. The plot is what happens in the story. Titles can also inform us of a work's theme. For instance, the title of Edgar Allan Poe's "The Tell-Tale Heart" informs readers of the story's theme of guilt before they even read about the repeated heartbeat the protagonist hears immediately before and constantly after committing and hiding a murder. Repetitive patterns of events or behaviors also give clues to themes. The same is true of symbols. For example, in F. Scott Fitzgerald's *The Great Gatsby,* for Jay Gatsby the green light at the end of the dock symbolizes Daisy Buchanan and his own dreams for the future. More generally, it is also understood as a symbol of the American Dream, and narrator Nick Carraway explicitly compares it to early settlers' sight of America rising from the ocean.

THEMATIC DEVELOPMENT

THEME IN THE GREAT GATSBY

In *The Great Gatsby,* F. Scott Fitzgerald portrayed 1920s America as greedy, cynical, and rife with moral decay. Jay Gatsby's lavish weekly parties symbolize the reckless excesses of the Jazz Age. The growth of bootlegging and organized crime in reaction to Prohibition is symbolized by the character of Meyer Wolfsheim and by Gatsby's own ill-gotten wealth. Fitzgerald symbolized social divisions using geography. The "old money" aristocrats like the Buchanans lived on East Egg, while the "new money" bourgeois like Gatsby lived on West Egg. Fitzgerald also used weather, as many authors have, to reinforce narrative and emotional tones in the novel. Just as in *Romeo and Juliet,* where William Shakespeare set the confrontation of Tybalt and Mercutio and its deadly consequences on the hottest summer day under a burning sun, in *The Great Gatsby,* Fitzgerald did the same with Tom Wilson's deadly confrontation with Gatsby. Both works are ostensible love stories carrying socially critical themes about the destructiveness of pointless and misguided behaviors—family feuds in the former, pursuit of money in the latter.

Review Video: Thematic Development
Visit mometrix.com/academy and enter code: 576507

THEME IN LES MISÉRABLES

In Victor Hugo's novel *Les Misérables,* the overall metamorphosis of protagonist Jean Valjean from a cynical ex-convict into a noble benefactor demonstrates Hugo's theme of the importance of love and compassion for others. Hugo also reflects this in more specific plot events. For example, Valjean's love for Cosette sustains him through many difficult periods and trying events. Hugo illustrates how love and compassion for others beget the same in them: Bishop Myriel's kindness to Valjean eventually inspires him to become honest. Years later, Valjean, as M. Madeleine, has rescued Fauchelevent from under a fallen carriage, Fauchelevent returns the compassionate act by giving Valjean sanctuary in the convent. M. Myriel's kindness also ultimately enables Valjean to rescue Cosette from the Thénardiers. Receiving Valjean's father-like love enables Cosette to fall in love with and marry Marius, and the love between Cosette and Marius enables the couple to forgive Valjean for his past crimes when they are revealed.

THEME IN "THE TELL-TALE HEART"

In one of his shortest stories, "The Tell-Tale Heart," Poe used economy of language to emphasize the murderer-narrator's obsessive focus on bare details like the victim's cataract-milky eye, the sound of a heartbeat, and insistence he is sane. The narrator begins by denying he is crazy, even citing his extreme agitation as proof of sanity. Contradiction is then extended: the narrator loves the old man, yet kills him. His motives are irrational—not greed or revenge, but to relieve the victim of his "evil eye." Because "eye" and "I" are homonyms, readers may infer that eye/I symbolizes the old man's identity, contradicting the killer's delusion that he can separate them. The narrator distances himself from the old man by perceiving his eye as separate, and dismembering his dead body. This backfires when he imagines the victim's heartbeat, which is really his own, just before he kills him and frequently afterward. Guilty and paranoid, he gives himself away. Poe predated Freud in exploring the paradox of killing those we love and the concept of projecting our own processes onto others.

Theme in the Works of William Faulkner and Charles Dickens

William Faulkner contrasts the traditions of the antebellum South with the rapid changes of post-Civil War industrialization in his short story "A Rose for Emily." Living inside the isolated world of her house, Emily Grierson denies the reality of modern progress. Contradictorily, she is both a testament to time-honored history and a mysterious, eccentric, unfathomable burden. Faulkner portrays her with deathlike imagery even in life, comparing her to a drowned woman and referring to her skeleton. Emily symbolizes the Old South; as her social status is degraded, so is the antebellum social order. Like Miss Havisham in Charles Dickens' *Great Expectations,* Emily preserves her bridal bedroom, denying change and time's passage. Emily tries to control death through denial, shown in her necrophilia with her father's corpse and her killing of Homer Barron to stop him from leaving her, then also denying his death. Faulkner uses the motif of dust throughout to represent not only the decay of Emily, her house, and Old Southern traditions, but also how her secrets are obscured from others.

Theme in Moby-Dick

The great White Whale in *Moby-Dick* plays various roles to different characters. In Captain Ahab's obsessive, monomaniacal quest to kill it, the whale represents all evil, and Ahab believes it his duty and destiny to rid the world of it. Ishmael attempts through multiple scientific disciplines to understand the whale objectively, but fails—it is hidden underwater and mysterious to humans—reinforcing Melville's theme that humans can never know everything; here the whale represents the unknowable. Melville reverses white's usual connotation of purity in Ishmael's dread of white, associated with crashing waves, polar animals, albinos—all frightening and unnatural. White is often viewed as an absence of color, yet white light is the sum total of all colors in the spectrum. In the same way, white can signify both absence of meaning, and totality of meaning incomprehensible to humans. As a creature of nature, the whale also symbolizes how 19th-century white men's exploitative expansionistic actions were destroying the natural environment.

Theme in The Old Man and the Sea

Because of the old fisherman Santiago's struggle to capture a giant marlin, some people characterize Ernest Hemingway's *The Old Man and the Sea* as telling of man against nature. However, it can more properly be interpreted as telling of man's role as part of nature. Both man and fish are portrayed as brave, proud, and honorable. In Hemingway's world, all creatures, including humans, must either kill or be killed. Santiago reflects, "man can be destroyed but not defeated," following this principle in his life. As heroes are often created through their own deaths, Hemingway seems to believe that while being destroyed is inevitable, destruction enables living beings to transcend it by fighting bravely with honor and dignity. Hemingway echoes Romantic poet John Keats' contention that only immediately before death can we understand beauty as it is about to be destroyed. He also echoes ancient Greek and Roman myths and the Old Testament with the tragic flaw of overweening pride or overreaching. Like Icarus, Prometheus, and Adam and Eve, the old man "went out too far."

Universal Themes

The Old Testament book of Genesis, the Quran, and the Epic of Gilgamesh all contain flood stories. Versions differ somewhat, yet marketed similarities also exist. Genesis describes a worldwide flood, attributing it to God's decision that mankind, his creation, had become incontrovertibly wicked in spirit and must be destroyed for the world to start anew. The Quran describes the flood as regional, caused by Allah after sending Nuh (notice the similarity in name to Noah) as a messenger to his people to cease their evil. The Quran stipulates that Allah only destroys those who deny or ignore messages from his messengers. In the Gilgamesh poems Utnapishtim, like Noah, is instructed to build a ship to survive the flood. Both men also send out birds afterward as tests, using doves and a raven, though with different outcomes. Many historians and archeologists believe a Middle Eastern tidal wave was a real basis for these stories. However, their universal themes remain the same: the flood was seen as God's way of wiping out humans whose behavior had become ungodly.

Theme of Overreaching

A popular theme throughout literature is the human trait of **reaching too far** or **presuming too much**. In Greek mythology, Daedalus constructed wings of feathers and wax that men might fly like birds. He permitted his son Icarus to try them, but cautioned the boy not to fly too close to the sun. The impetuous youth (in what psychologist David Elkind later named adolescence's myth of invincibility) ignored this, flying too close to the sun. The wax melted, the wings disintegrated, and Icarus fell into the sea and perished. In the Old Testament, God warned Adam and Eve not to eat fruit from the tree of knowledge of good and evil. Because they ignored this command, they were banished from Eden's eternal perfection, condemning them to mortality and suffering. The Romans were themselves examples of overreaching in their conquest and assimilation of most of the then-known world and their ultimate demise. In Christopher Marlowe's *Dr. Faustus* and Johann Wolfgang von Goethe's *Faust,* the protagonist sells his soul to the Devil for unlimited knowledge and success, ultimately leading to his own tragic end.

Story vs. Discourse

In terms of plot, "story" is the characters, places, and events originating in the author's mind, while "discourse" is how the author arranges and sequences events—which may be chronological or not. Story is imaginary; discourse is words on the page. Discourse allows a story to be told in different ways. One element of plot structure is relating events differently from the order in which they occurred. This is easily done with cause-and-effect; for example, in the sentence, "He died following a long illness," we know the illness preceded the death, but the death precedes the illness in words. In Kate Chopin's short story "The Story of an Hour" (1894), she tells some of the events out of chronological order, which has the effect of amplifying the surprise of the ending for the reader. Another element of plot structure is selection. Chopin omits some details, such as Mr. Mallard's trip home; this allows readers to be as surprised at his arrival as Mrs. Mallard is.

Plot and Meaning

Novelist E. M. Forster has made the distinction between story as relating a series of events, such as a king dying and then his queen dying, versus plot as establishing motivations for actions and causes for events, such as a king dying and then his queen dying from grief over his death. Thus, plot fulfills the function of helping readers understand cause-and-effect in events and underlying motivations in characters' actions, which in turn helps them understand life. This affects a work's meaning by supporting its ability to explain why things happen, why people do things, and ultimately the meaning of life. Some authors find that while story events convey meaning, they do not tell readers there is any one meaning in life or way of living, but rather are mental experiments with various meanings, enabling readers to explore. Hence stories may not necessarily be constructed to impose one definitive meaning, but rather to find some shape, direction, and meaning within otherwise random events.

Classic Analysis of Plot Structure

In *Poetics,* Aristotle defined plot as "the arrangement of the incidents." He meant not the story, but how it is structured for presentation. In tragedies, Aristotle found results driven by chains of cause and effect preferable to those driven by the protagonist's personality or character. He identified "unity of action" as necessary for a plot's wholeness, meaning its events must be internally connected, not episodic or relying on *deus ex machina* or other external intervention. A plot must have a beginning, middle, and end. Gustav Freytag adapted Aristotle's ideas into his Pyramid (1863). The beginning, today called the exposition, incentive, or inciting moment, emphasizes causes and de-emphasizes effects. Aristotle called the ensuing cause and effect *desis*, or tying up, today called complications which occur during the rising action. These culminate in a crisis or climax, Aristotle's *peripateia.* This occurs at the plot's middle, where cause and effect are both emphasized. The falling action, which Aristotle called the *lusis* or unraveling, is today called the dénouement. The resolution comes at the catastrophe, outcome, or end, when causes are emphasized and effects de-emphasized.

Review Video: Plot Line
Visit mometrix.com/academy and enter code: 944011

Analysis of Plot Structures Through Recurring Patterns

Authors of fiction select characters, places, and events from their imaginations and arrange them to create a story that will affect their readers. One way to analyze plot structure is to compare and contrast different events in a story. For example, in Kate Chopin's "The Story of an Hour," a very simple but key pattern of repetition is the husband's leaving and then returning. Such patterns fulfill the symmetrical aspect that Aristotle said was required of sound plot structure. In James Baldwin's short story, "Sonny's Blues," the narrator is Sonny's brother. In an encounter with one of Sonny's old friends early in the story, the brother initially disregards his communication. In a subsequent flashback, Baldwin informs us that this was the same way he had treated Sonny. In Nathaniel Hawthorne's "Young Goodman Brown," a pattern is created by the protagonist's recurrent efforts not to go farther into the wood. In Herman Melville's "Bartleby the Scrivener" and in William Faulkner's "Barn Burning," patterns are also created by repetition such as Bartleby's repeated refusals and the history of barn-burning episodes, respectively.

Literary Analysis

Analyzing Literary Texts

The best literary analysis shows special insight into at least one important aspect of a text. When **analyzing literary texts**, it can be difficult to find a starting place. Many texts can be analyzed several different ways, often leaving an overwhelming number of options for writers to consider. However, narrowing the focus to a particular element of literature can be helpful when preparing to analyze a text. Symbolism, themes, and motifs are common starting points for literary analysis. These three methods of analysis can lead to a holistic analysis of a text, since they involve elements that are often distributed throughout the text. However, not all texts feature these elements in a way that facilitates a strong analysis, if they are present at all. It is also common to focus on character or plot development for analysis. These elements are compatible with theme, symbolism, and allusion. Setting and imagery, figurative language, and any external contexts can also contribute to analysis or complement one of these other elements. The application of a critical, or literary, theory to a text can also provide a thorough and strong analysis.

Literary Theories and Criticism and Interpretation

Literary theory includes ideas that guide readers through the process of interpreting literature. Literary theory, as a subject, encompasses several specific, focused theories that lead readers to interpret or analyze literature through the context of the theory using the subjects and elements it involves. Some commonly used and discussed literary theories include **postcolonial theory**, **gender and feminist theory**, **structuralism**, **new historicism**, **reader-response theory**, and **sociological criticism**.

- **Postcolonial theory** involves the historical and geographical context of a work and leads readers to consider how colonization informs the plot, characters, setting, and other elements in the work.
- **Gender and feminist theory** invites readers to interpret a text by looking at its treatment of and suggestions about women and a culture's treatment of women. As with most literary theories, this information can be clearly stated or strongly implied in a work, but it may also be gleaned through looking closely at symbols, characters, and plot elements in a work.
- **Structuralism** uses the structure and organization of a work and the foundations of language to examine how and what a text conveys about the human experience and how those findings connect to common human experiences.
- **New historicism** heavily relies on the cultural and historical context of a work, including when it was written, where the author lives or lived, the culture and history of that location, and other works from the same culture. New historical readings seek to examine these details to expose the ideologies of the location and culture that influenced the work.
- **Reader-response theory** uses the individual reader's response to the text and experience while reading the text to examine the meaning of the reader's relationship with the text and what that relationship suggests about the reader or the factors impacting their experience.
- **Sociological criticism** considers the societies that are relevant to a text. The author's society and any reader's society are important to the text, as sociological criticism seeks to uncover what the text implies or reveals about those societies. This method of criticism can also involve studying the presentation of a society within the text and applying it to the author's society or their other writings.

Language

The Writing Process

Brainstorming

When choosing what to write about, activities like brainstorming can help inspire new ideas or help writers see how their ideas go together. **Brainstorming** means considering a variety of topics or ideas and is mainly used to find a creative approach to a subject or problem. A good first step in brainstorming is simple **free-association** with a topic. One way of doing this is sitting down with paper and pen and writing every thought that comes to mind about the topic in a word or phrase. It does not matter how helpful or good the thought seems at first; the writer should write down everything that comes to mind about the topic. Then, the writer should read the list over a few times. Next, he or she should look for patterns, repetitions, and clusters of ideas. This allows a variety of fresh ideas to come as the writer thinks about the topic.

Free Writing

Free writing is a more organized form of brainstorming. **Free writing** means taking a limited amount of time, like 2 to 3 minutes, to write everything that comes to mind about a topic in complete sentences. When the time is up, the writer should review everything he or she has written down. Many of the sentences may not make sense, but they may contain ideas and details that help the writer organize his or her ideas and prepare to plan the composition. Usually, free writing results in more useful ideas than brainstorming because the writer's thoughts and connections are written in complete sentences. However, both methods can be used together to help the writer prepare to plan and write a composition.

Mapping

One specific way to use graphic organizers is to map an essay. There are many different types of graphic organizers. One easy method to create one is to draw a circle in the middle of the page and write a broad topic in it. Then, draw smaller circles with related topics and ideas, or with topics that fit within the broad topic, written inside and draw line to connect each circle to the main circle. This method can show ideas that fit within the broad topic and will help guide the essay, or it can show which ideas may work better as the main topic of the essay.

Once the main idea and other ideas and details for the essay have been chosen, they can be used to map the essay. Mapping is another word for using a certain type of graphic organizer. These graphic organizers look like a map and organize ideas and details as they will appear in the essay. The essay map can have the main idea at the top or in the center. If the main idea is at the top, the supporting ideas will appear below it in a row, and any additional details will appear under the supporting idea they go with. If the main idea appears in the center, the supporting ideas may appear around it, and the additional details will appear around the supporting ideas they go with.

Planning

Planning is the process of organizing a piece of writing before writing a draft. At the beginning of planning, writers should decide **why they are writing** and **who will read what they write**. The writer must also choose a **genre**, which is the **type** of composition he or she will write. There are fiction genres, such as comedy, folklore, action, and mystery. There are also nonfiction genres, such as essays, reports, poems, and journals. To plan his or her composition, a writer may create an outline or a graphic organizer, such as a Venn diagram, a spider-map, or a flowchart. These methods should help the writer choose their topic, main ideas, and how to organize the composition. If the writer needs to do research for the composition, he or she may also do so as they plan. Planning helps writers organize all of their ideas and decide if they have enough information to begin their first draft. However, writers should remember that the decisions they make during planning may change later, so their plan does not have to be perfect.

Drafting

Writers may then use their plan, outline, or graphic organizer to compose their first draft. They may write more drafts after the first one to improve their writing. Writing multiple drafts can help writers think of different ways to state their ideas and correct mistakes that may be hard to fix without rewriting a section of the composition, or the whole composition. There is no "right" number of drafts, so different writers may write a different number of drafts. Writing drafts also makes it easier to write freely because a writer can improve his or her composition with each draft they write.

Revising, Editing, and Proofreading

Once a writer completes a draft, he or she can move on to revising, editing, and proofreading to improve the draft. **Revising** is making sure that the composition is right for the audience, is not missing important information, is on topic, and is well organized. The writer should also consider the composition's style when revising and ensure that it is appropriately formal or serious. Revising may happen after the first draft so that errors are not repeated in the next draft. Each draft should be revised before the next one is written so that no mistakes are missed. **Editing** comes next. Editing a composition includes steps like improving transitions between paragraphs and making sure each paragraph is on topic. While editing, the writer must pay attention to the words he or she uses and the way the information in each paragraph is organized. Writers may also fix grammar mistakes in the editing phase, since some errors will require a writer to rewrite large parts of their work. **Proofreading** means fixing misspelled words, errors in grammar, and any other small mistakes in the composition.

During the revising, editing, and proofreading steps, it can be helpful for writers to ask a peer to read their work, since he or she may notice mistakes or problems the writer missed before. A writer may also choose to read his or her own work aloud, or listen to someone else read it. Hearing a composition aloud can help writers find mistakes or opportunities for improvement in their work more easily. This happens because when something is read aloud, the person reading the text must pay closer attention to the words on the page. When a writer or a peer reads the composition, they should point out any sentence that confuses them the first time they read it. Most of these sentences can be revised in a way that makes it easier to read and understand.

Adding and Removing Information

While both revising and editing may involve changing the words in a composition, they can also involve adding or taking away words. When a writer has completed a draft and reread it, he or she may notice that something, such as a transition, important details, or an explanatory sentence, is missing. Simply changing the words to make the passage sound better will not solve this problem, so the writer must **add** whatever words and information is needed to make the passage make sense and achieve the writer's purpose.

In other cases, a writer may have words, a sentence, or sometimes an entire paragraph that gives unnecessary information or explains the information in a way that is confusing. When this happens, the extra words and information weaken the composition and must be **removed**. Sometimes, this is difficult for writers to do because it may require them to remove writing they are proud of or a fact they find interesting. Despite this, revising and editing are steps meant to improve and strengthen a composition, so the writer should change, add, or remove parts of his or her writing in a way that makes it better and achieves his or her purpose.

Revising Sentences

Sentence variety is important to consider when writing an essay. A variety of sentence lengths and types can make an essay more engaging, and different types of sentences can sometimes help readers better understand information. For example, a sentence containing a list may make more sense when written with a simple sentence structure, since writing a compound sentence containing a list may give the reader too much information at once. On the other hand, information that is closely related and can be connected with a conjunction should be written in a compound sentence, rather than a simple sentence, since a compound sentence helps the reader see that the information goes together.

Using only simple sentences often makes writing boring and bothersome to read. Writing using only compound sentences makes it difficult for writers to explain information well and difficult for readers to understand, since every sentence will include a coordinating conjunction. To check an essay for sentence variety, it is helpful to look at whether the essay contains different sentence structures and lengths. It is also important to pay attention to the way each sentence starts and avoid beginning with the same words or phrases.

Revising Vocabulary

When writing informational or argumentative texts, it is important to use **precise vocabulary**, or **word choice**, to explain your main idea and supporting details. Generalized vocabulary will not help the audience fully understand the points that you are attempting to make because it will not accurately explain your main idea and supporting details. Precise vocabulary is important to use because it will accurately describe the ideas that are central to your text. When you research a subject, make sure to familiarize yourself with any vocabulary that is involved in its explanation. Use context clues, dictionaries, or, if necessary, a technical dictionary to decode any words that you are not familiar with. Precise vocabulary also impacts the effectiveness of narrative text. Carefully choosing vocabulary to describe sensory details, or imagery, helps writers paint the best possible picture of the events they are describing through their writing.

Recursive Writing Process

Brainstorming, planning, drafting, revising, editing, and proofreading are all steps in the **writing process**. This process is helpful to remember when beginning a new composition, but once a writer has practiced these steps in this order, he or she can use the **recursive writing process**. The recursive writing process is the same as the normal writing process, but the steps in the recursive writing process do not have to happen in the same order. For example, one writer may need to repeat steps after completing other steps. A different writer may discover that he or she can practice the planning and revising steps as he or she writes a draft. The recursive writing process involves moving back and forth between planning, drafting, and revising, followed by more planning, more drafting, and more revising until the writer is happy with his or her work. Each writer can use the recursive writing process in their own way, as long as it helps them improve their work and write the best they can.

Review Video: Recursive Writing Process
Visit mometrix.com/academy and enter code: 951611

Essay Structure and Organization

Central Ideas and Supporting Details

In the first paragraph of a composition, writers include a sentence that explains the **central idea.** This sentence is also known as the **thesis**. The rest of the paragraph shows the reader why the topic of the essay is interesting and includes details that support the central idea. One way to understand the relationship between the central idea and supporting information is to think about a table: the tabletop is the central idea, and each of the table's legs is a supporting detail or group of details. All of the legs work together to support the tabletop and create a table, just like the supporting details work together to support the central idea and create a composition.

Introduction

The introduction is used to capture the reader's attention and announce the essay's central idea. Normally, the introduction contains about 3-5 sentences. An introduction can begin with an interesting quote, a question, a strong opinion, or something else that will **interest** the reader's and prompt them to keep reading. If the composition has a prompt, the introduction should **restate** or **summarize** some part of the prompt so that the reader will have an idea of what information will be in the essay. Finally, your introduction should include the **central idea**, the primary thing the essay will tell the reader.

Review Video: Introduction
Visit mometrix.com/academy and enter code: 961328

Body

In an essay's introduction, the writer states the central idea and prepares the reader for the information in the rest of the composition. In the body of the composition, the writer **explains**, **demonstrates**, and **gives more information about** the **central idea**. This is done using supporting details and examples that are relevant to the central idea of the composition. For example, if the composition's central idea is a vacation the writer took, the body will include descriptions of where the writer went, what they experienced, and what they thought of the trip. If the composition's central idea is the writer's opinion, the body will include examples and facts that show why he or she has formed that opinion. If composition's central idea is a topic and the writer wants to instruct the reader, the body will contain facts, explanations, and examples that help teach the reader about the central idea. A writer will use supporting details to explain the central idea throughout the body.

The body should also contain multiple paragraphs, and the order the writer puts these paragraphs in is important. Each paragraph should include at least one supporting detail, but a paragraph may include more than one if two or more supporting details work together to support the central idea. If the central idea is to describe something that happened, the paragraphs should match the order in which the events occurred. If the central idea is to present an opinion or instruct the reader, the paragraphs should be ordered in the way that would make the most sense to the reader. The order of body paragraphs is important because it can impact how easy a composition is to read.

Review Video: Drafting Body Paragraphs
Visit mometrix.com/academy and enter code: 724590

Choosing Supporting Details and Examples

When writing an informative or argumentative text, writers must choose supporting details carefully. Including details that are irrelevant, inaccurate, or vague does not strengthen the author's writing, while relevant, accurate, provable, and specific details do strengthen the author's writing. These details can make the writer's meaning clearer or give evidence that the author's points are true or logical. Such details may include examples or facts, such as statistics, statements from others who have authority on the subject, and common events or experiences. Choosing appropriate supporting details can also help the author show that they put effort into forming their ideas. This can also make the composition more intriguing and enjoyable to read, since the writer's own interest and insight will be apparent to the reader.

Paragraphs

After the introduction of a passage, the body paragraphs will explain and elaborate upon the central idea. While each paragraph should relate to the central idea of the composition, each paragraph should focus on one point or supporting detail. Normally, a paragraph has a good topic sentence that summarizes the paragraph's main point. A topic sentence is a sentence that gives an introduction to the paragraph and its contents. Topic sentences should contain information that is more specific than what is in the introduction and may include a supporting detail, but they should not contain explanations or examples.

The next sentences in the paragraph should support the topic sentence. These sentences can contain examples, explanations, or other specific information that supports the topic sentence, which supports the central idea of the composition. While a paragraph may be structured in any way, as long as it logically provides information that supports the central idea, it can be best to use a template or pattern to make sure that each paragraph is complete and well organized. For example, a good template to follow is topic sentence, evidence, explanation, conclusion. This means that after the topic sentence, the next sentence should provide evidence, like a quote or example, that supports the paragraph's main point. Next, the paragraph should include a sentence that explains how that evidence supports the paragraph's main point. If there are multiple examples or quotes, more than one sentence may be used to explain them. Finally, there should be a concluding sentence that helps the reader understand the paragraph and prepares them for the next one.

A paragraph must contain enough information to support its main point and the composition's central idea. A paragraph of two or three sentences will most likely not support the main point or central idea because it is not likely to contain enough information, explanation, or evidence. When a paragraph does not support the main point or central idea, it does not help the writer achieve their purpose or goal for writing the essay. A helpful, informative paragraph will often have somewhere from three to five sentences. Also, it is important that the sentences within the paragraph lead the reader through the information. Each paragraph should flow logically and stay on topic throughout.

Starting a New Paragraph

For most forms of writing, you will need to use multiple paragraphs. This means that deciding when to start a new paragraph is very important. Reasons for starting a new paragraph include:

- To separate the introduction and conclusion from the body paragraphs
- To move from one supporting detail or point to another
- To indicate an important shift in time or place
- To show a comparison, contrast, or cause and effect relationship

Transitions

Transitions between sentences and paragraphs guide readers from idea to idea and show relationships between sentences and paragraphs. Writers should use transitions carefully and only when they are truly helpful. They should also be selected to fit the author's purpose. Transitions can show relationships such as time, comparison, an order of events, and cause and effect. Transitions are often used at the beginning of a phrase, sentence, or paragraph, since this helps prepare the reader for the next piece of information.

Review Video: Transitions in Writing
Visit mometrix.com/academy and enter code: 233246

Types of Transitional Words

Time	Afterward, immediately, earlier, meanwhile, recently, lately, now, since, soon, when, then, until, before, etc.
Sequence	too, first, second, further, moreover, also, again, and, next, still, besides, finally
Comparison	similarly, in the same way, likewise, also, again, once more
Contrasting	but, although, despite, however, instead, nevertheless, on the one hand... on the other hand, regardless, yet, in contrast
Cause and Effect	because, consequently, thus, therefore, then, to this end, since, so, as a result, if... then, accordingly
Examples	for example, for instance, such as, to illustrate, indeed, in fact, specifically
Place	near, far, here, there, to the left/right, next to, above, below, beyond, opposite, beside
Repetition, Summary, or Conclusion	as mentioned earlier, as noted, in other words, in short, on the whole, to summarize, therefore, as a result, to conclude, in conclusion
Addition	and, also, furthermore, moreover

Review Video: Transition Words
Visit mometrix.com/academy and enter code: 707563

Conclusion

The conclusion of a composition should summarize the central idea and show that it has been explained well. A good conclusion shows the reader why the author's central idea is meaningful and important and how the supporting details should help the reader understand the central idea. The conclusion should also give the reader something to think about that is related to the central idea. For example, in the conclusion, the author can invite readers to think about how they feel or what they think after reading the composition. Some things to avoid when writing conclusions include:

- Introducing a completely new idea
- Apologizing for one's opinions or writing
- Repeating the central idea word for word rather than summarizing them
- Using the conclusion to summarize every detail in the composition

Review Video: Drafting Conclusions
Visit mometrix.com/academy and enter code: 209408

Grammar

Subjects and Predicates

Subjects

Every sentence needs a subject and a predicate. The **subject** of a sentence names who or what the sentence is about. The subject may be directly stated in a sentence, or the subject may be implied. The **complete subject** includes the simple subject and any **modifiers**, such as adjectives, articles, prepositions, and adverbs, that go with it. To find the complete subject, ask *Who* or *What* before the verb to complete the question. The answer, including any modifiers, is the complete subject. To find the **simple subject**, remove all of the modifiers in the complete subject.

Examples:

The small, red car is the one that he wants for Christmas. (simple subject: car; complete subject: The small, red car)

The young artist is coming over for dinner. (simple subject: artist; complete subject: The young artist)

Review Video: Subjects in English
Visit mometrix.com/academy and enter code: 444771

An imperative sentence is a sentence that gives someone instructions or makes a request to someone. In **imperative** sentences, the verb's subject is understood, but is not actually present in the sentence. For example, this about the sentence *Drive to the store.* This sentence is a command, and the subject is *you*. If the subject were directly stated, the sentence would be *You, drive to the store.* Another fact to consider is that, normally, the subject comes before the verb. However, the subject comes after the verb in sentences that begin with *There are* or *There was.*

Direct:

John knows the way to the park.	Who knows the way to the park?	John
The cookies need ten more minutes.	What needs ten minutes?	The cookies
By five o'clock, Bill will need to leave.	Who needs to leave?	Bill
There are five letters on the table for him.	What is on the table?	Five letters
There were coffee and doughnuts in the house.	What was in the house?	Coffee and doughnuts

Implied:

Go to the post office for me.	Who is going to the post office?	You
Come and sit with me, please?	Who needs to come and sit?	You

PREDICATES

In a sentence, there is always a predicate and a subject. The subject tells what the sentence is about, and the **predicate** explains or describes the subject.

Think about the sentence *He sings.* In this sentence, we have a subject, *He*, and a predicate, *sings*. This is all that is needed for a sentence to be complete. Most sentences contain more information, but if this is all the information that is given in a sentence, then it is a complete sentence.

Now, let's look at another sentence: *John and Jane sing on Tuesday nights at the dance hall.*

subject — predicate

John and Jane | sing on Tuesday nights at the dance hall.

Subject-Verb Agreement

Verbs **agree** with their subjects in number. In other words, singular subjects need singular verbs. Plural subjects need plural verbs. **Singular** is for **one** person, place, or thing. **Plural** is for **more than one** person, place, or thing. Subjects and verbs must also share the same point of view, as in first, second, or third person.

Review Video: Subject-Verb Agreement
Visit mometrix.com/academy and enter code: 479190

Number Agreement Examples:

Single Subject and Verb: Dan (singular subject) calls (singular verb) home.

Dan is one person. So, the singular verb *calls* is needed.

Plural Subject and Verb: Dan and Bob (plural subject) call (plural verb) home.

More than one person needs the plural verb *call.*

Person Agreement Examples:

First Person: I *am* walking.

Second Person: You *are* walking.

Third Person: He *is* walking.

Complications with Subject-Verb Agreement

Words Between Subject and Verb

Words that come between the simple subject and the verb do not affect subject-verb agreement.

Examples:

The joy (singular subject) of my life returns (singular verb) home tonight.

The phrase *of my life* does not affect the verb *returns.*

The question (singular subject) that still remains unanswered is (singular verb) "Who are you?"

Don't let the phrase "*that still remains…*" confuse you. The subject *question* goes with the verb *is.*

Compound Subjects

A compound subject is formed when two or more nouns joined by *and*, *or*, or *nor* act together as the subject of the sentence.

JOINED BY AND

When a compound subject is joined by *and*, it is treated as a plural subject and requires a plural verb.

Examples:

(plural subject: You and Jon) (plural verb: are) You and Jon are invited to come to my house.

(plural subject: pencil and paper) (plural verb: belong) The pencil and paper belong to me.

JOINED BY OR/NOR

For a compound subject joined by *or* or *nor*, the verb must agree in number with the part of the subject that is closest to the verb.

Examples:

(subject: Today or tomorrow) (verb: is) Today or tomorrow is the day.

(subject: Stan or Phil) (verb: wants) Stan or Phil wants to read the book.

(subject: the pen nor the book) (verb: is) Neither the pen nor the book is on the desk.

(subject: blanket or pillows) (verb: arrive) Either the blanket or pillows arrive this afternoon.

INDEFINITE PRONOUNS AS SUBJECT

An indefinite pronoun is a pronoun that does not refer to a specific noun. Different indefinite pronouns are used as a singular noun, a plural noun, or change depending on how they are used.

ALWAYS SINGULAR

Pronouns such as *each*, *either*, *everybody*, *anybody*, *somebody*, and *nobody* are always singular. This is because these pronouns always stand in for one person, place, or thing.

Examples:

(singular subject: Each) (singular verb: has) Each of the runners has a different bib number.

(singular verb: Is) (singular subject: either) Is either of you ready for the game?

Note: The words *each* and *either* can also be used as adjectives. For example, *each* person is unique. When one of these adjectives modifies the subject of a sentence, it is always a singular subject.

singular subject — singular verb
Everybody grows a day older every day.

singular subject — singular verb
Anybody is welcome to bring a tent.

Always Plural

Pronouns such as *both*, *several*, and *many* are always plural. This is because these pronouns always stand in for more than one person, place, thing, or idea.

Examples:

plural subject — plural verb
Both of the siblings were too tired to argue.

plural subject — plural verb
Many have tried, but none have succeeded.

Depend on Context

Pronouns such as *some*, *any*, *all*, *none*, *more*, and *most* can be either singular or plural depending on what they are representing in the context of the sentence.

Examples:

singular subject — singular verb
All of my dog's food was still there in his bowl.

plural subject — plural verb
By the end of the night, all of my guests were already excited about coming to my next party.

Other Cases Involving Plural or Irregular Form

Some nouns are **singular in meaning but plural in form**: news, mathematics, physics, and economics.

The *news is* coming on now.

Mathematics is my favorite class.

Some nouns are plural in form and meaning, and have **no singular equivalent**: scissors and pants.

Do these *pants come* with a shirt?

The *scissors are* for my project.

Note: Look to your **dictionary** for help when you aren't sure whether a noun with a plural form has a singular or plural meaning.

Example

Which word should go in the blank?

If Kelly is going to the party, Joan and Susan ____ going to the store.

a. Is
b. Are
c. Am
d. Was

Try using each choice in the sentence. Choice A, *is*, forms this sentence: If Kelly is going to the party, Joan and Susan is going to the store. There are two people, Joan and Susan, who are going to the store. This makes the subject of the clause plural. *Is* is a singular verb, meaning it does not agree with the subject and cannot be the answer.

Choice B, *are*, forms this sentence: If Kelly is going to the party, Joan and Susan are going to the store. The subject of the clause is still plural. But *are* is a plural verb! The subject and verb agree, so *are* is the correct answer.

Choice C, *am*, forms this sentence: If Kelly is going to the party, Joan and Susan am going to the store. *Am* is a singular verb, and it is also only used in first person, when the writer or speaker is referring to themself. The subject of the clause is plural, and the sentence is in third person, so *am* is not the correct answer.

Choice D, *was*, forms this sentence: If Kelly is going to the party, Joan and Susan was going to the store. *Was* is a singular verb, so it does not agree with the plural subject in this clause.

Complements

A complement is a noun, pronoun, or adjective that is used to give more information about the subject or verb in the sentence.

Direct Objects

A direct object is a noun or pronoun that takes or receives the **action** of a verb. A complete sentence does not need a direct object, so not all sentences will have them. When you are looking for a direct object, find the verb and ask *who* or *what.*

Examples:

I took *the blanket.*

Jane read *books.*

Indirect Objects

An indirect object is a word or group of words that show how an action had an **influence** on someone or something. If there is an indirect object in a sentence, then you always have a direct object in the sentence. When you are looking for the indirect object, find the verb and ask *to, for, whom*, or *what.*

Examples:

We taught the old dog (indirect object) a new trick (direct object).

I gave them (indirect object) a math lesson (direct object).

Review Video: Direct and Indirect Objects
Visit mometrix.com/academy and enter code: 817385

Pronoun-Antecedent Agreement

The **antecedent** is the noun that has been replaced by a pronoun. A pronoun and its antecedent **agree** when they have the same number (singular or plural) and gender (male, female, or neutral).

Examples:

Singular agreement: John (antecedent) came into town, and he (pronoun) played for us.

Plural agreement: John and Rick (antecedent) came into town, and they (pronoun) played for us.

To determine which is the correct pronoun to use in a compound subject or object, try each pronoun **alone** in place of the compound in the sentence. Your knowledge of pronouns will tell you which one is correct.

Example:

Bob and (I, me) will be going.

Test: (1) *I will be going* or (2) *Me will be going*. The second choice cannot be correct because *me* cannot be used as the subject of a sentence. Instead, *me* is used as an object.

Answer: Bob and I will be going.

When a pronoun is used with a noun immediately following (as in "we boys"), try the sentence **without the added noun**.

Example:

(We/Us) boys played football last year.

Test: (1) *We played football last year* or (2) *Us played football last year*. Again, the second choice cannot be correct because *us* cannot be used as a subject of a sentence. Instead, *us* is used as an object.

Answer: We boys played football last year.

Review Video: Pronoun Usage
Visit mometrix.com/academy and enter code: 666500

Review Video: Pronoun-Antecedent Agreement
Visit mometrix.com/academy and enter code: 919704

A pronoun should point clearly to the **antecedent**. Here is how a pronoun reference can be unhelpful if it is puzzling or not directly stated.

Unhelpful: Ron and Jim (antecedent) went to the store, and he (pronoun) bought soda.

Who bought soda? Ron or Jim?

Helpful: Jim (antecedent) went to the store, and he (pronoun) bought soda.

The sentence is clear. Jim bought the soda.

EXAMPLE

Tom printed his ticket to the concert, but he forgot ____ at home.

Which pronoun should go in the blank?

a. It
b. Them
c. Him
d. He

What is the antecedent that the missing pronoun must match? There are only four nouns in the sentence. They are *Tom*, *ticket*, *concert*, and *home*. Which one should the missing pronoun refer to? Tom is the one who forgot something, so the pronoun does not refer to Tom. The concert is not at Tom's home, so he cannot forget the concert at home. It is also not logical to say that Tom forgot his home at home The antecedent must be *ticket*.

Choice A says that the missing pronoun is *it*. The pronoun refers to *ticket*, which is a singular noun. A ticket is also a nonliving thing. The missing pronoun is also the object in the second clause. *It* is singular, refers to nonliving nouns, and can be used as the object. Choice A is correct.

Choice B says that the missing pronoun is *them*. The pronoun refers to the singular noun *ticket*. While *them* can be used to refer to nonliving nouns and can be the object of a sentence, it is a plural pronoun. Choice B is incorrect.

Choice C says that the missing pronoun is *him*. The missing pronoun refers to a nonliving thing, not a human. *Him* is an objective personal pronoun and is singular, but it only refers to living nouns. *Him* cannot represent *ticket*, so choice C is incorrect.

Choice D says that the missing pronoun is *he*. The missing pronoun refers to a nonliving noun and is the object of the second sentence. While *he* is a singular pronoun, it can only be used as the subject of a sentence and only refers to living nouns. Choice D is incorrect.

PHRASES

A phrase is a group of words that functions as a single part of speech, usually a noun, adjective, or adverb. A **phrase** is not a complete thought, and does not contain a subject, but it adds detail or explanation to a sentence, or renames something within the sentence.

CLAUSES

A clause is a group of words that contains both a subject and a predicate (verb). There are two types of clauses: independent and dependent. An **independent clause** contains a complete thought, while a **dependent (or subordinate) clause** does not. A dependent clause includes a subject and a verb, and may also contain additional information, but it cannot stand as a complete thought without being joined to an independent clause. Dependent clauses function within sentences as adjectives, adverbs, or nouns.

Example:

I am running [independent clause] because I want to stay in shape [dependent clause].

The clause *I am running* is an independent clause: it has a subject and a verb, and it gives a complete thought. The clause *because I want to stay in shape* is a dependent clause: it has a subject and a verb, but it does not express a complete thought. This is due to the fact that it begins with *because*, which shows that there is more information needed to complete the thought. This dependent clause adds detail to the independent clause to which it is attached.

Review Video: Independent and Dependent Clauses
Visit mometrix.com/academy and enter code: 556903

SENTENCE STRUCTURE

Sentence structure is based on the type and number of clauses in the sentence. Two common sentence structures are simple sentences and compound sentences:

Simple: A simple sentence has one independent clause with no dependent clauses. A simple sentence may have a **compound subject** or a **compound verb**, or both.

Examples:

Judy [single subject] watered [single verb] the lawn.

Judy and Alan [compound subject] watered [single verb] the lawn.

Judy [single subject] watered [compound verb] the lawn and pulled [compound verb] weeds.

Judy and Alan [compound subject] watered [compound verb] the lawn and pulled [compound verb] weeds.

Compound: A compound sentence has two or more independent clauses with no dependent clauses. Usually, the independent clauses are joined with a comma and a coordinating conjunction or with a semicolon.

Examples:

The time has come [independent clause], and we are ready [independent clause].

I woke up at dawn [independent clause]; the sun was just coming up [independent clause].

Complex: A complex sentence has one independent clause and at least one dependent clause.

Examples:

Although he had the flu, (dependent clause) Harry went to work. (independent clause)

Marcia got married (independent clause) after she finished college. (dependent clause)

Review Video: Sentence Structure
Visit mometrix.com/academy and enter code: 700478

Sentence Fragments

Recall that a group of words must contain at least one **independent clause** in order to be considered a sentence. If it doesn't contain even one independent clause, it is called a **sentence fragment**.

Choosing the best steps for **repairing** a sentence fragment depends on what type of fragment it is. If the fragment is a dependent clause, it can sometimes be fixed by simply removing a subordinating word, such as *when*, *because*, or *if*, from the beginning of the fragment. Alternatively, a dependent clause can be joined to a closely related neighboring sentence. If the fragment is missing some required part, like a subject or a verb, it may be fixed by simply adding the missing part.

Examples:

Fragment: Because he wanted to sail the Mediterranean.

Removed subordinating word: He wanted to sail the Mediterranean.

Combined with another sentence: Because he wanted to sail the Mediterranean, he booked a Greek island cruise.

Example

Which of the following changes will NOT correct this sentence fragment?

Although she had found the coin first.

a. Remove *Although.*
b. Add a comma and *she let her brother keep it* after *first.*
c. Add *She let her brother keep the coin* before *although.*
d. Remove *first.*

Choice A suggests removing the word *although* to form the following sentence: She found the coin first. This option removes the subordinating conjunction to make the clause independent. The resulting sentence is complete, so removing *although* is an acceptable way to correct the fragment. Choice A is incorrect.

Choice B forms the following sentence: Although she had found the coin first, she let her brother keep it. A comma and an independent clause have been added to the sentence fragment to form a complex sentence. The resulting sentence is complete and written correctly, so choice B is incorrect.

Choice C forms the following sentence: She let her brother keep the coin although she had found the coin first. An independent clause has been added before the sentence fragment to form a complex sentence. This sentence is correctly written and complete, so choice C is an acceptable way to correct the fragment. Choice C is incorrect.

Choice D removes the word *first*, leaving *Although she had found the coin*. This is still a sentence fragment, since it is a single dependent clause. Choice D does not correct the fragment, so D is correct.

RUN-ON SENTENCES

Run-on sentences consist of multiple independent clauses that have not been joined together properly. Run-on sentences can be corrected in several different ways:

Join clauses properly: This can be done with a comma and coordinating conjunction, with a semicolon, or with a colon or dash if the second clause is explaining something in the first clause.

Example:

> **Incorrect**: I went on the trip, we visited lots of castles.
>
> **Corrected**: I went on the trip, and we visited lots of castles.

Split into separate sentences: This correction is best to use when the independent clauses are very long or when they are not closely related.

Example:

> **Incorrect**: The drive to New York takes ten hours, my uncle lives in Boston.
>
> **Corrected**: The drive to New York takes ten hours. My uncle lives in Boston.

Make one clause dependent: This is the easiest way to make the sentence correct and more interesting at the same time. It's often as simple as adding a subordinating word between the two clauses or before the first clause.

Example:

> **Incorrect**: I finally made it to the store and I bought some eggs.
>
> **Corrected**: When I finally made it to the store, I bought some eggs.

Reduce to one clause with a compound verb: If both clauses have the same subject, remove the subject from the second clause, and you now have just one clause with a compound verb.

Example:

> **Incorrect**: The drive to New York takes ten hours, it makes me very tired.
>
> **Corrected**: The drive to New York takes ten hours and makes me very tired.

Note: While these are the simplest ways to correct a run-on sentence, often the best way is to completely reorganize the thoughts in the sentence and rewrite it.

COMMA SPLICES

A comma splice is a specific error that may appear in a run-on sentence. When a sentence has two independent clauses, but the clauses are joined with only a comma, a **comma splice** is formed. Remember that if two independent clauses are joined with a comma, a coordinating conjunction is also needed. Most of the solutions for fixing run-on sentences can also be used to correct a comma splice.

Review Video: Fragments and Run-on Sentences
Visit mometrix.com/academy and enter code: 541989

EXAMPLE

Rick wants to go see a movie tomorrow he would miss his sister's recital.

Identify the change that would NOT correct this run-on sentence.

a. Add a comma after *tomorrow.*
b. Split it into two sentences between *tomorrow* and *he.*
c. Add a comma and *but* after *tomorrow.*
d. Add a subordinating conjunction to make one of the clauses dependent.

Choice A says to add a comma after *tomorrow.* This forms the following sentence: Rick wants to go see a movie tomorrow, he would miss his sister's recital. A comma has been used to join two independent clauses, but there is no coordinating conjunction. This choice forms a comma splice, so it is not an acceptable correction for this sentence. Choice A is the correct answer.

Choice B says to split the sentence into two sentences. This forms the following two sentences: Rick wants to go see a movie tomorrow. He would miss his sister's recital. Both of these sentences are complete. This is an acceptable way to correct the run-on sentence, so choice B is incorrect.

Choice C says to add a coordinating conjunction after *tomorrow.* This forms the following sentence: Rick wants to go see a movie tomorrow, but he would miss his sister's recital. A comma and a coordinating conjunction have been added between the two independent clauses. This is an acceptable way to correct a run-on sentence. Choice C is incorrect.

Choice D says to add a subordinating conjunction to make one of the sentences dependent. There are many new sentences that could be created by adding a subordinating conjunction. For example, consider the following sentence: Although Rick wants to go see a movie tomorrow, he would miss his sister's recital. Alternatively, the following sentence could also be created: Rick wants to go see a movie tomorrow even though he would miss his sister's recital. Both of these sentences have an independent clause and a dependent clause. These sentences are both complete and written correctly, so choice D is incorrect.

EXAMPLE

Identify the sentence that has a comma splice.

a. Tom stopped at the store to buy supplies and his family met him at the campsite.
b. The ball rolled into the living room quietly, but it still startled the dog.
c. Theresa brought her mom some flowers, her mom did not have a vase.
d. Sweet potatoes, pecans, and brown sugar are all ingredients in my cousin's sweet potato casserole.

Choice A has two independent clauses joined by a coordinating conjunction. This is incorrect because there should be a comma before the coordinating conjunction. While the sentence is written incorrectly, there is no comma, so this sentence does not have a comma splice. Choice A is incorrect.

Choice B has two independent clauses joined by a comma and a coordinating conjunction. This is the correct way to write a compound sentence, so there is no error here. Choice B is incorrect.

Choice C has two independent clauses joined by a comma. This is incorrect because independent clauses should be joined together by a comma and a coordinating conjunction. When the comma is present without a coordinating conjunction between two independent clauses, a comma splice is formed. This means that choice C is correct.

Choice D is a simple sentence that contains one independent clause. The only commas used in this sentence are used to separate items in a list. There are no clauses that need to be joined or errors related to commas, so choice D does not contain a comma splice. Choice D is incorrect.

THE EIGHT PARTS OF SPEECH

NOUNS

When you talk about a person, place, thing, or idea, you are talking about a **noun**. The two main types of nouns are **common** and **proper** nouns.

COMMON NOUNS

Common nouns are generic names for people, places, and things. Common nouns are not usually capitalized.

Examples of common nouns:

> *People*: boy, girl, worker, manager
>
> *Places*: school, bank, library, home
>
> *Things*: dog, cat, truck, car

PROPER NOUNS

Proper nouns name specific people, places, or things. All proper nouns are capitalized.

Examples of proper nouns:

> *People*: Abraham Lincoln, George Washington, Martin Luther King, Jr.
>
> *Places*: Los Angeles, California; New York; Asia
>
> *Things*: Statue of Liberty, Earth, Lincoln Memorial

Note: When referring to the planet that we live on, capitalize *Earth*. When referring to the dirt, rocks, or land, lowercase *earth*.

SINGULAR AND PLURAL NOUNS

Singular nouns name **one** person, place, thing, or idea. **Plural nouns** name **more than one** person, place, thing, or idea. Most nouns have both a singular and plural form. Many plural nouns are spelled like the singular noun with an *-s* at the end, but this is not true for all plural nouns. Singular nouns that already end in an *s*, *o*, *ch*, *sh*, or *x* usually end in *-es* when they are in the plural form. Singular nouns that end in a consonant followed by the letter *y* will usually lose the *y* and end in *-ies* in the plural form, and words that end with the letter *f* or *fe* will usually lose the *f* and end in *-ves*.

Some plural nouns have much different spellings than their singular form, and some plural nouns are spelled the same as their singular form. There are more rules for spelling plural nouns, but these are the most common spelling changes.

Examples of singular nouns:

> Typical nouns: dog, pencil, girl, store, hope, stingray
>
> Nouns ending in *s*, *o*, *ch*, *sh*, or *x*: mass, hero, lunch, polish, fox
>
> Nouns ending in a consonant and *y*: puppy, baby, fairy, sky
>
> Nouns ending in *f* or *fe*: self, life, calf, hoof

Examples of plural nouns:

> Typical nouns: dogs, pencils, girls, stores, hopes, stingrays

Nouns ending in *s, o, ch, sh*, or *x*: masses, heroes, lunches, polishes, foxes

Nouns ending in a consonant and *y*: puppies, babies, fairies, skies

Nouns ending in a vowel and *f* or *fe*: selves, lives, calves, hooves

COLLECTIVE NOUNS

Collective nouns are the names for a group of people, places, or things that function like singular nouns. The following are examples of collective nouns: *class, company, dozen, group, herd, team,* and *public*. Collective nouns usually require an article, such as *a, an*, and *the*, which shows that the noun is a single unit. For example, a choir is a group of singers. Even though there are many singers in a choir, the word choir describes a single group. If we refer to the members of the group, and not the group itself, it is no longer a collective noun.

Incorrect: The *choir are* going to compete nationally this year.

Correct: The *choir is* going to compete nationally this year.

Incorrect: The *members* of the choir *is* competing nationally this year.

Correct: The *members* of the choir *are* competing nationally this year.

PRONOUNS

Pronouns are words that are used to stand in for nouns. There are several different types of pronouns, but the two main types are subjective and objective pronouns. **Subjective** nouns and pronouns that those that are the subject of a sentence. **Objective** nouns and pronouns are those that are an object in a sentence. Another important type of pronoun is the personal pronoun, which refers to people. Personal pronouns can be subjective or objective. **Possessive** nouns and pronouns show possession or ownership. Pronouns can also be singular or plural.

Singular

Subjective	Objective	Possessive
I	Me	My, Mine
You	You	Your, Yours
He	Him	His
She	Her	Her, hers
It	It	Its
Who	Whom	Whose

Plural

Subjective	Objective	Possessive
we	us	our, ours
you	you	your, yours
they	them	their, theirs

Reflexive: Reflexive pronouns are pronouns that function as the object of a sentence and refer to the subject. Examples of reflexive pronouns include *myself, yourself, himself, herself, itself, ourselves, yourselves*, and *themselves*.

Indefinite: Indefinite pronouns are used to refer to multiple nouns or an undefined noun. Examples of indefinite nouns include *all, any, each, everyone, either/neither, one, some*, and *several*.

Relative: Relative pronouns are used to connect relative clauses that specify or describe a noun to the rest of the sentence. Examples of relative pronouns include *which*, *who*, *whom*, and *whose*.

Review Video: Nouns and Pronouns
Visit mometrix.com/academy and enter code: 312073

VERBS

If you want to write a sentence, then you need a verb. Without a verb, you have no sentence. The verb of a sentence indicates action or being. In other words, the verb shows something's action or state of being or the action that has been done to something.

TRANSITIVE AND INTRANSITIVE VERBS

A **transitive verb** is a verb whose action (e.g., drive, run, jump) indicates a receiver (e.g., car, dog, kangaroo). **Intransitive verbs** do not indicate a receiver of an action. In other words, the action of the verb does not point to a subject or object.

> **Transitive**: He plays the piano. | The piano was played by him.
>
> **Intransitive**: He plays. | John plays well.

ACTION VERBS AND LINKING VERBS

Action verbs show what the subject is doing. In other words, an action verb shows action. **Linking verbs** link the subject of a sentence to a noun or pronoun. They can also link a subject to an adjective, so the linking verb helps create a description. You always need a verb if you want a complete sentence. However, linking verbs on their own cannot be a complete sentence. Any verb that shows a condition and connects to a noun, pronoun, or adjective that describes the subject of a sentence is a linking verb.

Action: He sings. | Run! | Go! | I talk with him every day. | She reads.

Linking:

> Incorrect: I am.
>
> Correct: I am John. | I smell roses. | I feel tired.

Review Video: Action Verbs and Linking Verbs
Visit mometrix.com/academy and enter code: 743142

VOICE

Transitive verbs come in active or passive **voice**. If something does an action or is acted upon, then you will know whether a verb is active or passive. When the subject of the sentence is doing the action, the verb is in **active voice**. When the subject is acted upon, the verb is in **passive voice**.

> **Active**: Jon drew the picture. (The subject *Jon* is doing the action of *drawing a picture*.)
>
> **Passive**: The picture is drawn by Jon. (The subject *picture* is receiving the action from Jon.)

EXAMPLE

Which of the following sentences is written in passive voice?

a. The alligator quickly swam through the swamp.
b. She dug up the hidden treasure.
c. The vase was painted by an artist.
d. The bag held many apples.

In choice A, the subject is *alligator*, the verb is *swam*, and the object is *swamp*. Did the subject or the object do the action in this sentence? The alligator swam and acted upon the swamp. The subject did the action, so choice A is in active voice.

In choice B, the subject is *she*, the verb is *dug*, and the object is *hidden treasure*. Did the subject or the object do the action? She dug and acted upon the hidden treasure. The subject did the action, so choice B is in active voice.

In choice C, the subject is *vase*, the verb is *was painted*, and the object is *artist*. Did the subject or the object do the action? The vase simply existed. The painter painted and acted upon the vase. The object did the action, so choice C is in passive voice. Choice C is correct.

In choice D, the subject is *bag*, the verb is *held*, and the object is *apples*. Did the subject or the object do the action? The bag held and acted upon the apples. The subject did the action, so choice D is in active voice.

Verb Tenses

A verb **tense** shows the different form of a verb to point to the time of an action. The present and past tense are indicated by the verb's form. An action in the present, *I talk,* can change form for the past: *I talked.* However, for future tense, an auxiliary, or helping, verb is sometimes needed to show the change in form. When writing a composition, it is important to use verb tenses consistently. Choose the best tense for the composition and do not switch to a different tense unless it is necessary or appropriate for a particular sentence or paragraph.

Present: I talk
Past: I talked
Future: I will talk

Present: The action happens at the current time.

Example: He *walks* to the store every morning.

Past: The action happened in the past.

Example: He *walked* to the store an hour ago.

Future: The action is going to happen later.

Example: I *will walk* to the store tomorrow.

Review Video: Verb Tenses
Visit mometrix.com/academy and enter code: 269472

Irregular Verbs

While most verbs gain the suffix -ed when used in the past tense, irregular verbs receive different spelling changes when they are written in the past tense. For example, *walk* is a regular verb, and it becomes *walked* when written in the past tense. However, *run* is an irregular verb because it becomes *ran* when written in the past tense.

Example

My mother _____ me about the big nest of ants near the sandbox. I thanked her for telling me!

Which of the following verbs should go in the blank?

a. Warn
b. Warned
c. Will warn
d. Warns

First, look at the sentences. The first sentence does not have enough information to show which tense it is in. However, the second sentence says that the child thanked the mother. The verb here is *thanked*, which is the past-tense form of *thank*. Because the second sentence is in the past tense, it makes sense to say that the first sentence is also in past tense.

Choice A says that the missing verb is *warn. Warn* is a present-tense verb, but it can be used in the future tense if a helping verb is present. However, this sentence is in past tense, so it needs a past-tense verb. Choice A is wrong.

Choice B says that the missing verb is *warned. Warned* is a past-tense verb, and it logically completes the sentence. Choice B is correct!

Choice C says that the missing verb is *will warn. Will warn* is a future-tense verb, meaning that it describes an action that will occur in the future. However, since the speaker already thanked his or her mother for the warning, it is not logical to use a future-tense verb in the blank. Choice C is incorrect.

Choice D says that the missing verb is *warns. Warn* is usually used with plural subjects, and *warns* used with single subjects. *Warns* can be used in the future or present tense, but it cannot be used in the past tense. Since the sentence is in the past tense, it needs a past-tense verb, so D is incorrect.

Adjectives

An **adjective** is a word that is used to modify a noun or pronoun. An adjective answers a question: *Which one? What kind?* or *How many?* Usually, adjectives come before the words that they modify, but they may also come after a linking verb.

Which one? The *third* suit is my favorite.

What kind? This suit is *navy blue.*

How many? I am going to buy *four* pairs of socks to match the suit.

Review Video: Descriptive Text
Visit mometrix.com/academy and enter code: 174903

Comparison with Adjectives

Some adjectives are relative, and other adjectives are absolute. Adjectives that are **relative** can show the comparison between things. **Absolute** adjectives can also show comparison, but they do so in a different way. Let's say that you are reading two books. You think that one book is perfect, and the other book is not exactly perfect. It is not possible for one book to be more perfect than the other. Either you think that the book is perfect, or you think that the book is imperfect. In this case, perfect and imperfect are absolute adjectives.

Relative adjectives will show the different **degrees** of something or someone to something else or someone else. The three degrees of adjectives include positive, comparative, and superlative.

The **positive** degree is the normal form of an adjective.

Example: This work is *difficult*. | She is *smart*.

The **comparative** degree compares one person or thing to another person or thing.

Example: This work is *more difficult* than your work. | She is *smarter* than me.

The **superlative** degree compares more than two people or things.

Example: This is the *most difficult* work of my life. | She is the *smartest* lady in school.

Review Video: Adjectives
Visit mometrix.com/academy and enter code: 470154

Adverbs

An **adverb** is a word that is used to **modify,** or describe, a verb, adjective, or another adverb. Usually, adverbs answer one of these questions: *When? Where? How?* and *Why?* The negatives *not* and *never* are considered adverbs. Adverbs that modify adjectives or other adverbs **strengthen** or **weaken** the words that they modify.

Examples:

He walks *quickly* through the crowd.

The water flows *smoothly* on the rocks.

Note: Adverbs are usually indicated by the suffix *-ly*, which has been added to the root word. For instance, *quick* can be made into an adverb by adding *-ly* to construct *quickly*. Some words that end in *-ly* do not follow this rule and can function as other parts of speech. Examples of adjectives ending in *-ly* include: *early, friendly, holy, lonely, silly,* and *ugly*. To know if a word that ends in *-ly* is an adjective or adverb, check your dictionary. Also, while many adverbs end in *-ly*, you need to remember that not all adverbs end in *-ly*.

Examples:

He is *never* angry.

You are *too* irresponsible to travel alone.

Types of Adverbs

Different types of adverbs are used to describe particular aspects of a verb, adjective, or other adverb. The following are examples of common types of adverbs:

Time: Some adverbs show when something was done, such as *yesterday*, *today*, or *in two days*.

Manner: Some adverbs show the way something was done, such as *hurriedly*, *neatly*, *grumpily*, or *loudly*.

Frequency: Some adverbs show how often something was done, such as *seldom*, *often*, *never*, or *often*.

Degree: Some adverbs show how much or to what degree something was done, such as *completely*, *barely*, *highly*, or *halfway*.

Conjunctive: Conjunctive adverbs are used similarly to conjunctions, as they connect different ideas, but they can connect ideas from different clauses or sentences. Some examples of conjunctive adverbs are *however*, *alternatively*, *likewise*, and *then*.

Comparison with Adverbs

The rules for comparing adverbs are the same as the rules for adjectives.

The **positive** degree is the standard form of an adverb.

> Example: He arrives *soon.* | She speaks *softly* to her friends.

The **comparative** degree compares one person or thing to another person or thing.

> Example: He arrives *sooner* than Sarah. | She speaks *more softly* than him.

The **superlative** degree compares more than two people or things.

> Example: He arrives *soonest* of the group. | She speaks the *most softly* of any of her friends.

Review Video: Adverbs
Visit mometrix.com/academy and enter code: 713951

Prepositions

A **preposition** is a word placed before a noun or pronoun that shows the relationship between an object and another word in the sentence.

Common prepositions:

about	before	during	on	under
after	beneath	for	over	until
against	between	from	past	up
among	beyond	in	through	with
around	by	of	to	within
at	down	off	toward	without

Examples:

> The napkin is *in* the drawer.
>
> The Earth rotates *around* the Sun.
>
> The needle is *beneath* the haystack.
>
> Can you find "me" *among* the words?

Prepositional Phrases

One important thing to know about prepositions is that they form special phrases, called prepositional phrases. A **prepositional phrase** begins with a preposition and ends with a noun or pronoun that is the object of the preposition. Normally, the prepositional phrase functions as an **adjective** or an **adverb** within the sentence.

Examples:

> prepositional phrase
> The picnic is on the blanket
>
> prepositional phrase
> I am sick with a fever today.

prepositional phrase

Among the many flowers, John found a four-leaf clover.

Be careful not to mistake the object in a prepositional phrase as the subject of a sentence. The subject of the sentence will not be found in a prepositional phrase because a prepositional phrase is used to describe how an object is related to the subject. Prepositional phrases do not influence subject-verb agreement.

Review Video: Prepositions
Visit mometrix.com/academy and enter code: 946763

Example

Which of the following could NOT complete the sentence?

She went ____ the cave.

a. Sadly
b. Into
c. From
d. Through

Choice A says that the missing word is *sadly*. The blank is between *went* and *the cave*, meaning that the missing word will connect these pieces of the sentence. While *sadly* could be used here to show how the girl felt, there would still be missing information. A preposition is needed here to show whether she entered, exited, or stood outside of the cave. *Sadly* is an adverb, so A is the correct answer.

Choice B says that *into* would complete the sentence. Does *into* complete the sentence without leaving missing information? To say *she went into the cave* is a logical, complete sentence. Choice B is incorrect.

Choice C says that the missing word is *from*. This creates the sentence *she went from the cave*. Since she could have left the cave to go somewhere else, this is also a logical, complete sentence. Choice C is incorrect.

Choice D says that *through* would complete the sentence. The sentence would read *she went through the cave*. Since she could have explored the whole cave or found an exit on the other side of it, *through* can logically complete the sentence. Choice D is incorrect.

Example

Identify the prepositional phrase in the following sentence.

Mable visited the store to buy some vegetables.

a. To buy
b. Visited the store
c. The store to buy
d. To buy some vegetables

Remember the pieces of a prepositional phrase. Prepositional phrases should begin with a preposition and end with a noun or pronoun. Considering these rules, can any of the answer choices be eliminated? Choice B and choice C can be eliminated because neither choice begins with a preposition!

That leaves choices A and D. Choice A says that the prepositional phrase is *to buy*. This does start with a preposition, and it does give more information about Mable's trip to the store. However, it does not end with a noun or pronoun. Choice D says that the prepositional phrase is *to buy some vegetables*. Choice D begins with a preposition and ends with a noun, and it explains why Mabel went to the store.

Choice D is the only choice that has all of the pieces of a prepositional phrase, so D is correct!

Example

A band with 15 members _____ performing at my restaurant tonight.

Identify the verb that best completes the sentence.

a. Were
b. Is
c. Are
d. Are not

This question is asking which verb should go in the blank. There are a couple of reasons why choosing the correct verb for this sentence may be confusing. First of all, there are two nouns that appear before the verb. Second, one of these nouns is singular and one is plural.

The first step is to determine which noun goes with the verb. The two nouns are *band* and *members*. While *members* is closest to the blank, it is part of a prepositional phrase that describes *band*. The subject of the sentence is *band*, so the verb must agree with *band*.

Is *band* singular or plural? The sentence says that the band has multiple members, but there is only one band. *Band* is a collective noun, meaning that it is a singular noun. This means that the correct verb will also be singular. With this in mind, can any of the answer choices be eliminated?

Choices A, C, and D are all plural verbs. Even though the blank appears after a plural noun, this noun is part of a prepositional phrase. The verb should match the singular subject *band*. The only choice with a singular verb is choice B, so B is the correct answer.

Conjunctions

Conjunctions join words, phrases, or clauses and they show the connection between the joined pieces. **Coordinating conjunctions** connect equal parts of sentences. Coordinating conjunctions can also be used to create compound subjects and compound predicates, in addition to compound sentences.

Coordinating Conjunctions

The **coordinating conjunctions** include: *and, but, yet, or, nor, for,* and *so*

Compound Subjects:

compound subject

Terry *and* Marissa went to the movies last Saturday.

compund subject

Either pumpkin pie *or* apple pie would be a good dessert to bring to Thanksgiving dinner.

compound subject

Neither the clownfish *nor* the goldfish liked the new fish food very much.

Compound Predicates:

compound predicate

Veronica left school *and* picked up her sister from soccer practice.

compound predicate

The cat did not take a nap *or* play with the dog yesterday.

Compound Sentences:

The rock was small, *but* it was heavy.

She drove in the night, *and* he drove in the day.

Bill dressed nicely today, *for* he must give an important presentation this afternoon.

Correlative Conjunctions

Some examples of **correlative conjunctions** are: *either...or* | *neither...nor* | *not only...but also.* When one correlative conjunction is used, its matching correlative conjunction will be used later in the sentence.

Examples:

Either you are coming *or* you are staying.

He *not only* ran three miles *but also* swam 200 yards.

Review Video: Coordinating and Correlative Conjunctions
Visit mometrix.com/academy and enter code: 390329

Subordinating Conjunctions

Subordinating conjunctions link dependent clauses, clauses with either a subject or a predicate, to independent clauses, clauses with both a subject and a predicate, to form a complex sentence. The subordinating conjunction will always be at the beginning of the dependent clause. When the dependent clause is at the beginning of the sentence, it will end with a comma. When the independent clause is at the beginning of the sentence, no comma is needed.

Common **subordinating conjunctions** include:

after	since	whenever
although	so that	where
because	unless	wherever
before	until	whether
in order that	when	while

Examples:

I am hungry *because* I did not eat breakfast.

He went home *when* everyone left.

While her brother ate dinner, she played his favorite video game.

Review Video: Subordinating Conjunctions
Visit mometrix.com/academy and enter code: 958913

End Punctuation

Periods

Use a period to end all sentences except direct questions and exclamations. Periods are also used for abbreviations.

Examples: 3 p.m. | 2 a.m. | Mr. Jones | Mrs. Stevens | Dr. Smith | Bill, Jr. | Pennsylvania Ave.

Note: An abbreviation is a shortened form of a word or phrase.

Question Marks

Question marks should be used following a **direct question**. A polite request can be followed by a period instead of a question mark.

Direct Question: What is for lunch today? | How are you? | Why is that the answer?

Polite Requests: Can you please send me the item tomorrow. | Will you please walk with me on the track.

Review Video: Question Marks
Visit mometrix.com/academy and enter code: 118471

Exclamation Marks

Exclamation marks are used after a word group or sentence that shows much feeling or has special importance. Exclamation marks should not be overused. They are saved for proper **exclamatory interjections**.

Example: We're going to the finals! | You have a beautiful car! | "That's crazy!" she yelled.

Review Video: Exclamation Points
Visit mometrix.com/academy and enter code: 199367

Commas

The comma is a punctuation mark that can help you understand connections in a sentence. Not every sentence needs a comma. However, if a sentence needs a comma, you need to put it in the right place. A comma in the wrong place or a missing comma will make a sentence's meaning unclear. These are some of the rules for commas:

Use Case	Example
Before a **coordinating conjunction** joining independent clauses in compound sentences	Bob caught three fish, and I caught two fish.
Between **items in a series**	I will bring the turkey, the pie, and the coffee.
After a **dependent clause** that **begins a complex sentence**	Before she left, Ashley turned off all of the lights in her house.
After **transition words**	Consequently, Joel's mother grounded him.
After an **introductory phrase**	After the final out, we went to a restaurant to celebrate.
After a **prepositional phrase** at the **beginning of a sentence**	At 10 in the evening, Georgia finally arrived home from work.
After an **adverbial clause**	Studying the stars, I was awed by the beauty of the sky.
Before and after **nonessential modifiers**	John Frank, who coaches the team, was promoted today.
Before and after **nonessential appositives**	Thomas Edison, an American inventor, was born in Ohio.
Before and after **nonrestrictive phrases** or **clauses**	His favorite movie, which premiered before he was born, is over three hours long.
After **absolute phrases**	Relieved the test was over, Leah dropped her pencil and slouched in her chair.

Commas for Setting Off Nonessential Words, Phrases, and Clauses

Identifying where to place commas for nonessential words, phrases, and clauses is sometimes tricky. If the word, phrase, or clause is necessary for the sentence to be complete or logical, then it is essential, or restrictive. Additionally, if the word, phrase, or clause cannot be removed without changing the meaning of the sentence, then it is essential. Nonessential words, phrases, and clauses are those that give unnecessary information or do not flow smoothly with the rest of the words in the sentence. These words usually can also be logically placed in more than one spot in the sentence. **Appositives** are often nonessential words or phrases. They are most often used to specify which person or thing is being discussed. An appositive is an additional name or description that may be essential or nonessential.

Review Video: When To Use a Comma
Visit mometrix.com/academy and enter code: 786797

Example

The singer growing more exhausted with every song decided to stop dancing and stood still while singing.

Identify the nonrestrictive phrase that should be set off by commas in the above sentence.

a. The singer growing more exhausted
b. Decided to stop dancing
c. Growing more exhausted with every song
d. Stop dancing and stood still

Choice A says that *the singer growing more exhausted* is the nonrestrictive phrase. Is the sentence still a complete sentence without this phrase? No, because choice A includes the subject, *the singer*. Choice A is not the nonrestrictive phrase.

Choice B says that *decided to stop dancing* is the nonrestrictive phrase. Does the sentence make sense without this phrase? No, removing this phrase leaves the following sentence: The singer growing more exhausted with every song and stood still while singing. This is not a logical sentence, so choice B is not the nonrestrictive phrase.

Choice C says that *growing more exhausted with every song* is the nonrestrictive phrase. Removing this phrase leaves the following sentence: The singer decided to stop dancing and stood still while singing. This sentence makes sense and has the same meaning as the original sentence. This phrase gives extra information that is not essential to the sentence, so choice C is the nonrestrictive phrase. Choice C is correct.

Choice D says that *stop dancing and stood still* is the nonrestrictive phrase. Removing this phrase leaves the following sentence: The singer growing more exhausted with every song decided to while singing. This sentence is now missing important information. What did the singer decide to do while singing? The remaining sentence is now missing the verb. Removing choice D makes the sentence incomplete, so choice D is not the nonrestrictive phrase.

EXAMPLE

My friends found a stray cat, which is white and brown and brought it to my house.

Identify the best place for an additional comma in the sentence above?

a. After *friends*
b. After *white*
c. After *brown*
d. After *it*

Choice A says another comma should be added after *friends*. This would set off *found a stray cat*. Can this information be removed from the sentence? No, because the sentence would not make sense without this information. The phrase tells what the friends found. Choice A is incorrect.

Choice B says another comma should be added after *white*. This would set off *which is white*. These words cannot be removed from the sentence because the remaining sentence is not logical. Choice B is incorrect.

Choice C says another comma should be added after *brown*. This would set off the clause *which is white and brown*. Can this information be removed from the sentence? Yes, it can! This information is not necessary for the sentence to make sense, and it does not flow with the rest of the sentence. When this information is removed, the remaining sentence is logical and complete, and it flows well. Choice C is correct.

Choice D says another comma should be added after *it*. This would set off *which is white and brown and brought it*. These words cannot be removed from the sentence because the remaining words do not form a logical sentence. Choice D is incorrect.

SEMICOLONS

The semicolon is used to connect major sentence pieces of equal value. Some rules for semicolons include:

Use Case	Example
Between closely connected independent clauses **not connected with a coordinating conjunction**	You are right; we should go with your plan.
Between independent clauses **linked with a transitional word**	I think that we can agree on this; however, I am not sure about my friends.
Between items in a **series that has internal punctuation**	I have visited New York, New York; Augusta, Maine; and Baltimore, Maryland.

Review Video: How to Use Semicolons
Visit mometrix.com/academy and enter code: 370605

EXAMPLE

Which of the following sentences is NOT written correctly?

a. My sister burned the lasagna we were going to eat for dinner; we went out to eat instead of cooking something else.
b. The ball rolled into the ditch, therefore, it was muddy and wet when he retrieved it.
c. She has lived in many cities, including Nashville, Tennessee; San Diego, California; and Salt Lake City, Utah.
d. He hung the picture in the wrong spot; now there is a distracting hole in the wall.

Choice A is a compound sentence. The semicolon is used to separate two independent clauses. There is no coordinating conjunction in the sentence. This sentence correctly uses a semicolon, so choice A is incorrect.

Choice B is a compound sentence. In a compound sentence, either a coordinating conjunction or a semicolon can be used to separate the independent clauses. This sentence includes a transitional word, but it uses neither a semicolon nor a coordinating conjunction. To revise this sentence, *therefore* can be replaced by a coordinating conjunction, or the first comma can be replaced with a semicolon This sentence is written incorrectly, so choice B is the correct answer.

Choice C is a sentence that includes a list. Remember that semicolons can be used to separate items in a list when at least one of the items includes a comma. In this sentence, a list of cities is given. Since a comma is required to separate the name of a city from the name of the state it is in, each of the items in the list contain a comma. This means that each full city name must be separated by a semicolon. This sentence is written correctly, so choice C is incorrect.

Choice D is a compound sentence and does not contain a coordinating conjunction. Semicolons can be used to separate independent clauses in a compound sentence instead of a coordinating conjunction. This sentence uses a semicolon correctly, so choice D is incorrect.

COLONS

The colon is used to call attention to the words that follow it. A colon must come after a **complete independent clause**. The rules for colons are as follows:

Use Case	Example
After an independent clause to **make a list**	I want to learn many languages: Spanish, German, and Italian.
For **explanations**	There is one thing that stands out on your resume: responsibility.
To give a **quote**	He started with an idea: "We are able to do more than we imagine."
After the **greeting in a formal letter**	To Whom It May Concern:
Show **hours and minutes**	It is 3:14 p.m.
Separate a **title and subtitle**	The essay is titled "America: A Short Introduction to a Modern Country."

Review Video: Using Colons
Visit mometrix.com/academy and enter code: 868673

EXAMPLE

Which of the following sentences does NOT use a colon correctly?

a. Your reports must be submitted by 10:30 p.m.
b. Terrence: his best friend, is graduating from college on Saturday.
c. Shelly had three tasks to complete before her mother returned: empty the dishwasher, walk the dog, and tidy the living room.
d. Brian was excited to write a report over his favorite book: *Frankenstein*.

Choice A uses a colon to separate the hour from the minute. Colons are necessary when writing hours and minutes. This colon is used correctly and is in the right place, so choice A is incorrect.

Choice B uses a colon to separate a nonessential appositive. This is not an acceptable use for a colon because it is not used in a time, and it does not follow an independent clause. Also, nonessential appositives that appear in the middle of a sentence should only be set off by commas. This is an incorrect use for a colon, so choice B is the correct answer.

Choice C uses a colon to separate an independent clause from a list. This is an acceptable use for a colon. This colon is appropriately used and is in the right place, so choice C is incorrect.

Choice D uses a colon for explanation. This is an acceptable use for a colon when the word, phrase, or clause being separated follows an independent clause. The independent clause should also introduce, or describe, the information following the colon. Choice D correctly uses a colon, so it is incorrect.

PARENTHESES

Parentheses are used for additional information. Also, they can be used to put labels for letters or numbers in a series. Parentheses should not be used very often. If they are overused, parentheses can be a distraction instead of a help.

Examples:

Extra Information: The rattlesnake (see Image 2) is a dangerous snake of North and South America.

Series: Include in the email (1) your name, (2) your address, and (3) your question for the author.

Review Video: Parentheses
Visit mometrix.com/academy and enter code: 947743

EXAMPLE

Which of the following CANNOT be set off by parentheses?

a. A short list of examples
b. A reference to a graph or chart that is relevant to the text
c. An essential phrase in a sentence
d. A number used to label an item in a series

Remember that parentheses are used to set off extra information from the rest of the sentence. Extra words set off by parentheses are often not meant to be read with the rest of the sentence in the same way as words set off by commas. Usually, the words in parenthesis do not impact the meaning of the other words in the sentence. Instead, they can include additional information that is relevant to the sentence or guide the reader to that information.

Choice A says that parentheses cannot be used to set off a short list of examples. Examples are used to elaborate on information and help the reader better understand it. Examples often do not impact the meaning of the sentence. When there are only a few examples and they do not affect the sentence's meaning, they can be set off by parentheses.

Choice B says that parentheses cannot be used to set off a reference to a graph or chart. References like these are used to lead the reader to look at a graph or chart so he or she will see important information. This keeps the writer from placing the image in between sections of text. When references are in parentheses, they are not meant to impact the meaning of the sentence. References to graphs and charts can be set off by parentheses.

Choice C says that parentheses cannot be used to set off essential phrases in a sentence. When a phrase is essential to a sentence, it should not be set off by any punctuation marks. Essential phrases cannot be set off by parentheses, so choice C is correct.

Choice D says that parentheses cannot be used to set off numbers used as labels. Sometimes, when a list appears in a sentence, the items may be referred to in a different location. In these cases, it can be helpful when the items are labeled. The labels are meant to guide the readers to the information, not to change the meaning of the sentence. Numbers used to label items in a series can be set off by parentheses.

Quotation Marks

Use quotation marks to close off **direct quotations** of a person's written or spoken words, which are also called **dialogue**. Do not use quotation marks around indirect quotations. An indirect quotation gives someone's message without using the person's exact words. Use **single quotation marks** to close off a quotation inside a quotation.

> **Direct Quote**: Nancy said, "I am waiting for Henry to arrive."
>
> **Indirect Quote**: Henry said that he is going to be late to the meeting.
>
> **Quote inside a Quote**: The teacher asked, "Has everyone read Martin Luther King's 'I Have a Dream' speech?"

Quotation marks should be used around the titles of **short works**: newspaper and magazine articles, poems, short stories, songs, television episodes, and radio programs. Titles of **long works** should be italicized when they are part of a typed composition or underlined when they are part of a handwritten composition.

Examples:

> "Rip Van Winkle" (short story by Washington Irving)
>
> "O Captain! My Captain!" (poem by Walt Whitman)

Review Video: Quotation Marks
Visit mometrix.com/academy and enter code: 884918

APOSTROPHES

An apostrophe is used to show **possession** or the **deletion of letters in contractions**. An apostrophe is not needed with the possessive pronouns *his, hers, its, ours, theirs, whose*, and *yours*.

Singular Nouns: David's car | a book's theme | my brother's board game

Plural Nouns that end with -*s*: the scissors' handle | boys' basketball

Plural Nouns that end without -*s*: Men's department | the people's adventure

Review Video: Apostrophes
Visit mometrix.com/academy and enter code: 213068

Review Video: Punctuation Errors in Possessive Pronouns
Visit mometrix.com/academy and enter code: 221438

APOSTROPHES IN CONTRACTIONS

Contractions are combinations of words. Contractions involve taking two words, removing at least one letter from one of the words, putting an apostrophe in its place, and removing the space. For example, *does not* can be written as the contraction *doesn't*. The *o* is removed from *not* and is replaced with an apostrophe, which represents the removed letter, so it appears as *n't*. The space after does is then removed, turning *does not* into the contraction *doesn't*. Some more examples of contractions are listed below.

First Word	Second Word	Contraction
Can	Not	Can't
Do	Not	Don't
She	Will	She'll
They	Will	They'll
He	Is	He's
It	Is	It's
They	Are	They're
I	Am	I'm

Not all words can be used to form contractions, but many small, commonly used words can.

CAPITALIZATION

One important part of using correct grammar is properly capitalizing words. Usually, only nouns will be capitalized, but there are some exceptions. The most important capitalization rule is that the first word of every sentence, no matter what part of speech it is, should be capitalized. Another exception is that the pronoun *I* should always be capitalized.

Proper nouns are always capitalized, but sometimes it can be tricky to decide whether or not a noun is a proper noun. Some words that are usually common nouns may become proper nouns when used with other words or phrases. Also, when words that are not nouns are used with a noun, or when a group of words are used together as one noun, those words may also need to be capitalized.

TITLES OF BOOKS, STORIES, AND ESSAYS

Most of the words in titles of things like books, stories, and essays should be capitalized, but some should not. The very first word in a title should always be capitalized. Any other word in a title that is a noun, pronoun, adjective, verb or adverb should be capitalized. Articles, such as *a* or *the*, should not be capitalized. Short conjunctions and prepositions are usually not capitalized.

ABBREVIATIONS, INITIALS, AND ACRONYMS

Abbreviations are shortened versions of other words. When an abbreviation shortens, or abbreviates, a word that should be capitalized, the abbreviation's first letter should also be capitalized. When the shortened word is a noun that is not capitalized, the abbreviation should be in lowercase. Initials are usually written using the first letter from multiple words. For example, John Fitzgerald Kennedy is commonly referred to by his initials, JFK. Acronyms also use the first letter from multiple words, but they are different from initials because they form words on their own. For example, NASA is an acronym for National Aeronautics and Space Administration. Some acronyms, like NASA, omit small words, such as *and*, *of*, and *for*. When initials and acronyms are used for proper nouns, each letter should be capitalized.

The types of words and phrases in the chart below are proper nouns and should always be capitalized:

	Description	Example
Historical Periods	A range of time in history that is related to specific events or circumstances	During the Romantic Period, many authors and poets wrote about their emotions.
Historical Events	Names of important events that happened in history	Napoleon Bonaparte led France after the French Revolution.
Historical Documents	Titles of important papers or compositions that are connected to historical events	The Mayflower Compact was written to create rules and expectations for the colony in Plymouth.
Languages	Names of the different languages that people speak	I want to learn to speak Cantonese, Spanish, and German.
Races and Ethnicities	Words often used to describe a person's heritage or cultural group	Malia taught her granddaughter how to hula so she could share a tradition of her Native Hawaiian heritage with her.
Nationalities	Words that describe which country a person is from	My teacher who moved to Canada last year is Romanian.
Organizations	Titles of official groups formed by people	Fewer than half of the states in America have a team in the National Basketball Association.

EXAMPLE

> Allison and Claire enjoy studying art from the beginning of the renaissance. They started a club so they and other students can learn more about it. Allison and Claire named the club Early Renaissance Art Club, which can be abbreviated to ERA Club. The students that joined elected Claire as the president and Allison as the vice president. The club's first meeting will take place after Christmas vacation.

Which of the following changes should be made in the passage?

a. In the first sentence, *Renaissance* should be capitalized.
b. In the third sentence, *ERA* should be written as *Era*.
c. In the fourth sentence, *president* and *vice president* should be capitalized.
d. In the last sentence, *Christmas* should be in lowercase.

Choice A says that *Renaissance* should be capitalized in the first sentence of the passage. The Renaissance is a historical period, so *Renaissance* is a proper noun that should always be capitalized. Choice A is correct.

Choice B says that *ERA* should be written as *Era*. In the third sentence of the passage, the word *era* is used as an acronym. Remember that all letters in an acronym should be capitalized. The correct capitalization is *ERA*, so choice B is incorrect.

Choice C says that *president* and *vice president* should be capitalized. Titles for people are capitalized when they are used as part of a person's name or in the place of a person's name. In this passage, these titles are not used as part of anyone's name or in place of anyone's name, so they should be in lowercase. Choice C is incorrect.

Choice D says that *Christmas* should be in lowercase. The passage says that the first meeting will be held after Christmas break. Even though *Christmas* is used to describe when the students are getting a vacation from school, it is the name of a holiday. Names of holidays are always capitalized, so choice D is incorrect.

Word Confusion

To, Too, and Two

To can be an adverb or a preposition for showing direction, purpose, and relationship. A dictionary can also be used to see the many other ways to use *to* in a sentence.

> Examples: I went to the store. | I want to go with you.

Too is an adverb that means *also, as well, very,* or *in excess.*

> Examples: I can walk a mile too. | You have eaten too much.

Two is a number.

> Example: You have two minutes left.

There, Their, and They're

There can be an adjective, adverb, or pronoun. Often, *there* is used to show a place or to start a sentence.

> Examples: I went there yesterday. | There is something in his pocket.

Their is a pronoun that is used to show ownership.

> Examples: He is their father. | This is their fourth apology this week.

They're is a contraction of *they are.*

> Example: Did you know that they're in town?

Its and It's

Its is a possessive pronoun that shows ownership.

> Example: The guitar is in its case.

It's is a contraction of *it is.*

> Example: It's an honor and a privilege to meet you.

Affect and Effect

There are two main reasons that *affect* and *effect* are so often confused: 1) both words can be used as either a noun or a verb, and 2) unlike most homophones, their usage and meanings are closely related to each other. Here is a quick explanation of the four usage options:

Affect (n): feeling, emotion, or mood that is displayed

Example: The patient had a flat *affect.* (i.e., his face showed little or no emotion)

Affect (v): to alter, to change, to influence

Example: The sunshine *affects* the plant's growth.

Effect (n): a result, a consequence

Example: What *effect* will this weather have on our schedule?

Effect (v): to bring about, to cause to be

Example: These new rules will *effect* order in the office.

Example

Choose the correct spelling from each pair of homophones in the following passage.

> I found a unique tree in the forest. (It's/Its) trunk is blue, and it has (two/too) many branches to count. I brought some of my friends to see it, but the tree did not seem to (affect/effect) them. While (their/they're) not fascinated by the strange tree, I am!

The first pair of homophones is *it's* and *its.* Remember that the contraction *it's* is used in place of *it is. Its* is a possessive pronoun that shows a thing's ownership or possession. An easy way to decide whether *it's* or *its* is correct is to see how the sentence sounds with *it is,* instead. *It is trunk is blue* does not make sense. *Its trunk is blue* means that the tree has a blue trunk, so *its* is the correct choice.

The next pair of homophones is *two* and *too. Two* only means the number two. *Too* can mean *also* or *in excess.* Which of these makes the most sense in this sentence? *Two many branches to count* or *too many branches to count*? The correct meaning is that there is an abundance of branches, so *too* is the correct choice for this pair.

The third pair of homophones is *affect* and *effect.* Since both of these words can be used as a noun or verb, identifying the correct part of speech is a helpful first step. The part of speech is a verb, since the correct word will show what *the tree* does to *them. Affect* as a verb means to change or influence. *Effect* as a verb means to lead to or cause something to happen. Replace the homophone with these synonyms. Seeing the tree cannot cause or lead the speaker's friends to exist, but it can change them or influence them. *Affect* is the correct choice for this pair.

The last pair of homophones is *their* and *they're. Their* is a possessive pronoun used to show that multiple people or things own something. *They're* is a contraction used in place of *they are.* Replace the homophone with *they are.* Does the sentence make sense? It does because they, the speaker's friends, are not fascinated by the tree. Saying *their not fascinated* does not make sense. *They're* is the correct choice for this pair.

Vocabulary

Word Roots and Prefixes and Suffixes

Affixes

Affixes in the English language are morphemes that are added to words to create related but different words. Derivational affixes form new words based on and related to the original words. For example, the affix *–ness* added to the end of the adjective *happy* forms the noun *happiness.* Inflectional affixes form different grammatical versions of words. For example, the plural affix *–s* changes the singular noun *book* to the plural noun *books*, and the past tense affix *–ed* changes the present tense verb *look* to the past tense *looked.* Prefixes are affixes placed in front of words. For example, *heat* means to make hot; *preheat* means to heat in advance. Suffixes are affixes placed at the ends of words. The *happiness* example above contains the suffix *–ness.* Circumfixes add parts both before and after words, such as how *light* becomes *enlighten* with the prefix *en-* and the suffix *–en.* Interfixes create compound words via central affixes: *speed* and *meter* become *speedometer* via the interfix *–o–*.

Review Video: Affixes
Visit mometrix.com/academy and enter code: 782422

Word Roots, Prefixes, and Suffixes to Help Determine Meanings of Words

Many English words were formed from combining multiple sources. For example, the Latin *habēre* means "to have," and the prefixes *in-* and *im-* mean a lack or prevention of something, as in *insufficient* and *imperfect.* Latin combined *in-* with *habēre* to form *inhibēre,* whose past participle was *inhibitus.* This is the origin of the English word *inhibit,* meaning to prevent from having. Hence by knowing the meanings of both the prefix and the root, one can decipher the word meaning. In Greek, the root *enkephalo-* refers to the brain. Many medical terms are based on this root, such as encephalitis and hydrocephalus. Understanding the prefix and suffix meanings (*-itis* means inflammation; *hydro-* means water) allows a person to deduce that encephalitis refers to brain inflammation and hydrocephalus refers to water (or other fluid) in the brain.

Review Video: Root Words in English
Visit mometrix.com/academy and enter code: 896380

Review Video: Determining Word Meanings
Visit mometrix.com/academy and enter code: 894894

Prefixes

Knowing common prefixes is helpful for all readers as they try to determining meanings or definitions of unfamiliar words. For example, a common word used when cooking is *preheat.* Knowing that *pre-* means in advance can also inform them that *presume* means to assume in advance, that *prejudice* means advance judgment, and that this understanding can be applied to many other words beginning with *pre-*. Knowing that the prefix *dis-* indicates opposition informs the meanings of words like *disbar, disagree, disestablish,* and many more. Knowing *dys-* means bad, impaired, abnormal, or difficult informs *dyslogistic, dysfunctional, dysphagia,* and *dysplasia.*

Suffixes

In English, certain suffixes generally indicate both that a word is a noun, and that the noun represents a state of being or quality. For example, *-ness* is commonly used to change an adjective into its noun form, as with *happy* and *happiness, nice* and *niceness,* and so on. The suffix *–tion* is commonly used to transform a verb into its noun form, as with *converse* and *conversation or move* and *motion*. Thus, if readers are unfamiliar with the second form of a word, knowing the meaning of the transforming suffix can help them determine meaning.

Prefixes for Numbers

Prefix	Definition	Examples
bi-	two	bisect, biennial
mono-	one, single	monogamy, monologue
poly-	many	polymorphous, polygamous
semi-	half, partly	semicircle, semicolon
uni-	one	uniform, unity

Prefixes for Time, Direction, and Space

Prefix	Definition	Examples
a-	in, on, of, up, to	abed, afoot
ab-	from, away, off	abdicate, abjure
ad-	to, toward	advance, adventure
ante-	before, previous	antecedent, antedate
anti-	against, opposing	antipathy, antidote
cata-	down, away, thoroughly	catastrophe, cataclysm
circum-	around	circumspect, circumference
com-	with, together, very	commotion, complicate
contra-	against, opposing	contradict, contravene
de-	from	depart
dia-	through, across, apart	diameter, diagnose
dis-	away, off, down, not	dissent, disappear
epi-	upon	epilogue
ex-	out	extract, excerpt
hypo-	under, beneath	hypodermic, hypothesis
inter-	among, between	intercede, interrupt
intra-	within	intramural, intrastate
ob-	against, opposing	objection
per-	through	perceive, permit
peri-	around	periscope, perimeter
post-	after, following	postpone, postscript
pre-	before, previous	prevent, preclude
pro-	forward, in place of	propel, pronoun
retro-	back, backward	retrospect, retrograde
sub-	under, beneath	subjugate, substitute
super-	above, extra	supersede, supernumerary
trans-	across, beyond, over	transact, transport
ultra-	beyond, excessively	ultramodern, ultrasonic

Negative Prefixes

Prefix	Definition	Examples
a-	without, lacking	atheist, agnostic
in-	not, opposing	incapable, ineligible
non-	not	nonentity, nonsense
un-	not, reverse of	unhappy, unlock

Extra Prefixes

Prefix	Definition	Examples
for-	away, off, from	forget, forswear

Prefix	Definition	Examples
fore-	previous	foretell, forefathers
homo-	same, equal	homogenized, homonym
hyper-	excessive, over	hypercritical, hypertension
in-	in, into	intrude, invade
mal-	bad, poorly, not	malfunction, malpractice
mis-	bad, poorly, not	misspell, misfire
neo-	new	Neolithic, neoconservative
omni-	all, everywhere	omniscient, omnivore
ortho-	right, straight	orthogonal, orthodox
over-	above	overbearing, oversight
pan-	all, entire	panorama, pandemonium
para-	beside, beyond	parallel, paradox
re-	backward, again	revoke, recur
sym-	with, together	sympathy, symphony

Below is a list of common suffixes and their meanings:

Adjective Suffixes

Suffix	Definition	Examples
-able (-ible)	capable of being	toler*able*, ed*ible*
-esque	in the style of, like	picturesque, grotesque
-ful	filled with, marked by	thankful, zestful
-ific	make, cause	terrific, beatific
-ish	suggesting, like	churlish, childish
-less	lacking, without	hopeless, countless
-ous	marked by, given to	religious, riotous

Noun Suffixes

Suffix	Definition	Examples
-acy	state, condition	accuracy, privacy
-ance	act, condition, fact	acceptance, vigilance
-ard	one that does excessively	drunkard, sluggard
-ation	action, state, result	occupation, starvation
-dom	state, rank, condition	serfdom, wisdom
-er (-or)	office, action	teach*er*, elevat*or*, hon*or*
-ess	feminine	waitress, duchess
-hood	state, condition	manhood, statehood
-ion	action, result, state	union, fusion
-ism	act, manner, doctrine	barbarism, socialism
-ist	worker, follower	monopolist, socialist
-ity (-ty)	state, quality, condition	acid*ity*, civil*ity*, twen*ty*
-ment	result, action	Refreshment
-ness	quality, state	greatness, tallness
-ship	position	internship, statesmanship
-sion (-tion)	state, result	revi*sion*, expedi*tion*
-th	act, state, quality	warmth, width
-tude	quality, state, result	magnitude, fortitude

VERB SUFFIXES

Suffix	Definition	Examples
-ate	having, showing	separate, desolate
-en	cause to be, become	deepen, strengthen
-fy	make, cause to have	glorify, fortify
-ize	cause to be, treat with	sterilize, mechanize

NUANCE AND WORD MEANINGS

SYNONYMS AND ANTONYMS

When you understand how words relate to each other, you will discover more in a passage. This is explained by understanding **synonyms** (e.g., words that mean the same thing) and **antonyms** (e.g., words that mean the opposite of one another). As an example, *dry* and *arid* are synonyms, and *dry* and *wet* are antonyms.

There are many pairs of words in English that can be considered synonyms, despite having slightly different definitions. For instance, the words *friendly* and *collegial* can both be used to describe a warm interpersonal relationship, and one would be correct to call them synonyms. However, *collegial* (kin to *colleague*) is often used in reference to professional or academic relationships, and *friendly* has no such connotation.

If the difference between the two words is too great, then they should not be called synonyms. *Hot* and *warm* are not synonyms because their meanings are too distinct. A good way to determine whether two words are synonyms is to substitute one word for the other word and verify that the meaning of the sentence has not changed. Substituting *warm* for *hot* in a sentence would convey a different meaning. Although warm and hot may seem close in meaning, warm generally means that the temperature is moderate, and hot generally means that the temperature is excessively high.

Antonyms are words with opposite meanings. *Light* and *dark*, *up* and *down*, *right* and *left*, *good* and *bad*: these are all sets of antonyms. Be careful to distinguish between antonyms and pairs of words that are simply different. *Black* and *gray*, for instance, are not antonyms because gray is not the opposite of black. *Black* and *white*, on the other hand, are antonyms.

Not every word has an antonym. For instance, many nouns do not. What would be the antonym of *chair*? During your exam, the questions related to antonyms are more likely to concern adjectives. You will recall that adjectives are words that describe a noun. Some common adjectives include *purple*, *fast*, *skinny*, and *sweet*. From those four adjectives, *purple* is the item that lacks a group of obvious antonyms.

Review Video: Synonyms and Antonyms
Visit mometrix.com/academy and enter code: 105612

DENOTATIVE VS. CONNOTATIVE MEANING

The **denotative** meaning of a word is the literal meaning. The **connotative** meaning goes beyond the denotative meaning to include the emotional reaction that a word may invoke. The connotative meaning often takes the denotative meaning a step further due to associations the reader makes with the denotative meaning. Readers can differentiate between the denotative and connotative meanings by first recognizing how authors use each meaning. Most non-fiction, for example, is fact-based and authors do not use flowery, figurative language. The reader can assume that the writer is using the denotative meaning of words. In fiction, the author may use the connotative meaning. Readers can determine whether the author is using the denotative or connotative meaning of a word by implementing context clues.

Review Video: Connotation and Denotation
Visit mometrix.com/academy and enter code: 310092

Nuances of Word Meaning Relative to Connotation, Denotation, Diction, and Usage

A word's denotation is simply its objective dictionary definition. However, its connotation refers to the subjective associations, often emotional, that specific words evoke in listeners and readers. Two or more words can have the same dictionary meaning, but very different connotations. Writers use diction (word choice) to convey various nuances of thought and emotion by selecting synonyms for other words that best communicate the associations they want to trigger for readers. For example, a car engine is naturally greasy; in this sense, "greasy" is a neutral term. But when a person's smile, appearance, or clothing is described as "greasy," it has a negative connotation. Some words have even gained additional or different meanings over time. For example, *awful* used to be used to describe things that evoked a sense of awe. When *awful* is separated into its root word, awe, and suffix, -ful, it can be understood to mean "full of awe." However, the word is now commonly used to describe things that evoke repulsion, terror, or another intense, negative reaction.

> **Review Video: Word Usage in Sentences**
> Visit mometrix.com/academy and enter code: 197863

Using Context to Determine Meaning

Context Clues

Readers of all levels will encounter words that they have either never seen or have encountered only on a limited basis. The best way to define a word in **context** is to look for nearby words that can assist in revealing the meaning of the word. For instance, unfamiliar nouns are often accompanied by examples that provide a definition. Consider the following sentence: *Dave arrived at the party in hilarious garb: a leopard-print shirt, buckskin trousers, and bright green sneakers.* If a reader was unfamiliar with the meaning of garb, he or she could read the examples (i.e., a leopard-print shirt, buckskin trousers, and bright green sneakers) and quickly determine that the word means *clothing*. Examples will not always be this obvious. Consider this sentence: *Parsley, lemon, and flowers were just a few of the items he used as garnishes.* Here, the word *garnishes* is exemplified by parsley, lemon, and flowers. Readers who have eaten in a variety of restaurants will probably be able to identify a garnish as something used to decorate a plate.

> **Review Video: Reading Comprehension: Using Context Clues**
> Visit mometrix.com/academy and enter code: 613660

Using Contrast in Context Clues

In addition to looking at the context of a passage, readers can use contrast to define an unfamiliar word in context. In many sentences, the author will not describe the unfamiliar word directly; instead, he or she will describe the opposite of the unfamiliar word. Thus, you are provided with some information that will bring you closer to defining the word. Consider the following example: *Despite his intelligence, Hector's low brow and bad posture made him look obtuse.* The author writes that Hector's appearance does not convey intelligence. Therefore, *obtuse* must mean unintelligent. Here is another example: *Despite the horrible weather, we were beatific about our trip to Alaska*. The word *despite* indicates that the speaker's feelings were at odds with the weather. Since the weather is described as *horrible*, then *beatific* must mean something positive.

Substitution to Find Meaning

In some cases, there will be very few contextual clues to help a reader define the meaning of an unfamiliar word. When this happens, one strategy that readers may employ is **substitution**. A good reader will brainstorm some possible synonyms for the given word, and he or she will substitute these words into the sentence. If the sentence and the surrounding passage continue to make sense, then the substitution has revealed at least some information about the unfamiliar word. Consider the sentence: *Frank's admonition rang in her ears as she climbed the mountain.* A reader unfamiliar with *admonition* might come up with some substitutions like *vow, promise, advice, complaint,* or *compliment.* All of these words make general sense of the sentence, though their meanings are diverse. However, this process has suggested that an admonition is some sort of message. The substitution strategy is rarely able to pinpoint a precise definition, but this process can be effective as a last resort.

Occasionally, you will be able to define an unfamiliar word by looking at the descriptive words in the context. Consider the following sentence: *Fred dragged the recalcitrant boy kicking and screaming up the stairs.* The words *dragged*, *kicking*, and *screaming* all suggest that the boy does not want to go up the stairs. The reader may assume that *recalcitrant* means something like unwilling or protesting. In this example, an unfamiliar adjective was identified.

Additionally, using description to define an unfamiliar noun is a common practice compared to unfamiliar adjectives, as in this sentence: *Don's wrinkled frown and constantly shaking fist identified him as a curmudgeon of the first order.* Don is described as having a *wrinkled frown and constantly shaking fist*, suggesting that a *curmudgeon* must be a grumpy person. Contrasts do not always provide detailed information about the unfamiliar word, but they at least give the reader some clues.

WORDS WITH MULTIPLE MEANINGS

When a word has more than one meaning, readers can have difficulty determining how the word is being used in a given sentence. For instance, the verb *cleave*, can mean either *join* or *separate*. When readers come upon this word, they will have to select the definition that makes the most sense. Consider the following sentence: *Hermione's knife cleaved the bread cleanly.* Since a knife cannot join bread together, the word must indicate separation. A slightly more difficult example would be the sentence: *The birds cleaved to one another as they flew from the oak tree.* Immediately, the presence of the words *to one another* should suggest that in this sentence *cleave* is being used to mean *join*. Discovering the intent of a word with multiple meanings requires the same tricks as defining an unknown word: look for contextual clues and evaluate the substituted words.

CONTEXT CLUES TO HELP DETERMINE MEANINGS OF WORDS

If readers simply bypass unknown words, they can reach unclear conclusions about what they read. However, looking for the definition of every unfamiliar word in the dictionary can slow their reading progress. Moreover, the dictionary may list multiple definitions for a word, so readers must search the word's context for meaning. Hence context is important to new vocabulary regardless of reader methods. Four types of context clues are examples, definitions, descriptive words, and opposites. Authors may use a certain word, and then follow it with several different examples of what it describes. Sometimes authors actually supply a definition of a word they use, which is especially true in informational and technical texts. Authors may use descriptive words that elaborate upon a vocabulary word they just used. Authors may also use opposites with negation that help define meaning.

EXAMPLES AND DEFINITIONS

An author may use a word and then give examples that illustrate its meaning. Consider this text: "Teachers who do not know how to use sign language can help students who are deaf or hard of hearing understand certain instructions by using gestures instead, like pointing their fingers to indicate which direction to look or go; holding up a hand, palm outward, to indicate stopping; holding the hands flat, palms up, curling a finger toward oneself in a beckoning motion to indicate 'come here'; or curling all fingers toward oneself repeatedly to indicate 'come on', 'more', or 'continue.'" The author of this text has used the word "gestures" and then followed it with examples, so a reader unfamiliar with the word could deduce from the examples that "gestures" means "hand motions." Readers can find examples by looking for signal words "for example," "for instance," "like," "such as," and "e.g."

While readers sometimes have to look for definitions of unfamiliar words in a dictionary or do some work to determine a word's meaning from its surrounding context, at other times an author may make it easier for readers by defining certain words. For example, an author may write, "The company did not have sufficient capital, that is, available money, to continue operations." The author defined "capital" as "available money," and heralded the definition with the phrase "that is." Another way that authors supply word definitions is with appositives. Rather than being introduced by a signal phrase like "that is," "namely," or "meaning," an appositive comes after the vocabulary word it defines and is enclosed within two commas. For example, an author may write, "The Indians introduced the Pilgrims to pemmican, cakes they made of lean meat dried and mixed with fat, which proved greatly beneficial to keep settlers from starving while trapping." In this example, the appositive phrase following "pemmican" and preceding "which" defines the word "pemmican."

DESCRIPTIONS

When readers encounter a word they do not recognize in a text, the author may expand on that word to illustrate it better. While the author may do this to make the prose more picturesque and vivid, the reader can also take advantage of this description to provide context clues to the meaning of the unfamiliar word. For example, an author may write, "The man sitting next to me on the airplane was obese. His shirt stretched across his vast expanse of flesh, strained almost to bursting." The descriptive second sentence elaborates on and helps to define the previous sentence's word "obese" to mean extremely fat. A reader unfamiliar with the word "repugnant" can decipher its meaning through an author's accompanying description: "The way the child grimaced and shuddered as he swallowed the medicine showed that its taste was particularly repugnant."

OPPOSITES

Text authors sometimes introduce a contrasting or opposing idea before or after a concept they present. They may do this to emphasize or heighten the idea they present by contrasting it with something that is the reverse. However, readers can also use these context clues to understand familiar words. For example, an author may write, "Our conversation was not cheery. We sat and talked very solemnly about his experience and a number of similar events." The reader who is not familiar with the word "solemnly" can deduce by the author's preceding use of "not cheery" that "solemn" means the opposite of cheery or happy, so it must mean serious or sad. Or if someone writes, "Don't condemn his entire project because you couldn't find anything good to say about it," readers unfamiliar with "condemn" can understand from the sentence structure that it means the opposite of saying anything good, so it must mean reject, dismiss, or disapprove. "Entire" adds another context clue, meaning total or complete rejection.

SYNTAX TO DETERMINE PART OF SPEECH AND MEANINGS OF WORDS

Syntax refers to sentence structure and word order. Suppose that a reader encounters an unfamiliar word when reading a text. To illustrate, consider an invented word like "splunch." If this word is used in a sentence like "Please splunch that ball to me," the reader can assume from syntactic context that "splunch" is a verb. We would not use a noun, adjective, adverb, or preposition with the object "that ball," and the prepositional phrase "to me" further indicates "splunch" represents an action. However, in the sentence, "Please hand that splunch to me," the reader can assume that "splunch" is a noun. Demonstrative adjectives like "that" modify nouns. Also, we hand someone some*thing*—a thing being a noun; we do not hand someone a verb, adjective, or adverb. Some sentences contain further clues. For example, from the sentence, "The princess wore the glittering splunch on her head," the reader can deduce that it is a crown, tiara, or something similar from the syntactic context, without knowing the word.

SYNTAX TO INDICATE DIFFERENT MEANINGS OF SIMILAR SENTENCES

The syntax, or structure, of a sentence affords grammatical cues that aid readers in comprehending the meanings of words, phrases, and sentences in the texts that they read. Seemingly minor differences in how the words or phrases in a sentence are ordered can make major differences in meaning. For example, two sentences can use exactly the same words but have different meanings based on the word order:

- "The man with a broken arm sat in a chair."
- "The man sat in a chair with a broken arm."

While both sentences indicate that a man sat in a chair, differing syntax indicates whether the man's or chair's arm was broken.

> **Review Video: Syntax**
> Visit mometrix.com/academy and enter code: 242280

DETERMINING MEANING OF PHRASES AND PARAGRAPHS

Like unknown words, the meanings of phrases, paragraphs, and entire works can also be difficult to discern. Each of these can be better understood with added context. However, for larger groups of words, more context is needed. Unclear phrases are similar to unclear words, and the same methods can be used to understand their meaning. However, it is also important to consider how the individual words in the phrase work together. Paragraphs are a bit more complicated. Just as words must be compared to other words in a sentence, paragraphs must be compared to other paragraphs in a composition or a section.

DETERMINING MEANING IN VARIOUS TYPES OF COMPOSITIONS

To understand the meaning of an entire composition, the type of composition must be considered. **Expository writing** is generally organized so that each paragraph focuses on explaining one idea, or part of an idea, and its relevance. **Persuasive writing** uses paragraphs for different purposes to organize the parts of the argument. **Unclear paragraphs** must be read in the context of the paragraphs around them for their meaning to be fully understood. The meaning of full texts can also be unclear at times. The purpose of composition is also important for understanding the meaning of a text. To quickly understand the broad meaning of a text, look to the introductory and concluding paragraphs. Fictional texts are different. Some fictional works have implicit meanings, but some do not. The target audience must be considered for understanding texts that do have an implicit meaning, as most children's fiction will clearly state any lessons or morals. For other fiction, the application of literary theories and criticism may be helpful for understanding the text.

RESOURCES FOR DETERMINING WORD MEANING AND USAGE

While these strategies are useful for determining the meaning of unknown words and phrases, sometimes additional resources are needed to properly use the terms in different contexts. Some words have multiple definitions, and some words are inappropriate in particular contexts or modes of writing. The following tools are helpful for understanding all meanings and proper uses for words and phrases.

- **Dictionaries** provide the meaning of a multitude of words in a language. Many dictionaries include additional information about each word, such as its etymology, its synonyms, or variations of the word.
- **Glossaries** are similar to dictionaries, as they provide the meanings of a variety of terms. However, while dictionaries typically feature an extensive list of words and comprise an entire publication, glossaries are often included at the end of a text and only include terms and definitions that are relevant to the text they follow.
- **Spell Checkers** are used to detect spelling errors in typed text. Some spell checkers may also detect the misuse of plural or singular nouns, verb tenses, or capitalization. While spell checkers are a helpful tool, they are not always reliable or attuned to the author's intent, so it is important to review the spell checker's suggestions before accepting them.
- **Style Manuals** are guidelines on the preferred punctuation, format, and grammar usage according to different fields or organizations. For example, the Associated Press Stylebook is a style guide often used for media writing. The guidelines within a style guide are not always applicable across different contexts and usages, as the guidelines often cover grammatical or formatting situations that are not objectively correct or incorrect.

Types of Essays

ESSAYS

Essays usually focus on one topic, subject, or goal. There are several types of essays, including informative, persuasive, and narrative. An essay's structure and formality depend on the type of essay and its goal. While narrative essays typically do not include outside sources, other types of essays often require some research and the use of primary and secondary sources.

The basic format of an essay typically has three major parts: the introduction, the body, and the conclusion. The body is further divided into the writer's main points. Most essays will have at least three main points, but essays that go into more depth can have almost any number of main points.

An essay's introduction should answer three questions:

1. What is the **subject** of the essay?

   If an essay is about a book, the answer would include the title and author of the book, as well as any additional information needed, such as the subject or argument of the book.

2. How does the essay **discuss** the subject?

   To answer this, the writer briefly summarizes the main points and the evidence supporting them to let readers know how the essay is organized and what information they can expect to read.

3. What will the essay **prove**?

   This information is in the thesis statement, usually the opening paragraph's last sentence, which clearly states the writer's message.

The body elaborates on all the main points related to the thesis, introducing one main point at a time, and includes supporting evidence with each main point. Each body paragraph should state the point in a topic sentence, which is usually the first sentence in the paragraph. The paragraph should then explain the point's meaning, support it with quotations or other evidence, and then explain how this point and the evidence are related to the thesis. The writer should then repeat this procedure in a new paragraph for each additional main point.

The conclusion restates the content of the introduction, including the thesis, to remind the reader of the essay's main argument or subject. The essay writer may also summarize the highlights of the argument or description contained in the body of the essay, following the same organization originally used in the body. For example, a conclusion might look like: Point 1 + Point 2 + Point 3 = Thesis, or Point 1 → Point 2 → Point 3 → Thesis Proof. Good organization makes essays easier for writers to compose and provides a guide for readers to follow. Well-organized essays hold attention better and are more likely to get readers to believe or agree with the writer.

USING SOURCES IN ESSAYS

Sometimes writers use information from others in their work. This is most common in expository and persuasive writing. For an expository essay, a writer may not know all of the information that he or she needs to finish the composition. The writer may use other people's work to find the missing information and complete the composition. Persuasive writers may do research to find facts or statements from others that support their own beliefs and make their writing more persuasive. In both cases, research helps the writer find information that **supports** his or her **original work**.

Outside information must be relevant, true, and helpful to be appropriate for a composition. Writers must also be careful not to use too much outside information, since this can make the composition unoriginal. If a writer does use outside information, it is extremely important that the writer mention in the composition where the information came from. If the writer forgets or chooses not to say where the information came from, he or she has stolen someone else's work and presented it as their own. Doing this is called **plagiarism**.

INFORMATIONAL TEXTS

Informational texts, also called instructional or expository texts, are compositions written to inform the reader about a specific topic. An informational essay can inform readers in a variety of ways, such as giving them instructions, telling them facts about the topic, or teaching them why something happens. Informational texts should be logical, meaning that they should present information in an order that the reader can easily understand, and they should include the right amount of information so the writer successfully informs his or her audience of new information.

Informational texts should also focus on a **central idea**. In the introduction of an informational text, there may be a sentence or two that clearly state the essay's central idea. This sentence, or sentences, is called a **thesis statement**. The central idea should be clear throughout the composition. By emphasizing the central idea in the introduction, body, and conclusion, the writer can ensure that the central idea is clear. One way to make sure that the central idea is emphasized is to think about the purpose of each part of the essay. The introduction prepares the reader by telling them what the rest of the essay is about, so the central idea should be **introduced** in this section. The body tells the reader the information the writer wants to tell the audience, so this **explains** the central idea and facts about it to the reader. The conclusion is used to **remind** the reader of how the information in the body is related and **restates** the central idea one final time.

STRUCTURES OR ORGANIZATIONAL PATTERNS IN INFORMATIONAL TEXTS

Informational text can be **descriptive**, meaning that it gives information that can be experienced through the five senses, or it answers the questions what, who, when, where, and why. One common method of organizing informational text is to put it in a certain sequence, or order. **Chronological** texts include events in the order that they occurred, from start to finish. **How-to**, or **instructional**, texts organize information into a series of instructions in the order in which the steps should be followed. **Comparison-contrast** structures of informational text describe different ideas to their readers by pointing out how things or ideas are similar and how they are different. **Cause and effect** structures of informational text describe events that occurred and the causes or reasons for those events. **Problem and solution** structures of informational texts introduce and describe problems and offer one or more solutions for each problem described.

Review Video: Organizational Methods to Structure Text
Visit mometrix.com/academy and enter code: 606263

ARGUMENTATIVE WRITING

In argumentative writing, the writer expresses a belief or opinion that he or she wants to lead readers to agree with. When writing an argumentative composition, the writer should first identify the **topic** his or her opinion is about. The topic may be serious or fun, as long as there is one clear topic in the composition. The next step is for the writer to determine his or her opinion on the topic and determine why he or she holds that opinion. In order to persuade others to agree with their opinion, the writer must be able to give readers reasons to support the opinion. If the writer does not know why he or she has an opinion, it will be difficult to convince readers to agree. In addition to having reasons that support their opinion, writers should prepare examples that support each of these reasons in order to strengthen their composition.

Once the writer has determined his or her topic, opinion, and reasons for having the opinion, he or she is ready to begin writing an argumentative essay. In the introduction, the writer should capture the reader's interest, introduce the topic, and reveal his or her opinion about the topic. In the body of the composition, the writer should remind the reader of the opinion and give his or her reasons for holding the opinion. If the writer has any examples, facts, or other information that supports his or her opinion or reasons for believing it, these should also be included in the body. Writers may also use a body paragraph to mention opposing opinions or beliefs and explain why they disagree with them. As in other compositions, the conclusion should remind the reader of the essay's topic and purpose, as well as remind the reader how the opinion has been explained and supported. The conclusion should also invite the reader to continue thinking about the topic and writer's opinion. This can be done through questions or statements that lead readers to consider whether or not they agree with the author's opinion or what their own opinions are.

Review Video: Argumentative Writing
Visit mometrix.com/academy and enter code: 561544

Informative vs. Persuasive Writing

Informative writing, also called explanatory or expository writing, is written to show that something is true or factual, while **persuasive** writing is written to lead the reader to agree with something that may or may not be true or factual. While persuasive text is written to **persuade** readers to agree with the author's position, informative text simply **provides information** to readers. Informative writing **informs** readers about why or how something is as it is. This can include offering new information, explaining how a process works, or describing a concept for readers.

Review Video: Informational Text
Visit mometrix.com/academy and enter code: 924964

Facts and Opinions

Writers and readers must always be aware of the difference between fact and opinion. A **fact** can be tested and proven to be true. An **opinion**, on the other hand, is someone's personal thoughts or feelings. Opinions are often not changed by information. If an author writes that a newborn elephant is about five times taller than a newborn giraffe, then he or she is stating a fact. If the author writes that giraffes are more interesting than elephants, then he or she is giving an opinion because this cannot be proven to be true or false. Opinions are often supported by facts. For instance, the author might use a comparison between the way that giraffes eat and the way elephants eat as evidence of how giraffes are more interesting. An opinion supported by facts tends to be more convincing. On the other hand, when authors support their opinions with other opinions, readers should seriously think about and read the argument carefully to see whether it is logical and trustworthy.

Review Video: Distinguishing Fact and Opinion
Visit mometrix.com/academy and enter code: 870899

Narrative Writing

Put simply, **narrative** writing tells a story. Narratives should tell stories in such a way that the readers learn something or gain understanding about a related topic or idea. Personal narratives are narratives writers create about personal experiences that were meaningful to them. Narratives should start with the story's actions or events, rather than long descriptions or introductions. However, the narrative should still include descriptions at points where they will entertain the reader or help the reader visualize or better understand the scene. To write an effective description, writers should include sensory details, asking themselves what they saw, heard, felt or touched, smelled, and tasted during the experiences they describe. In narrative writing, the details should be **concrete** rather than **abstract**. Concrete details are those that can be experienced through one of the five senses, while abstract details are not able to be experienced in this way. Using concrete details enables readers to imagine everything that the writer describes. Writers should make sure that there is a point to each story by describing what they learned from the experience they narrate.

Personal Narratives

A **personal narrative** is a story about something that happened to the writer. **Personal narrative essays** are structured the same as other types of essays, as they have an introduction, body paragraphs, and a conclusion. Like other essays, the introduction of a personal narrative should contain a hook, or an opening sentence that interests the reader and prompts them to read the rest of the narrative. The introduction may also provide context for the story told in the personal narrative. One significant difference between personal narratives and other essays is that the body paragraphs of a personal narrative should contain sensory details, or imagery. A good personal narrative will give the reader a clear picture of the events and engage their emotions, and sensory details are effective at achieving these goals. The body should describe the events in chronological order, and the story should be completed in the last body paragraph. The conclusion will summarize the main idea of the personal narrative and may include information such as the writer's brief reflection on the events, how the events taught or changed the writer, or any relevant events that have happened since the events in the narrative.

Sensory Details

Writers need to use vivid descriptions when writing descriptive essays. Narratives should also include descriptions of characters, things, and events. Writers should remember to describe not only the visual detail of what someone or something looks like, but details from other senses, as well. For example, they can contrast the feeling of a sea breeze to the feeling of a mountain breeze, describe how they think something inedible would taste, and compare sounds they hear in the same location at different times of day and night. Readers have trouble visualizing images or imagining sensory impressions and feelings from abstract descriptions, so concrete descriptions make these more real.

Informational Text Example

Below is a prompt for an informational text. There is also an example of an essay that addresses the prompt. There are multiple drafts of this essay to show what kinds of changes a writer may make during the writing process to improve his or her work.

PROMPT:

Do you ever dream of going to a new city, state, or even country? Write about one place you want to travel to on vacation. Be sure to share why you would like to visit that place.

Rough Draft

Imagine traveling into the city or the beach and being transported back in time. This is what it must be like to live in Greece. The old buildings, beautiful beaches, and Greek foods are reasons I want to visit Greece.

Several buildings from ancient Greece are still standing, and they can easily be enjoyed by visitors and the people of Greece today. Some of the most famous ones, like the Parthenon, are located throughout the capital. This means that even when you are sitting in an air-conditioned restaurant in Athens, you can still see what is left of history. There are also tours that teach visitors more about these structures and the events that happened at each one. Though seeing these structures is not the only reason I would like to visit Greece, they would be enough of a reason for me to visit.

In addition to the scenery, another reason to visit Greece is to try real Greek and Mediterranean foods. I have tried a few Greek foods, like baklava and pita bread, and I enjoyed them. While these foods are available in America, I think they are probably made a little differently in Greece. I am interested in seeing what the differences are and trying new things. I hope I can visit Greece soon, because I am getting hungry just thinking about the food there!

Greece has a variety of beaches, as some are small with rocky structures and some look like normal beaches. The water is also different from some American waters because Greece is next to the Mediterranean Sea. Also, many historical events and myths took place on some of the beaches. I would love to sit on one of those beaches and try to imagine ships or characters from myths coming to the shore! The beaches in Greece are beautiful, but I think they also sound fun and interesting!

Walking through historical structures, visiting unique beaches, and eating new foods there is my dream. If I only ever have the chance to go on one vacation, I hope it is to Greece!

Revised Draft

Imagine traveling into the city or the beach and being transported back in time. This is what it must be like to live in Greece. The remaining historical sites that are still there allow visitors to see two cultures side by side. The old buildings, beautiful beaches, and Greek foods are reasons I want to visit Greece.

Several buildings from ancient Greece are still standing, and they can easily be enjoyed by visitors and the people of Greece today. Some of the most famous ones, like the Parthenon, are located throughout the capital. This means that even when you are sitting in an air-conditioned restaurant in Athens, you can still see what is left of history. There are also tours that teach visitors more about these structures and the events that happened at each one. Though seeing these structures is not the only reason I would like to visit Greece, they would be enough of a reason for me to visit.

Greece has a variety of beaches, as some are small with rocky structures and some look like normal beaches. The water is also different from some American waters because Greece is next to the Mediterranean Sea. Also, many historical events and myths took place on some of the beaches. I would love to sit on one of those beaches and try to imagine ships or characters from myths coming to the shore! The beaches in Greece are beautiful, but I think they also sound fun and interesting!

In addition to the scenery, a third reason to visit Greece is to try real Greek and Mediterranean foods. I have tried a few Greek foods, like baklava and pita bread, and I enjoyed them. While these foods are available in America, I think they are probably made a little differently in Greece. I am interested in seeing what the differences are and trying new things. I hope I can visit Greece soon, because I am getting hungry just thinking about the food there!

Greece is a special place where the old and the new come together. Walking through historical structures, visiting unique beaches, and eating new foods there is my dream. If I only ever have the chance to go on one vacation, I hope it is to Greece!

Revised Draft Notes

Remember the purpose of the revising stage of the writing process. When revising, it is important to look at the whole composition. Do all of the paragraphs strengthen the composition? Do the introduction and conclusion help the reader understand the central idea and main points?

In this revision, nothing has been removed, but there are some additions. Look at the underlined words. In the introduction, a sentence has been added. Why? Previously, the introduction had only a hook and a thesis. The sentences were well written, but the writer did not provide a connection between the hook and the thesis. The new sentence connects the ideas in both sentences and introduces some of the main points the writer will discuss in the essay.

In the conclusion, another sentence has been added. This sentence strengthens the composition by creating a transition from the body to the conclusion. Before, the conclusion began abruptly by listing the three main points from the body of the essay. This sentence makes the essay flow better by giving the reader a transition from the body to the conclusion. This sentence reminds the reader of composition's central idea before repeating the writer's main points and sharing his or her hopes.

Finally, the third and fourth paragraphs have been switched. Why is that? Before, the writer discussed ancient buildings, then food, then the beaches. This revised draft discusses buildings, then beaches, then food. This new order puts the more closely related points, the scenery of the buildings and beaches, closer together in the essay. This helps the reader by making the organization of the essay more logical.

EDITED DRAFT

Imagine traveling into the city or the beach and being transported back in time. This is what it must be like to live in Greece, since the remaining historical sites ~~that are still there~~ allow visitors to see two cultures side by side. The ~~old~~ ancient buildings, beautiful beaches, and Greek foods are reasons I want to visit Greece.

Several buildings from ancient Greece are still standing, and they can easily be enjoyed by visitors and the people of Greece today. Some of the most famous ones, like the Parthenon, are located throughout the capital. This means that even when you are sitting in an air-conditioned restaurant in Athens, you can still see ~~what is left~~ glimpses of history. There are also tours that teach visitors more about these structures and the events that happened at each one. ~~Though seeing these structures is not the only reason I would like to visit Greece, they would be enough of a reason for me to visit.~~ Seeing these structures alone is enough of a reason for me to visit Greece!

Another reason I want to travel to Greece is to see the beaches there. There are a variety of beaches, as some are small with rocky structures and some look like ~~normal~~ typical beaches. The water is also different from some American waters because Greece is next to the Mediterranean Sea. Also, many historical events and myths took place on some of the beaches. I would love to sit on one of those beaches and try to imagine ships or characters from myths coming to the shore! The beaches in Greece are beautiful, but I think they also sound fun and interesting!

In addition to the scenery, a third reason to visit Greece is to try ~~real~~ authentic Greek and Mediterranean foods. I have tried a few Greek foods, like baklava and pita bread, and I enjoyed them. While these foods are available in America, I think they are probably made a little differently in Greece, so I am interested in seeing what the differences are and trying new things. I hope I can visit Greece soon, because I am getting hungry just thinking about the food there!

Greece is a special place where the old and the new come together. Walking through historical structures, visiting unique beaches, and eating new foods there is my dream. If I only ever have the chance to go on one vacation, I hope it is to Greece!

EDITED DRAFT NOTES

Since the writer has revised his or her work, the next step is to edit the composition. Remember that editing is very similar to revising, but editing usually includes paying attention to each paragraph, instead of the whole composition. Look at the changes that were made to each paragraph.

There are small changes throughout this draft. First, look at the introduction. Before, the introduction had four sentences that were about the same length. In this draft, the second and third sentences have been combined to make a longer sentence. This creates more sentence variety in the introduction, which makes the composition more entertaining for the writer's audience. A few words have been crossed out, as well. *That are still there* has been replaced with *remaining*. This change makes the writing more concise and formal. Also, *old* has been replaced with *ancient*. This clarifies what kind of buildings the writer is describing by using a word that more specifically describes the age of the buildings.

In the next paragraph, *what is left* has been replaced with *glimpses*. This change makes the writing more concise by using one word instead of three. Furthermore, this change makes the writing more interesting and entertaining by using a better vocabulary word. At the end of the paragraph, the last sentence has been condensed. Most of the sentences in this paragraph are long. Shortening this sentence adds sentence variety to this paragraph and makes the concluding sentence more concise. Overall, these changes make the paragraph easier to read by eliminating unnecessary words and using better vocabulary.

There are a few more changes left in the third and fourth paragraphs. A transition has been added to the beginning of the third paragraph. Now, the writer introduces the next main point before describing the beaches. This makes the essay flow better overall and making it easier for the writer's audience to read. *Normal* has been replaced with *typical*. Since there are so many different beaches in the world, there are not really any normal beaches. *Typical* is a much clearer word. Now, the reader knows that the writer is trying to distinguish the beaches in Greece from the type of beaches that he or she sees most often.

In the next paragraph, *real* has been replaced with *authentic*. The food the writer has tried in America has been real food, not fake food, so this is poor word choice. Now, *authentic* clarifies the writer's meaning that the food will be closer to its original Greek or Mediterranean style. These changes in word choice improve the clarity of the essay by using specific words that better communicate the writer's points. Finally, the third and fourth sentences have been joined together. This increases sentence variety by adding a longer sentence to this paragraph.

Final Draft

Imagine traveling into the city or the beach and being transported back in time. This is what it must be like to live in Greece, since the remaining historical sites allow visitors to see two cultures side by side. The ancient buildings, beautiful beaches, and Greek foods are reasons I want to visit Greece.

Several buildings from ancient Greece are still standing, and they can easily be enjoyed by visitors and the people of Greece today. Some of the most famous ones, like the Parthenon, are located throughout the capital. This means that even when you are sitting in an air-conditioned restaurant in Athens, you can still see glimpses of history. There are also tours that teach visitors more about these structures and the events that happened at each one. Seeing these structures alone is enough of a reason for me to visit Greece!

Another reason I want to travel to Greece is to see the beaches there. There are a variety of beaches, as some are small with rocky structures and some look like typical beaches. The water is also different from some American waters because Greece is next to the Mediterranean Sea. Also, many historical events and myths took place on some of the beaches. I would love to sit on one of those beaches and try to imagine ships or characters from myths coming to the shore! The beaches in Greece are beautiful, but I think they also sound fun and interesting!

In addition to the scenery, a third reason to visit Greece is to try authentic Greek and Mediterranean foods. I have tried a few Greek foods, like baklava and pita bread, and I enjoyed them. While these foods are available in America, I think they are probably made a little differently in Greece, so I am interested in seeing what the differences are and trying new things. I hope I can visit Greece soon, because I am getting hungry just thinking about the food there!

Greece is a special place where the old and the new come together. Walking through historical structures, visiting unique beaches, and eating new foods there is my dream. If I only ever have the chance to go on one vacation, I hope it is to Greece!

Final Draft Evaluation

The essay answers the prompt and is on topic throughout the composition. The central idea is clear and is stated in the introduction, supported in the body, and restated in the conclusion. The thesis statement restates parts of the prompt and gives the reader a preview of the rest of the essay. The body uses well-structured paragraphs to explain the supporting details and examples and connects them to the central idea. The conclusion also emphasizes the central idea and supporting details and invites the reader to consider what they have read.

The essay is also interesting and written with a variety of sentence types. It uses transitions and good paragraph structure to make the essay easy for the reader to understand. The introduction also uses a hook to get the reader's attention and help him or her relate to the information in the essay. Not only does this essay answer the prompt and have appropriate structure, but it also makes use of good, engaging, and interesting details.

Reading Practice Test #1

Refer to the passage "'The Boy Musician'" to answer questions 1-8.

"The Boy Musician"

by Kate Dickinson Sweetser

(1) Johannes Chrysostemus Wolfgangus Theophilus Mozart—what a burden to be put upon a baby's tiny shoulders!

(2) If there is any truth underlying the belief that a name can in some measure foreshadow a child's future, then surely Wolfgang Mozart, who was born in Salzburg in 1756, came honestly by his heritage of greatness. When he was only a day old, he received the five-part name, to which was later added his confirmation name of Sigismundus. But as soon as he could choose for himself, the little son of Marianne and Leopold Mozart from his store of names, selected Wolfgang, to which he added Amadeus, by which combination he was always known, and the name is forever linked with the memory of a great genius.

(3) Almost before he could talk plainly the little fellow showed himself to be a musical prodigy, and when he was scarcely three years old, he would steal into the room where his father was giving a lesson on the harpsichord to Anna (or "Nannerl," as she was called), the sister five years older than himself. While she was being taught, Wolfgang would listen and watch with breathless attention.

(4) One day when the lesson was over, he begged his father to teach him too, but Leopold Mozart only laughed as he answered, glancing down into the child's serious face looking so intently into his:

(5) "Wait, my little man, thou art but a baby yet. Wait awhile, my Wolferl!" and the disappointed little musician crept away, but as soon as Nannerl and his father had left the room, the tiny fellow crept back again, went to the harpsichord and standing on tiptoe, touched the keys with his chubby fingers stretched wide apart until he reached and played *a perfect chord*! Leopold Mozart was in another part of the house, but his sensitive ear caught the sound, and he rushed back to find his baby on tiptoe before the harpsichord, giving the first hint of his marvelous ability.

(6) At once the proud and excited father began to give him lessons, and always, too, from that day, whenever Nannerl had her lesson, Wolfgang perched on his father's knee, and listened with rapt absorption, and often when the lesson was over, he would repeat what she had played in exact imitation of her manner of playing.

(7) Leopold Mozart, who was himself a talented musician, saw with pride almost beyond expression, that both of his children inherited his musical ability, and soon felt that Wolfgang was a genius. When the boy was only four, his father, to test his powers, tried to teach him some minuets. To his perfect astonishment, Wolfgang played after him in a most extraordinary manner, not merely striking the notes correctly, but marking the rhythm with accurate expression, and to learn and play each minuet the little fellow required only half an hour.

(8) When he was five years old, one day his father entered the sitting-room of their home and found Wolfgang bending over a table, writing so busily that he did not hear his father enter, or see that he was standing beside him. Wolfgang's chubby little hand held the pen awkwardly, but held it with firm determination while it travelled back and forth across a large sheet of

paper on which he was scribbling a strange collection of hieroglyphics, with here and there a huge blot, testifying to his haste and inexperience in the use of ink.

(9) What was he trying to do? His father's curiosity finally overcame him and he asked:

(10) "What are you doing, Wolfgang?" The curly head was raised with an impatient gesture.

(11) "I am composing a concerto for the harpsichord. I have nearly finished the first part."

(12) "Let me see it."

(13) "No, please, I have not yet finished."

(14) But even as he spoke, the eager father had taken up the paper and carried it over to where a friend stood, and they looked it over together, exchanging amused glances at the queer characters on it. Presently Leopold Mozart, after looking carefully at it, said:

(15) "Why it really seems to be composed by rule! But it is so difficult that no one could ever play it."

(16) "Oh, yes, they could, but it must be studied first," exclaimed little Wolfgang eagerly, and running to the harpsichord, he added:

(17) "See, this is the way it begins," and he was able to play enough of it, to show what his idea in writing it had been, and his father and the friend who had before exchanged glances of amusement, now looked at each other with wonder not untouched with awe.

1. What theme is developed in the passage based on the interaction between Wolfgang Mozart and his father Leopold?

a. The qualities of a genius can surprise even their parents.
b. Children may work very hard to receive their parents' approval.
c. Siblings often battle for their parents' attention.
d. Children avoid disobeying their parents for fear of punishment.

2. How does the author's use of a third-person omniscient point of view impact the reader's understanding of the events in the story?

a. The reader understands how the author of the passage has been inspired by Wolfgang Mozart.
b. The reader knows how both Wolfgang Mozart and his father feel about the concerto Wolfgang has written.
c. The reader understands why Leopold Mozart thinks that three-year-olds are too young to learn music.
d. The reader knows how the historical time period the passage is set in creates conflict.

3. Part A: What can the reader infer about Leopold Mozart based on the passage?

a. Leopold Mozart was only proud of Wolfgang and not of Nannerl.
b. Leopold Mozart thought his children should be of a certain age before learning music.
c. Leopold Mozart felt upset that his son was a better musician than he was.
d. Leopold Mozart taught Wolfgang how to write musical compositions.

Part B: What leads the reader to infer this about Leopold Mozart?

a. Leopold only helped Wolfgang with lessons and didn't teach Nannerl at all.
b. Leopold avoided playing music in front of Wolfgang because he was afraid his son would outperform him.
c. Leopold helped develop and correct his musical notation for the concerto he was composing.

d. Wolfgang had to wait to have lessons despite requesting to at a young age, yet his older sister already was receiving lessons.

4. Which best explains how the story's setting influenced Wolfgang Mozart's value of music?

a. The story is set in a time period that took place before music was recorded.
b. The story is set in a household where Wolfgang Mozart could only speak to his family.
c. The story is set in a time period where children were commonly given lengthy names.
d. The story is set in a household where Wolfgang Mozart observed his talented father.

5. Which sentence from the passage best demonstrates that the passage is historical fiction?

a. Leopold Mozart was in another part of the house, but his sensitive ear caught the sound, and he rushed back to find his baby on tiptoe before the harpsichord, giving the first hint of his marvelous ability.
b. When he was five years old, one day his father entered the sitting-room of their home and found Wolfgang bending over a table, writing so busily that he did not hear his father enter, or see that he was standing beside him.
c. If there is any truth underlying the belief that a name can in some measure foreshadow a child's future, then surely Wolfgang Mozart, who was born in Salzburg in 1756, came honestly by his heritage of greatness.
d. While she was being taught, Wolfgang would listen and watch with breathless attention.

6. Read the dictionary entry (adapted from Merriam-Webster) for the word *chord*.

chord \ [kawrd] \ noun
1. a feeling or emotion
2. a line segment that connects two points on a curve
3. a group of three or more tones that produce harmony
4. a thin rope made of interwoven strands

Which definition is the best match for how chord is used in paragraph 5?

a. Definition 1
b. Definition 2
c. Definition 3
d. Definition 4

7. What is the most likely reason that the author included the information in paragraphs 4 and 5?

a. To highlight how much Wolfgang Mozart wanted to learn music
b. To show that Wolfgang Mozart could never have made great music without his father's influence
c. To detail the inspirations for Wolfgang Mozart's earliest musical compositions
d. To suggest that Wolfgang Mozart was motivated to be a better musician than his sister

8. How does the author's use of terms like "my little man" and "my Wolferl" contribute to the tone in paragraph 5?

a. It creates a warning tone.
b. It creates a hopeful tone.
c. It creates an affectionate tone.
d. It creates a friendly tone.

Refer to the passage "The Trouble with Tests" to answer questions 9-15.

The Trouble with Tests

(1) Lisa was a good student. She studied hard, diligently did her homework, and turned in assignments on time. Whenever she had to take a test, however, Lisa had a problem. Her hands

began to sweat, and her stomach began to churn. She felt dizzy and breathless and sick. As a result, Lisa couldn't focus and always did poorly on tests. Her grades suffered, and so did her confidence level.

(2) Lisa's problem is a common one. Often called test anxiety, it includes any unusual stress symptoms that occur during tests. Symptoms can be as mild as light nausea or a headache or as severe as vomiting or uncontrollable shaking. Millions of students deal with test anxiety every year, but few realize it can be improved through three simple steps.

(3) The first step to improving test anxiety is practicing better study habits. Proper preparation is an important step to overcoming test anxiety. It is important to develop regular study times and avoid last minute "cramming" for a test. Studying heavily on the day of or night before a test can actually increase test anxiety in most students. The better option is to devote at least a half-hour block of time to reviewing class materials each day. This can help embed information in the brain, making it more accessible at test time.

(4) Using memory games and tools is another way to improve study habits. Using these tools and games can help students better retain information. It also makes learning more fun, which can reduce stress levels. Flashcards with key points or ideas can be very helpful when used alone or with a study partner. Mnemonic devices—silly sayings to help students recall complex concepts—are also helpful tools for reducing stress and improving test performance. An example of a mnemonic device is "Every Good Boy Deserves Fudge" to help music students remember the note names for the lines of the treble clef staff (EGBDF).

(5) The second step to reducing test anxiety is to use relaxation techniques. The first relaxation technique that is useful for test anxiety is visualization. This involves choosing a favorite place or event. When test anxiety symptoms appear, students can close their eyes and visualize themselves in that favorite place or at that favorite event. The students should focus on sensory information—sights, sounds, smells, etc. This refocuses the attention of the brain and reduces anxiety.

(6) Another relaxation technique that works well for test anxiety is deep breathing. When the body is under stress, breathing becomes shallower, causing the heart rate to increase and the blood pressure to rise. Conscious deep breathing helps increase oxygen flow to the body, reducing the heart rate and blood pressure. To practice deep breathing, simply draw air in through the nose for five seconds, and then release the air through the mouth, blowing out steadily for five seconds. Done with eyes open or closed, deep breathing exercises reduce stress and relax the body.

(7) The third step to reducing test anxiety is positive self-talk. Often, test anxiety is the result of or is compounded by a lack of faith in abilities. Students can overcome this through positive self-talk and self-affirmation. Before each test, a student should repeat, "I can do this"—or some similar positive mantra—over and over. This can be done out loud or silently; either way, it creates a positive attitude and outlook that can reduce anxiety.

(8) The self-affirmation of celebrating success is key to overcoming test anxiety. Students should share test-taking victories with friends and loved ones. Students should also feel proud when they do well on a test. Every success is a blow to the obstacle of test anxiety. As with anything else, practice makes perfect, and celebrating success helps a student practice triumph over test anxiety.

(9) Test anxiety is a real problem, not an imagined issue or an excuse. It can be overcome, however, through three basic steps. First, students must use study tools and good habits for proper preparation. Second, students must use relaxation techniques—such as visualization

and deep breathing—to help release stress from the body. Finally, students must engage in positive self-talk and celebrate successes to create an atmosphere of triumph. When all three of these steps are consistently practiced, test anxiety will become a thing of the past.

9. Which of the following gives the best summary of "The Trouble with Tests"?

a. Lisa is an example of a student with test anxiety. She had distressing symptoms but was able to reduce her test anxiety after trying three simple steps consistently. As a result, she was able to do well on tests.
b. Many students suffer from test anxiety, and the main cause is poor study habits. Rather than "cramming," students should study a half-hour each day by using flashcards, memory games, and tools. These make learning more fun and distract from anxious thoughts of upcoming tests.
c. Some symptoms of test anxiety include sweating, nausea, headache, and dizziness. It's important to consider using relaxation techniques like deep breathing, as these can slow the heart rate and help reduce the body's stress response, relieving the symptoms of test anxiety.
d. Although test anxiety is common, there are simple strategies that can reduce it. These strategies include forming better study habits through preparation, tools, and games; using relaxation techniques like visualization and deep breathing; and using positive self-talk and celebrating successes.

10. Reread paragraph 7 in "The Trouble with Tests." What does *mantra* mean?

a. A deep breathing technique
b. A good-luck charm
c. A type of criticism
d. A repeated phrase

11. Which sentence from "The Trouble with Tests" best shows that, though test anxiety is common, students may feel alone in their experiences?

a. As a result, Lisa couldn't focus and always did poorly on tests.
b. Millions of students deal with test anxiety every year, but few realize it can be improved through three simple steps.
c. Studying heavily on the day of or night before a test can actually increase test anxiety in most students.
d. When test anxiety symptoms appear, students can close their eyes and visualize themselves in that favorite place or at that favorite event.

12. Paragraphs 4 and 8 support which key idea?

a. Other people can play a role in helping with test anxiety.
b. Games and tools can aid in remembering important concepts.
c. Doing well on a test confirms that a student is improving at managing their test anxiety.
d. It's important to share even small successes on tests.

13. Which sentence best states the controlling idea of "The Trouble with Tests"?

a. Test anxiety is common, but it can be reduced or eliminated by using specific strategies.
b. Students like Lisa are not just imagining the stressful symptoms that tests cause.
c. Having better study habits can significantly improve test anxiety.
d. A student with test anxiety should use the help of other people rather than suffering alone.

14. The passage "The Trouble with Tests" uses an organizational structure that:

a. Convinces the reader to try improving their study habits
b. Shows a cause-and-effect relationship between test anxiety and grades
c. Outlines a step-by-step process to overcome test anxiety
d. Reveals why some students do not experience test anxiety

15. Based on the information in "The Trouble with Tests," what can the reader conclude?

a. Forming good study habits is the most important way to reduce test anxiety.
b. Test anxiety is unlikely to go away on its own.
c. Teachers don't always understand test anxiety in their students.
d. The stress symptoms of test anxiety might indicate a bigger health problem.

Refer to the passage "Just Trying to Help" to answer questions 16-19.

Just Trying to Help

(1) One afternoon, Sharon was making a short film for a school project. She had worked all week to create costumes and props that would make the film stand out. She was excited to put everything in place and get started. However, just as she was about to start filming, she realized that she did not have a place to put the camera.

(2) "Oh gosh, how am I going to film anything?" Sharon said to herself just as her little sister, Emma, walked past her room.

(3) "What's wrong, Sharon?" Emma asked, concerned.

(4) Sharon chuckled and answered, "Oh, it's not a big deal. I have to make a video for school, and I just realized that I don't have a good place to put the camera." She paused, thinking. "I don't think mom and dad have a tripod, and I don't want to ask them to buy one."

(5) "Oh," Emma frowned. She looked around the room and saw Sharon's bookshelf. "You could take the books off and make a tower and put the camera on top!"

(6) Sharon laughed again. "No, I need to be able to point the camera up and down at different angles, and I can't do that if I put it on the stack of books."

(7) Emma frowned again, but then smiled. "Oh, I know! I can hold the camera!"

(8) "Oh, I wish you could, but I don't think you can hold it up high enough for some of the scenes. And I don't have a chair that would be safe for you to stand on. I'm sorry, Emma. But thank you for trying to help."

(9) Tears filled Emma's eyes and she began to walk away.

(10) "Hey, come back!" Sharon called. Emma turned around and began to sniffle. "What's wrong?" Sharon asked her.

(11) "I want to be able to help you!" Emma explained. "But I'm too little and I don't know how."

(12) "Oh, Emma." Sharon crouched down to hug her. "I'm glad you want to help me. Maybe there's a way you can. Let me think for a minute."

(13) Sharon and Emma sat on the floor, both looking at the props and costumes that were waiting to be used. Sharon sat up, looked at Emma, and smiled. "I think I've got it! What if you are the one in the video? Then I can hold the camera! What do you think about that?"

(14) Emma walked over to the costumes and put one on over her outfit. It was very loose, and she hung her head. "All of the costumes are too big. And I don't know what I'm supposed to do or say."

(15) At that moment, Sharon and Emma's dad walked by. "What are you two up to?" he asked. Sharon explained the problem, and he said, "Hm, yeah, you would have to remake all of the costumes. But here's an idea! What if I hold the camera? Then you can use the costumes you already have."

(16) "But then Emma can't help," Sharon said.

(17) "That's alright, Sharon," Emma said as she sat next to her. "But can I watch? Can I be your audience?"

(18) "Of course you can! Wow, I think this will work. Thanks, Dad!"

(19) They spent the afternoon filming scenes for the project. Sharon and Emma's dad held the video camera, and they brought Sharon's ideas to life. Emma sat and watched Sharon, laughing at the funny scenes and encouraging Sharon when she made mistakes.

(20) When they were done, Emma said to Sharon, "That was fun! Thank you for letting me stay and watch, even though I couldn't help."

(21) "You're very welcome," Sharon answered. "Thank you for laughing at some of the scenes. That let me know that they were actually funny. And thanks for cheering me on when I messed up. That helped me stay confident in what I was doing." She paused and added, "In the end, you were a huge help after all!"

16.Which two inferences can the reader make about Sharon and Emma's relationship based on the passage? Select all that apply.

a. Sharon and Emma compete for their father's attention.
b. Emma wants to be like Sharon when she is older.
c. Sharon and Emma have a close and supportive relationship.
d. Sharon is frustrated with Emma's lack of help.
e. Sharon and Emma are considerate of each other's feelings.

17. How does Emma's desire to help Sharon affect the resolution of the conflict?

a. It causes Emma to come up with other ideas on how she can help Sharon.
b. It demonstrates Emma's sadness when she realizes she is too little to help.
c. It allows Emma to still be involved and help her sister as she watches the filming.
d. It highlights that Emma felt discouraged once she put the costume on and saw it was too big.

18. Which piece of Emma's dialogue from the passage most clearly shows the conflict Emma experiences?

a. "What's wrong, Sharon?"
b. "But can I watch? Can I be your audience?"
c. "Oh, I know! I can hold the camera!"
d. "But I'm too little and I don't know how."

19. Which of the following gives the best summary of "Just Trying to Help"?

a. Emma was upset that she couldn't help her big sister, Sharon, with a video project. Once Emma and Sharon's dad asks what's going on, he is able to help, and Emma enjoys watching Sharon film scenes for the project.

b. Emma, Sharon, and their dad spend the afternoon filming scenes for Sharon's school project. Sharon had worked hard on costumes and props. After the filming, she tells Emma how thankful she is that Emma could be her audience for the project.

c. Sharon encounters problems with where to put the camera when trying to make a video for school. Her little sister, Emma, wants to help, but neither Sharon nor Emma's ideas are achievable. The girls' dad steps in to help hold the camera and Emma is finally able to help Sharon by being the audience.

d. Sharon was trying to make a video for school. She had costumes and props but needed a place to put the camera. Sharon wished that her little sister Emma could help, but neither of them could think of a solution for where to put the camera to successfully film the scenes.

Refer to the passage "Deeds of Kindness" to answer questions 20-23.

Deeds of Kindness

by Epes Sargent

Suppose the little Cowslip
—Should hang its golden cup
And say, "I'm such a little flower
—I'd better not grow up!"
How many a weary traveller
—Would miss its fragrant smell,
How many a little child would grieve
—To lose it from the dell!

Suppose the glistening Dewdrop
—Upon the grass should say,
"What can a little dewdrop do?
—I'd better roll away!"
The blade on which it rested,
—Before the day was done,
Without a drop to moisten it,
—Would wither in the sun.

Suppose the little Breezes,
—Upon a summer's day,
Should think themselves too small to cool
—The traveller on his way:
Who would not miss the smallest
—And softest ones that blow,
And think they made a great mistake
—If they were acting so?

How many deeds of kindness
—A little child can do,
Although it has but little strength
—And little wisdom too!
It wants a loving spirit
—Much more than strength, to prove

How many things a child may do
—For others by its love.

20.Based on the poem "Deeds of Kindness," which of the following statements would the poet most likely agree with?

a. Every act of kindness is significant.
b. Doing a kind deed with a friend is a good way to help others.
c. Being kind can help you succeed in reaching your goals.
d. Kind actions can bring people together for a common cause.

21. How do the rhyme scheme, meter, and short line lengths contribute to the effect of this poem?

a. They are consistent throughout the poem, so the poem is easy for children to memorize.
b. They make it read similarly to poetry for children, which highlights the poem's message.
c. They are unique and make the poem special, so people are likely to remember its message.
d. They make the poem sound the way the images described in it sound in real life.

22. What is the most likely reason that the author includes the last stanza in the poem "Deeds of Kindness"?

a. To contrast the characteristics of a child to items found in nature
b. To suggest that children are not yet wise enough to help others
c. To convince the reader that appreciating nature starts in childhood
d. To highlight that even small children can make a difference

23. What purpose does the use of extended metaphor serve in the poem "Deeds of Kindness"?

a. It explains what it is like to be a part of nature by comparing the reader to flowers.
b. It shows the value of children by comparing them to small delights in nature.
c. It exaggerates the meaning of what it is to be kind by comparing actions to objects.
d. It provides the point of view of nature by comparing people to plants.

Refer to the passages "Just Trying to Help" and "Deeds of Kindness" to answer questions 24-26.

24. Which of the following ideas is supported by both "Just Trying to Help" and "Deeds of Kindness"?

a. No person or thing is too little to be helpful.
b. Doing kind deeds for your family members is rewarding.
c. A problem can be solved when multiple people step in to help.
d. Ignoring things that seem small and insignificant can have a cost.

25. How is the depiction of the items in nature in "Deeds of Kindness" different from the depiction of Emma in "Just Trying to Help"?

a. In "Deeds of Kindness," there is a focus on how the items in nature feel, while in "Just Trying to Help," there is not a focus on Emma's feelings.
b. In "Deeds of Kindness," there is no mention of family, while in "Just Trying to Help," a family disagreement is described.
c. In "Deeds of Kindness," the items in nature are described along with their purposes, while "Just Trying to Help" shows Emma as she tries to find a purpose.
d. In "Deeds of Kindness," the items in nature make many attempts to be helpful, but in "Just Trying to Help," Emma only tries to help once.

26. Read the following from "Deeds of Kindness."

Suppose the little Breezes
---Upon a summer's day
Should think themselves too small to cool
---The traveler on his way

Which sentence from "Just Trying to Help" shows the same idea as this excerpt?

a. When they were done, Emma said to Sharon, "That was fun! Thank you for letting me stay and watch, even though I couldn't help."
b. Emma frowned again, but then smiled. "Oh, I know! I can hold the camera!"
c. "I want to be able to help you!" Emma explained. "But I'm too little and I don't know how."
d. Tears filled Emma's eyes and she began to walk away.

Refer to the passage "Mammie" to answer questions 27-34.

Mammie

Cast of Characters

- Anthony – Mandie's husband
- Mandie – Anthony's wife
- Mammie – Anthony's mother

SCENE 1

[MAMMIE's kitchen; the appliances are old, and a farmhouse table dominates the small room. MANDIE is clinging to ANTHONY. They are alone in the kitchen.]

MANDIE: Please don't leave me here with... her. She doesn't like me.

ANTHONY: Of course she likes you. Don't be silly. Why wouldn't she like you?

MANDIE: Oh, I don't know. She just doesn't. You don't know how she can be.

ANTHONY: Don't I? I only lived with her for the first 20 years of my life.

MANDIE: (*pleading*) Anthony, you can't go. Just take me with you. We can come back for dinner, just like you promised Mammie.

ANTHONY: (*taking* MANDIE *firmly by the shoulders*) No, Mandie. You're here, and you're staying. I'll only be gone for an hour or so. I promise to be back for dinner.

MANDIE: But Anthony—

ANTHONY: Shush! She'll hear you—Mammie!

[MAMMIE *enters, straightening her apron. She looks* MANDIE *up and down.* ANTHONY *moves to kiss* MAMMIE'S *cheek and* MANDIE *reluctantly does the same.*]

MAMMIE: Hello, Anthony. Hello, Amanda.

ANTHONY: Well, Mammie, I'm afraid it's hello and goodbye for me. I'm off to my meeting. (*He kisses* MANDIE.) You two girls have fun. I'll be back for dinner.

[ANTHONY exits.]

SCENE 2

[MANDIE *and* MAMMIE *look at each other for several seconds. The silence becomes uncomfortable. Finally,* MAMMIE *turns her back on* MANDIE *and begins preparing dinner. She takes pots, pans, and ingredients out of the cupboards.*]

MANDIE: (*clearing her throat*) So, um, what are you making for dinner?

MAMMIE: (*without turning around*) Baked chicken. Rice. Asparagus.

MANDIE: Oh. (*Pauses*) Could I help with something?

[MAMMIE *wordlessly takes out a large pot and a bag of rice. She hands the items to* MANDIE *and turns back to her work.*]

MAMMIE: You can make the rice.

[MANDIE *stands very still, holding the rice and the pot. She bites her lip. She looks very frightened. Finally,* MAMMIE *turns around to face* MANDIE.]

MAMMIE: Well, child? What is it?

MANDIE: (*looking at the floor*) I-I don't know how to make rice.

MAMMIE: Don't know how to make rice? Don't be silly. Everyone knows how to make rice.

MANDIE: (*starting to cry*) Everyone... except... me!

[MAMMIE *sighs and wipes her hands on her apron. She comes over and takes the pot and the rice away from* MANDIE. *She sets them on the table and gently chucks Mandie under the chin.*]

MAMMIE: Come, child. It's nothing to cry over. Hush now. What can you cook?

MANDIE: (*sniffling*) I can make brownies, I guess.

MAMMIE: Good. (*Patting* MANDIE *awkwardly on the shoulder*) Get to work, then.

[MANDIE *starts opening cupboard doors and pulling out ingredients.* MAMMIE *hands her a mixing bowl and measuring cups.*]

MANDIE: Thank you.

[*They work in silence for a while. After* MAMMIE *puts the chicken in the oven and puts the rice on to cook, she turns and watches* MANDIE *work. Her face softens.*]

MAMMIE: I suppose it's just as well, you know. Anthony always did like brownies better than rice. (*She smiles and sits at the table.*) I remember when he was little, he always used to stick his finger into the middle brownie as soon as I took the pan from the oven. He always burned himself something terrible, but he couldn't let anyone else have that soft, gooey center brownie.

MANDIE: (*giggling*) He still does that.

MAMMIE: (*shocked*) No! A big, grown man like Anthony?

MANDIE: Every time I make a batch of brownies.

[MANDIE *pours the batter into a brownie pan.* MAMMIE *watches her intently.*]

MAMMIE: (*motioning to the chair beside her*) Come, child. Have a seat. Tell me more about my Anthony.

SCENE 3

[MANDIE *and* MAMMIE *are sitting at the table, chatting.* ANTHONY *reenters and looks surprised to see them sitting together.*]

ANTHONY: (*kissing* MANDIE) Hello, ladies. Something smells good. (*He looks around.*) And is that a pan of brownies waiting to go into the oven?

MANDIE: Yes, Anthony. Now, go make yourself comfortable in the living room. We'll call you for dinner.

ANTHONY: (*bewildered*) Well, okay... I guess. Are you sure you don't want me to stay in here?

MANDIE: I'm sure. We have work to do. Now, go on.

[ANTHONY leaves, shaking his head and muttering to himself.]

MAMMIE: Besides, we can't talk about him when he's here!

[*They both laugh and move to finish the dinner preparations, chatting amiably.*]

THE END

27. What is the author's main purpose in writing this play?

a. To show that shared experiences can help build connections
b. To emphasize the importance of getting along as a family
c. To highlight the negative effects of disharmony between people
d. To display a picture of an everyday American family

28. How does the setting of this play influence Mammie's character?

a. It gives her a space to be a traditional wife and mother.
b. It causes her to become tough and resilient.
c. It forces her to rely on her intelligence and education.
d. It portrays her character as uptight and orderly.

29. Read these lines from the play.

MANDIE: Please don't leave me here with... her. She doesn't like me.
ANTHONY: Of course she likes you. Don't be silly. Why wouldn't she like you?
MANDIE: Oh, I don't know. She just doesn't. You don't know how she can be.

What can the reader predict based on these lines?

a. Mammie will welcome Mandie into her home.
b. Mandie will be uncomfortable around Mammie.
c. Anthony will let Mandie leave with him.
d. Mandie will try to win Mammie over.

30. How did Mandie and Mammie's behavior help resolve the conflict of the play?

a. Mammie was honest and said she hated Mandie, and Mandie accepted this.
b. Mammie and Mandie agree to do things differently but not argue.
c. Mandie is vulnerable, and Mammie sees she needs to support her.
d. Mandie makes Mammie realize she must like her because she is her family.

31. How does the author use irony in this play?

a. By making the women work together to accomplish a goal even though they dislike one another
b. By shocking Anthony with the fact that the women's new bond centers on his brownie habit
c. By making Mandie stop caring about what Mammie thought and then having Mammie start caring for her
d. By having the women bond in the same place Mandie confessed she was scared to be alone with Mammie

32. How does the use of action and silence in this play contribute to the development of Mammie's character?

a. It hints at events in Mammie's life that have formed her character.
b. It shows she is a poor communicator with most people.
c. It demonstrates the awkwardness of her relationship with Mandie.
d. It shows her love for Anthony even though she is not as fond of his wife.

33. Which event most likely encouraged Mandie and Mammie to bond with each other?

a. Anthony came home and was shocked by their behavior.
b. They both were able to cook something for dinner.
c. They realized they share a funny experience related to Anthony.
d. They spend a lot of time in silence before speaking to each other.

34. Which line from the play best demonstrates Mammie's critical tendencies?

a. Baked chicken. Rice. Asparagus.
b. Don't know how to make rice? Don't be silly. Everyone knows how to make rice.
c. Come, child. It's nothing to cry over. Hush now. What can you cook?
d. Besides, we can't talk about him when he's here!

Refer to the passage "Puck" to answer questions 35-42.

Puck

(1) It was the second week of an unseasonably cool July. The sun had finally made a rare weekend appearance, and the suburban neighborhood sizzled with possibility. As the day slipped lazily into evening, sunbaked residents trickled back to their homes from the lakeshore, the park, and the community pool. The air smelled of sunscreen, charcoal smoke, sweat, and overcooked meat.

(2) Will Jensen tossed a football across the yard to his best friend, Troy Coons. Dusk was settling around them, but the thought of retreating to the confines of the house seemed like a waste of the evening.

(3) "Can you believe we're going to college in a few weeks?" Troy asked, lobbing the ball back to Will.

(4) "What I can't believe is that you and I will be 600 miles apart," Will said, catching the ball easily. "I don't think we've gone more than three days without seeing each other since kindergarten."

(5) "Except for when you had chicken pox," Troy said. "And the time I went to Hawaii with my grandparents. Remember how we begged them to let you come in my luggage?"

(6) Will laughed and tossed the ball back. "Those things don't count," he argued.

(7) The ball went sideways, and Troy lunged for it, tripping over a ragged little terrier lounging lazily on the lawn. Troy collapsed in a tangled heap and the ball bounced down, just beyond his outstretched hand.

(8) "Puck!" Troy groaned. "No dogs on the field!"

(9) Will sauntered over and scooped up the little dog. He plopped down onto the crisp brown grass and laughed at Troy. Will reached over and rolled the ball toward Troy.

(10) "Don't blame Puck for your clumsiness," Will said, idly scratching the dog's fuzzy scalp. "How was he supposed to know you'd come stumbling through his daydreams?"

(11) Troy chuckled. Then they sat in silence as darkness swirled around them. Light glowed from windows thrown hopefully open to the faint breeze. Above them, the stars winked in the charcoal sky. In the distance, leftover fireworks crackled and fizzed. The night was ripe with memories to be made.

(12) "Are you taking Puck with you?" Troy finally asked, breaking the silence.

(13) "Nah. No dogs in the dorm. Besides, Puck would hate being locked up in a room. He's spent the last sixteen years being king of the castle. He'll be happier here. That way he can greet me whenever I make it back home."

(14) Will lifted Puck and held him in mid-air. Puck wriggled playfully and licked Will's nose with his doughy, pink tongue. Will laughed and set him down.

(15) "I sure will miss him, though," Will said, wiping Puck's saliva from his nose. "Puck's been a part of every memory I've had since I was really little."

(16) Troy faked a sniffle. "Stop, man. Just stop. I'm tearing up over here."

(17) Will punched Troy's arm good-naturedly. "Shut up!"

(18) A low, loud car careened around the corner, shattering the stupor of the summer night. Puck ran barking toward the car as it wove across the street like a wayward pinball.

(19) Seized with sudden panic, Will scrambled to his feet. "Puck, no! Come back!"

(20) As Will reached the sidewalk, Puck darted into the street. In a terrible, slow-motion montage, Will heard the tires squeal and Puck's bark turn to a startled yelp. Then the car sped away, and silence smothered the chaos.

(21) Will ran into the street. People peeked from doorways and windows, searching for the source of the commotion. Will fell beside Puck's limp body. Puck whimpered quietly and struggled to lick Will's hand. Then he was still.

(22) "No, Puck! No!" Will screamed. Shock rang in his ears, and he was dizzy with emotion. Troy put a hand on Will's shoulder, but Will shook it off. He didn't want to be comforted. He wanted to wallow and writhe in the pool of sadness that was overtaking him.

(23) Every memory he had with Puck flooded his mind. This was not how it was supposed to be. Puck was supposed to be waiting for him when he came home from college. He was supposed to watch out the window as Will drove away and be there wagging with excitement whenever Will came home. He was supposed to be the constant in Will's changing life. This was not part of the plan.

(24) Will stayed in the road for a long time, crouched over Puck. He felt numb, empty, and emotionless. Finally, Will's mother led him gently from the street. Troy and Will's father gathered Puck's body carefully into a sheet. Neighbors watched in sympathy as the sorrowful party crossed the lawn.

(25) They walked in silence as darkness swirled around them. Lights still glowed from windows thrown hopefully open to the faint breeze. Above them, stars still winked in the charcoal sky. In the distance, leftover fireworks still crackled and fizzed. Everything was the same, and nothing was the same. Puck was gone. And Will knew things would never really be the same again.

35. Which sentence from the passage best portrays Will and Troy's relationship as lighthearted?

a. Troy faked a sniffle. "Stop, man. Just stop. I'm tearing up over here."
b. "Can you believe we're going to college in a few weeks?" Troy asked, lobbing the ball back to Will.
c. "I sure will miss him, though," Will said, wiping Puck's saliva from his nose.
d. Troy put a hand on Will's shoulder, but Will shook it off.

36. What can the reader infer based on paragraph 4? Mark your answer for each inference below.

Inference	Supported by Paragraph 4	Not Supported by Paragraph 4
Troy and Will are excited to finally have some time apart from each other.		
Troy is ready to leave but Will wishes that he would not go without him.		
Troy and Will will miss each other while they are off at college.		
Troy is a little jealous that Will could take Puck with him to college.		
Troy and Will have had a strong connection since they first started school.		

37. Read the dictionary entry (from Oxford Languages and Merriam-Webster).

Montage

1. The process or technique of selecting, editing, and piecing together separate sections of film to form a continuous whole.
2. A sequence of film made using the technique of montage.
3. To combine into or depict in a montage.
4. A heterogeneous mixture.

Which definition best matches the way the word *montage* is used in paragraph 20?

a. Definition 1
b. Definition 2
c. Definition 3
d. Definition 4

38. Read this summary of "Puck":

> One summer evening, longtime friends Troy and Will enjoy time together outside. They talk about their next adventure that will be starting soon: going to college. Will explains how wonderful it will be to come home to his dog, Puck, on visits home from school. Shortly after, Puck dashes into the road where he is struck and killed by a car.

Which idea should be included to best summarize the passage?

a. The two have been friends since kindergarten.
b. Troy and Will are going to different colleges.
c. Will then realizes that everything has changed.
d. Will explains that the dorms do not allow dogs.

39. Based on the events in "Puck," which of the following best expresses the theme of the passage?

a. Change is inevitable.
b. College can be intimidating.
c. Teens cannot care for pets.
d. Happiness is forever.

40. What characteristics of the story help the reader identify it as realistic fiction?

a. The car in the passage is the same kind of car that exists in real life.
b. The characters are able to foresee what will happen to Puck.
c. The events that occur could potentially happen to a real person.
d. The setting is a cool summer evening after long periods of rain.

41. How does paragraph 18 foreshadow the accident?

a. It emphasizes Will and Puck's bond.
b. It creates a sense of danger.
c. It explains Puck's erratic behavior.
d. It demonstrates Troy's loyalty.

42. How does the author use figurative language in paragraph 22?

a. It uses irony and idioms to create a sense of humor.
b. It uses hyperbole and oxymorons to advance the plot.
c. It uses symbolism to create conflict between characters.
d. It uses imagery and metaphor to show a deep emotional impact.

Refer to the passage "Andy Grant's Pluck" to answer questions 43-46.

Andy Grant's Pluck

by Horatio Alger

(1) The house and everything about it seemed just as it did when he left at the beginning of the school term. But Andy looked at them with different eyes.

(2) Then he had been in good spirits, eager to return to his school work.

Now something had happened, he did not yet know what.

(3) Mrs. Grant was in the back part of the house, and Andy was in the sitting room before she was fully aware of his presence. Then she came in from the kitchen, where she was preparing supper.

(4) Her face seemed careworn, but there was a smile upon it as she greeted her son.

(5) "Then you got my telegram?" she said. "I didn't think you would be here so soon."

(6) "I started at once, mother, for I felt anxious. What has happened? Are you all well?"

(7) "Yes, thank God, we are in fair health, but we have met with misfortune."

(8) "What is it?"

(9) "Nathan Lawrence, cashier of the bank in Benton, has disappeared with twenty thousand dollars of the bank's money."

(10) "What has that to do with father? He hasn't much money in that bank."

(11) "Your father is on Mr. Lawrence's bond to the amount of six thousand dollars."

(12) "I see," answered Andy, gravely, "How much will he lose?"

(13) "The whole of it."

(14) This, then, was what had happened. To a man in moderate circumstances, it must needs be a heavy blow.

(15) "I suppose it will make a great difference?" said Andy, inquiringly.

(16) "You can judge. Your father's property consists of this farm and three thousand dollars in government bonds. It will be necessary to sacrifice the bonds and place a mortgage of three thousand dollars on the farm."

(17) "How much is the farm worth?"

(18) "Not over six thousand dollars."

(19) "Then father's property is nearly all swept away."

(20) "Yes," said his mother, sadly. "Hereafter he will receive no help from outside interest, and will, besides, have to pay interest on a mortgage of three thousand dollars, at six per cent."

(21) "One hundred and eighty dollars."

(22) "Yes."

(23) "Altogether, then, it will diminish our income by rather more than three hundred dollars."

(24) "Yes, Andy."

(25) "That is about what my education has been costing father," said Andy, in a low voice.

(26) He began to see how this misfortune was going to affect him.

(27) "I am afraid," faltered Mrs. Grant, "that you will have to leave school."

(28) "Of course I must," said Andy, speaking with a cheerfulness which he did not feel. "And in place of going to college I must see how I can help father bear this burden."

(29) "It will be very hard upon you, Andy," said his mother, in a tone of sympathy.

(30) "I shall be sorry, of course, mother; but there are plenty of boys who don't go to college. I shall be no worse off than they."

(31) "I am glad you bear the disappointment so well, Andy. It is of you your father and I have thought chiefly since the blow fell upon us."

(32) "Who will advance father the money on mortgage, mother?"

(33) "Squire Carter has expressed a willingness to do so. He will be here this evening to talk it over."

(34) "I am sorry for that, mother. He is a hard man. If there is a chance to take advantage of father, he won't hesitate to do it."

43. As it used in paragraph 1, the phrase *different eyes* means which of the following?

a. Andy's eyes have changed color
b. Andy now wears glasses
c. Andy sees that the mood in the house has changed
d. Andy is happy to be home

44. Read this sentence from paragraph 14:

To a man in moderate circumstances, it must needs be a heavy blow.

The author uses the metaphor a *heavy blow* to indicate which of the following?

a. Andy's father is in a difficult situation
b. Andy won't be able to go back to school
c. Andy's father has lost over six thousand dollars
d. Andy is disappointed about his family's problems

45. Which of these is the best summary of the selection?

a. Andy Grant comes home from school and discovers that his father has won six thousand dollars. He will use the money to buy equipment for the farm. Andy finds out that he will need to leave school in order to help his father on the farm and work for Squire Carter
b. Andy Grant goes home and discovers that his family has fallen upon misfortune. Nathan Lawrence, the bank's cashier, has stolen twenty thousand dollars of Andy's father's money. Now that Andy's family has lost so much money, they won't be able to pay for his education and he'll have to leave school
c. Andy Grant's father has lost six thousand dollars because Nathan Lawrence stole it. This loss will cost Andy's family a lot of money. Since Andy's family pays $300 a month for his school, he will have to stop going to school. Andy is very cheerful that he doesn't have to go to school. He decides to work for Squire Carter in order to help his family
d. Andy Grant's family has suffered a misfortune because the bank's cashier stole money, some of which belonged to Andy's father. Without the money, Andy's family will have trouble paying its bills, including Andy's school bills. Andy will have to stop going to school. Furthermore, his father will have to borrow money

46. What phrase or sentence from the selection best shows Andy's feelings about having to leave school?

a. He began to see how this misfortune was going to affect him
b. Speaking with a cheerfulness which he did not feel
c. And in place of going to college I must see how I can help father bear this burden
d. I am sorry for that, mother

Answers and Explanations for Reading Test #1

1. A: Throughout the passage, Wolfgang surprises his father with his abilities multiple times, such as when he plays a perfect chord at age three, plays minuets correctly after learning them in only a half hour, and creates a difficult harpsichord concerto at the age of five. These instances bring Leopold astonishment, wonder, and awe. This supports choice A, which is the correct answer. The passage does not suggest that Wolfgang had to work hard to receive Leopold's approval. In fact, Leopold was very proud of his son and recognized his talent, so choice B is incorrect. The passage does not support the idea that Wolfgang and his sister Nannerl had to battle for their parents' attention. The brother and sister receive music lessons together and their father is proud of both of them, so choice C is incorrect. The passage does not include any description of Wolfgang avoiding disobeying his father or fearing punishment from him, so choice D is incorrect.

2. B: Because of the third-person narration, the reader knows how both Wolfgang Mozart and his father, Leopold Mozart, feel about Wolfgang's concerto. For example, Wolfgang Mozart is "impatient" when his father interrupts him but then "eagerly" plays the first part of his composition. Leopold Mozart is at first "amused" and then is full of "wonder" and "awe" after seeing and hearing his young son's concerto. Knowing the thoughts and feelings of more than one character without them being stated in dialogue is common of a third-person omniscient point of view. Choice A is incorrect, as the author would use a first-person point of view with words such as "I" or "me" if she were describing how she had been inspired by Wolfgang Mozart. The passage does not clearly explain why Leopold Mozart thinks his son's age is too young to learn music, so choice C is incorrect. The passage does not include evidence that supports the idea that conflict is created because of the historical time period, so choice D is incorrect.

3. Part A: B: The passage reveals that Leopold Mozart gave lessons to Wolfgang's older sister, Nannerl, but told Wolfgang to wait when Wolfgang asked for lessons at age three. Based on this, the reader can infer that Leopold Mozart felt that three years old was too young to learn music. He only gave his young son lessons once he heard Wolfgang's talent. Although the passage is mainly about Wolfgang and describes him as a "genius," paragraph 7 states that Leopold saw "with pride almost beyond expression, that both of his children inherited his musical ability." This means that the reader cannot infer that Leopold was not also proud of Nannerl, so choice A is incorrect. The passage does not support the idea that Leopold was upset about his son Wolfgang's musical ability. There is only evidence of Leopold being proud of Wolfgang, so choice C is incorrect. Initially, Leopold is curious and amused when his son composes a piece of music. He is later filled with "wonder" and "awe" upon hearing Wolfgang play it. From Leopold's reactions, the reader cannot infer that he taught his son to write compositions, so choice D is incorrect.

Part B: D: The reader can infer that Leopold Mozart thought his children should be of a certain age before learning music because he told Wolfgang to wait when he was only three years old but was giving Wolfgang's older sister lesson.

4. D: The story is set in a household where Wolfgang Mozart spends time around his father, who is a talented musician. It is evident that Leopold Mozart values music since he teaches lessons to Nannerl, and later to Mozart. Since Wolfgang Mozart grew up surrounded by music, it is logical to assume that this influenced his appreciation of music, so choice D is correct. The time period of the story and the fact that music was not yet recorded did not directly influence Wolfgang Mozart's value for music. Someone can value music regardless of a given time period or how they listen to it, so choice A is incorrect. Although the passage mainly features Wolfgang Mozart and his family members, there is no evidence that he did not talk to other people besides his family, so choice B is incorrect. The fact that Wolfgang Mozart was given multiple names did not influence his beliefs on music, so choice C is incorrect.

5. C: Historical fiction stories take place in the past. They have characteristics that are appropriate for the given time period and include both historically accurate events and fictional events. Choice C tells the reader where (Salzburg) and when (1756) Wolfgang Mozart was born, which is a historically accurate event. It also tells the reader the setting of the passage, which shows the reader that this is a work of historical fiction. Choice A describes a character's reaction to an event, which is not unique to historical fiction, so this choice is incorrect. Choice B describes a scene that could happen in any type of fiction, not just historical fiction, so this choice is incorrect. Choice D describes a character's behavior that could occur in any genre of fiction or nonfiction, making this choice incorrect.

6. C: Paragraph 5 says that young Mozart touched the keys of the harpsichord to play "a perfect chord," which shows that *chord* is a musical term. This means that definition 3—three or more tones that produce harmony—is the best fit. Based on the way the word is used in paragraph 5, it would not make sense to say that Mozart played a feeling or emotion, so choice A is incorrect. The word *chord* is not used in the paragraph to describe a shape or line segment, so choice B is incorrect. Definition 4 describes a cord rather than a chord, and it does not describe something Mozart's father could have heard him playing musically, so choice D is incorrect.

7. A: In paragraph 5, Wolfgang Mozart's father tells him to wait to learn music, as he is "but a baby." However, Wolfgang Mozart creeps back into the room and plays a chord even though his father has told him no and he can only reach the keyboard by "standing on tiptoe." The paragraph highlights the fact that multiple challenges were standing in young Wolfgang Mozart's way, but he wanted to learn music anyway, so choice A is correct. Paragraphs 4 and 5 do not suggest that Wolfgang Mozart could have only made great music with his father's influence. In fact, the passage shows that his father initially told him he must wait to learn music because he was too young, so choice B is incorrect. The information in paragraphs 4 and 5 does not explain what inspired his earliest compositions, so choice C is incorrect. Paragraphs 4 and 5 do not suggest that Wolfgang Mozart wanted to be a better musician than his sister, so choice D is incorrect.

8. C: The language in paragraph 5 creates an affectionate tone. Leopold Mozart refers to his son, Wolfgang, as "my little man" and calls him by a nickname, "my Wolferl." This shows that even though Leopold Mozart told his son he was too young to learn music yet, he was doing so in a warm and loving manner, so choice C is correct. Although Leopold Mozart denied his son's request, he did so lovingly, not by giving a warning or using stern words, so choice A is incorrect. In this paragraph, Mozart is told that he must wait to learn music because he is so young. This disappoints Wolfgang rather than giving him hope, so choice B is incorrect. The warm and loving language in paragraph 5 is used by a father giving guidance to his son. His word choice is more personal and emotional than language used by friends, so choice D is incorrect.

9. D: This summary captures all the key ideas of the passage. It states that test anxiety is common but can be reduced with simple strategies, and it gives a list of the strategies given in the article. The passage opens with an example of a student with test anxiety, Lisa. However, the passage is not about Lisa. Also, this summary includes information that is not provided by the passage, so choice A is incorrect. Choice B leaves out key ideas and suggests that poor study habits are the main cause of test anxiety, so it is incorrect. Choice C leaves out key ideas in the passage since it only talks about relaxation techniques. It leaves out the other strategies and the main idea that test anxiety is common but can be managed, so choice C is incorrect.

10. D: "I can do this" is an example of a mantra, or a phrase that is repeated to benefit the speaker. In the context of the passage, a mantra can be used to reinforce that a student believes in his or her own abilities to do well on tests. Since a mantra is something with words that a student would repeat, it is not likely to be a deep breathing technique, so choice A is incorrect. A good-luck charm would be something a student would hold or carry for test anxiety, not something he or she would say, so choice B is incorrect. Choice C is incorrect because a mantra is described as something positive, and criticism is often negative.

11. B: Test anxiety is common. This is shown by the passage through the statement that millions of students deal with it. However, the fact that "few realize it can be improved" suggests that students still feel alone in dealing with their test anxiety. If students knew others shared their anxiety, they would be more likely to know about and share solutions, so choice B is correct. Choice A describes one student with test anxiety; it does not show that test anxiety is common or that students may feel alone, so it is incorrect. Choice C simply describes a common study habit that can increase test anxiety, so this choice is incorrect. Choice D describes a step that students can take to reduce test anxiety. This choice does not show that test anxiety is common or that students may feel alone in dealing with it, so it is incorrect.

12. A: Paragraphs 4 and 8 explain ways that other people can help a person manage test anxiety, such as using flashcards together and sharing test-taking victories, so choice A is correct. The use of games and tools is only supported by paragraph 4, so choice B is incorrect. Only paragraph 8 suggests that doing well on a test confirms an improvement in test anxiety management, not paragraph 4, so choice C is incorrect. The importance of sharing small successes is not supported by paragraph 4, only paragraph 8, so choice D is incorrect.

13. A: Choice A captures the controlling idea of the passage, which is that test anxiety is common but can be improved through the use of specific strategies. The use of Lisa as an example helps illustrate what it can be like for students who experience test anxiety. However, the idea that Lisa and others are experiencing a genuine type of anxiety is not the entire passage's controlling idea, so choice B is incorrect. Forming good study habits is just one specific strategy. Choice C gives a supporting detail from the passage, not the controlling idea, so it is incorrect. Going to other people for help with test anxiety is a supporting detail mentioned in the passage. Choice D leaves out important aspects of the controlling idea, so it is incorrect.

14. C: The passage is organized in a way that outlines a step-by-step process to overcome test anxiety. It does this by stating that there are three simple steps to achieve this and giving details that show how to do each step, so choice C is correct. The passage does discuss the value of improving study habits when aiming to improve test anxiety, but study habits are not the main topic of the passage, so choice A is incorrect. The passage does note that test anxiety can make a student's grades suffer, as illustrated with the example of Lisa, but the passage does not focus on the cause-and-effect relationship between test anxiety and students' grades, so choice B is incorrect. The passage does not reveal why some students do not experience test anxiety. It only highlights the ways that test anxiety can be overcome, so choice D is incorrect.

15. B: The passage provides three steps that can help a person overcome test anxiety when they are practiced consistently. This shows the reader that test anxiety is not likely to go away on its own, so choice B is correct. Forming good study habits is one of the steps, but it is not described as the most important way to reduce test anxiety, so choice A is incorrect. The passage does not explain text anxiety from a teacher's perspective, so choice C is incorrect. The symptoms of test anxiety are described, but the possibility that they could point to a bigger health problem is not discussed, so choice D is incorrect.

16. C, E: Based on the passage, the reader can infer that Sharon and Emma have a close and supportive relationship and consider each other's feelings. Emma offered to help Sharon in multiple ways when she gets frustrated. Sharon comforted Emma when Emma was sad about not being able to help. Emma was also eager to be Sharon's audience even though Emma couldn't help directly with the camera or by being in the video, and Sharon was thankful for Emma's help. The reader cannot infer that Sharon and Emma compete for their father's attention, as the passage does not give any evidence that supports this, so choice A is incorrect. While Emma wanted to help and support Sharon, the reader cannot infer that Emma wants to be like Sharon when she is older. None of Emma's dialogue or actions shows this, so choice B is incorrect. Sharon did not get frustrated with Emma not being able to help. In fact, Sharon tried to think of another way that Emma could help when Emma was sad about being too little to help, so choice D is incorrect.

17. C: Emma is motivated to help Sharon and tries to come up with ways to help. When her ideas do not work, she decides that she is okay with simply watching and being Sharon's audience. Emma's involvement ends up being very helpful to Sharon after all. So, even though Sharon would have been able to complete her project without Emma, Emma's desire to help causes the resolution to the conflict to be more helpful to Sharon than she expected. Emma does come up with different ideas for helping Sharon. However, since those ideas do not work, they add to the conflict rather than resolving it, so choice A is incorrect. Emma becomes sad in response to her developing conflict, wanting to help but being unable to. This is not part of the conflict resolution, so choice B is incorrect. Emma's discouragement upon finding that the costume is too big is part of the rising action rather than the conflict resolution, so choice D is incorrect.

18. D: Emma wanted to help Sharon, but she was too little to hold the camera or fit into the costumes. She did not know how else she could help, which made her feel upset. A conflict is a struggle that must be overcome. However, Emma asking Sharon what is wrong does not show what Emma is struggling with, so choice A is incorrect. Emma asking Sharon if she can watch and be the audience does not show the conflict Emma is experiencing, so choice B is incorrect. In choice C, Emma tries to provide a solution. Though this solution is not the best one for the problem at hand, this dialogue does not show a conflict that Emma is experiencing. It shows Sharon's conflict more clearly, as it shows that she needs someone to hold the camera. Choice C is incorrect.

19. C: Choice C is the most accurate summary of the events and conflict in the passage. The key concepts of the story's conflict and resolution are all present: Sharon's problem, Emma's desire to help, Emma's struggle to find a way to help, the girls' dad helping solve the problem, and Emma being able to help after all by being the audience. Choice A is incorrect, as it does not clearly describe the key ideas, conflict, and resolution of the passage and leaves out the fact that Emma was able to help after all. Choice B leaves out the story's conflict, which is that Emma wants to help Sharon but can't, so this choice is incorrect. Choice D is incorrect because it leaves out the resolution of the story.

20. A: The poet would most likely agree that every act of kindness is significant since the poem describes things that seem insignificant but highlights the difference they can make in the lives of others. While the poem highlights the value of deeds of kindness, it does not discuss doing kind deeds with a friend. The reader cannot predict that the poet would agree with the statement in choice B, so it is incorrect. The poem does not provide any evidence that being kind can help someone succeed in their goals, so the reader cannot predict that the poet would agree with this statement and choice C is incorrect. The poem does not support the idea that kind deeds unite people and bring them together for a cause, so choice D is incorrect.

21. B: This poem has a consistent rhythm and rhyme scheme, and it uses short lines. It also has a sing-song quality. These characteristics make this poem similar to many other poems written for children. This quality of the poem brings the reader's attention to the group that the poem is about: children. By doing this, the meter, structure, and rhyme highlight the poem's message, so choice B is correct. Choice A is incorrect because the consistency of the poem does not guarantee that it is easy to memorize. Choice C is incorrect because the rhyme scheme, meter, and line lengths used in this poem are not unique. They are commonly used in poetry. Choice D is incorrect because the rhyme scheme, meter, and line lengths do not cause the poem to sound like the elements of nature that the poem describes. The poem's sound is consistent, but the natural elements it describes are different from one another.

22. D: The last stanza highlights the fact that even small children can make a difference. It says that they can do deeds of kindness with a "loving spirit," even if they may have "little strength" or "little wisdom," so choice D is correct. It is not accurate to say that the poem contrasts children to things found in nature. Instead, it shows that though the cowslip, dewdrop, breezes, and little child may all seem small or insignificant, they can make a difference, so choice A is incorrect. While the last stanza states that a child may have "little wisdom," this is a detail that is used to contrast the fact that a child can still do loving and kind things for others. Therefore, the stanza is not suggesting that children are not wise enough to help others, so choice B is incorrect. The last stanza of the poem does not describe the value of appreciating nature or suggest that this starts in childhood, so choice C is incorrect.

23. B: A metaphor is a type of figurative language that compares two things. An extended metaphor continues throughout a work and uses more details than a standard metaphor. The purpose of the extended metaphor, which compares children to small delights in nature, is to show the value of children and how they can be helpful despite their age and experience. The extended metaphor is not used to explain what it is like to be a part of nature, and it does not compare the reader to the flowers mentioned in the poem, so choice A is incorrect. The extended metaphor does not use exaggeration; its language is literal and factual, so choice C is incorrect. The extended metaphor does not provide nature's point of view, and this is not the purpose of the poem, so choice D is incorrect.

24. A: Both passages suggest that no person or thing is too little to be helpful. In "Just Trying to Help," Emma was too little to help Sharon by holding the camera or wearing the costumes, but she was ultimately very helpful to Sharon by acting as an audience member. In "Deeds of Kindness," each of the four stanzas describes something that is small or little but is still helpful despite its size. While "Deeds of Kindness" does focus on kind deeds, it does not focus on kind deeds done for family members, so choice B is incorrect. Only "Just Trying to Help" shows multiple people working together to solve a problem, where "Deeds of Kindness" does not focus on solving problems or working together, so choice C is incorrect. Neither passage suggests that ignoring things that seem small can result in a cost. Instead, the passages suggest that things that seem small can be helpful, so choice D is incorrect.

25. C: In "Deeds of Kindness," the purpose of the items in nature are stated as each item is described. In "Just Trying to Help," Emma's purpose in the situation is not made clear until the end of the story. This makes choice C correct. "Just Trying to Help" does focus on Emma's feelings, as it shows that she felt sad and disappointed when she could not find a way to help, so choice A is incorrect. While family is only mentioned in "Just Trying to Help," the story does not center around a family disagreement, so choice B is incorrect. The items in nature do not make many attempts to be helpful. On the other hand, Emma came up with multiple ways to try to help Sharon in "Just Trying to Help," not just one, so choice D is incorrect.

26. C: Both the excerpt from the poem and choice C show something or someone thinking they are too small to help. Choice A shows how Emma feels after being a part of the activity. It does not show that she feels too small or little to help, so this choice is incorrect. Choice B shows one of Emma's ideas for helping, not her decision that she is too small to help, so this choice is incorrect. Choice D shows Emma's emotions upon not being able to help, but it does not make it clear that she felt she was too little to help, so this choice is incorrect.

27. A: This short play demonstrates that people can get along with each other better when they share common interests or experiences. Mandie and Mammie struggle to get along until Mammie realizes that she and Mandie do not have the same experiences. She realizes that she cannot assume what Mandie knows how to do when they are making dinner. Instead, she asks Mandie to cook something she knows how to make, so they are both able to make dinner together. As they are doing so, they learn that they have both had a similar experience with Anthony and bond over it. This demonstrates the idea in choice A, so it is correct. Choice B is incorrect because the play shows few effects of Mandie and Mammie's changed relationship. Choice C is incorrect because the play also only shows a couple of effects of the tension between Mandie and Mammie. The purpose of the play is not to show the impact of their relationship. Choice D is incorrect because this play only focuses on an out of the ordinary event and does not focus on a typical family.

28. A: The kitchen with old appliances and a large farmhouse table gives Mammie a place to be a traditional wife and mother, which she appears to be. It seems she values the older ways of doing things. Because the setting does not cause Mammie to live through challenging conditions, it does not make her tough or resilient. This makes choice B incorrect. Choice C is incorrect because the setting does not force Mammie to rely on her intelligence or education. While she does show that she has intelligence and knowledge, she is also able to use her emotions and other skills in the play. If Mammie were uptight and orderly, the setting would likely have mentioned things being clean and organized. These are not clear traits of the kitchen or dining table, so choice D is incorrect.

29. B: Based on Mandie's statement that Mammie doesn't like her and her comment that her husband does not "know how she can be," it can be concluded that Mammie will act in a way that makes Mandie uncomfortable.

Because it is clear that the two do not get along, it cannot be predicted that Mammie will welcome Mandie into her home, so choice A is incorrect. Choice C is incorrect because Anthony does not think Mammie dislikes Mandie. Therefore, the reader cannot assume that Anthony would take Mandie with him. Choice D is incorrect because these lines do not suggest that Mandie will make an attempt to get Mammie to like her. She seems to have resolved to let Mammie dislike her.

30. C: Mandie feels as though Mammie does not like her, so she does not want to spend time around her. While preparing dinner, Mandie is vulnerable and tearfully confesses that she does not know how to make rice. Mammie sees that Mandie needs care and support at this time. She cups her face and is calm and patient with her. She then gives Mandie a more appropriate task, and they later bond over it as they talk about Anthony. This makes choice C correct. Mammie did not say that she hated Mandie. While it is true Mammie seemed disinterested in her, there is no sign of hatred, so choice A is incorrect. At the end of the story, the women have bonded and enjoy time together. They do not discuss the different ways that they do things, so choice B is incorrect. Mandie does not use her position as Mammie's daughter-in-law to convince Mammie to like her, so choice D is incorrect.

31. D: At the beginning of the play, Mandie expresses to Anthony that she thinks his mother does not like her. She does this while they are standing in the kitchen. This is the same place where Mammie and Mandie later bond and enjoy their time together, so choice D is correct. The women do work together to achieve a goal: cooking dinner. However, the women grow to like each other as they are cooking, so choice A is incorrect. While it is true that they bonded over the way Anthony eats brownies, they did not explain this to Anthony, so he could not have been shocked by it. Additionally, this would not be an example of irony, so choice B is incorrect. The story does not suggest that Mandie no longer cares what Mammie thinks of her. Mammie shows care for Mandie just after Mandie begins crying, so choice C is incorrect.

32. C: Silence and action contribute to the development of Mammie's character by showing how awkwardly she behaves with Mandie. At the beginning of scene 2, she says very little to Mandie, and her behavior can easily be interpreted as rude. In reality, Mammie probably just does not know what to say to Mandie. Choice A is incorrect because Mammie's silence and actions do not suggest anything about her past. Choice B is incorrect because the play only shows Mammie behaving this way with Mandie, not with others. Choice D is incorrect because these behaviors do not suggest that she loves Anthony.

33. C: Mandie's relationship with Mammie begins to improve when Mammie tells Mandy that when Anthony was growing up, he loved to stick his finger into the middle brownie after she baked them, and Mandy replies by laughing about the fact that he still does it. After that, Mammie asks Mandie to come sit and talk with her about Anthony, which gives them an opportunity to get to know each other and learn to enjoy talking together. Choice A is incorrect because Anthony's reaction is a result of Mammie and Mandie's changed behavior. Choice B is incorrect because, while the task of cooking dinner put them in the same setting together, neither Mammie nor Mandie really relaxed or opened up until they began laughing about Anthony. Choice D is incorrect because their silence created more tension and distance between them.

34. B: Choice B clearly shows Mammie's critical tendencies because of the way she responds to Mandie's ignorance. She tells her to stop being silly because everyone knows how to cook rice. She is so sure that everyone should know this skill that she does not even consider that Mandie may not know how to do it. When Mandie does claim that she does not know how to cook rice, Mammie criticizes the idea and acts as though it is ridiculous. Choice A is incorrect because this line does not show that Mammie is critical. It only shows that she is short and does not have much else to say to Mandie. Choice C is incorrect because Mammie is attempting to comfort Mandie and correct the effects of her criticism. Choice D is incorrect because Mammie is joking about her son. She and Mandie are not necessarily saying things that are critical of Anthony.

35. A: Troy feels comfortable enough to tease Will by pretending to be overwhelmed with emotions and cry when Will talks about his relationship with his dog. This portrays their relationship as lighthearted. Choice B is part of their conversation about going away to college. This helps set the period of life the boys are in but does not describe their friendship. It is also an important topic and not one that they talk about lightly, so choice B is incorrect. Choice C portrays the relationship between Will and his dog, not Will and Troy, so it is incorrect. In choice D, it is clear that Troy cares for Will. However, this action is done out of concern for him, so it is not a lighthearted action. This means that choice D is incorrect.

36.

Inference	Supported by Paragraph 4	Not Supported by Paragraph 4
Troy and Will are excited to finally have some time apart from each other.		X
Troy is ready to leave but Will wishes that he would not go without him.		X
Troy and Will will miss each other while they are off at college.	X	
Troy is a little jealous that Will could take Puck with him to college.		X
Troy and Will have had a strong connection since they first started school.	X	

In paragraph 4, Will explains that he and Troy have not gone more than three days without seeing each other since they were in kindergarten, and he is in disbelief that they will soon be far away from one another. The passage also states that they are best friends. From this, the reader can infer that Will and Troy have had a strong connection since they first began school. This also supports the inference that Will and Troy will miss each other while they are at different colleges. While they express excitement about going to school, they do not express excitement about being apart from each other. The story includes no mention of Will not wanting Troy to go without him. They are going to different schools, and neither boy asks if he can go with the other. Troy does not ask Will if he is taking Puck until paragraph 12. When he does ask, it seems to be out of curiosity and an effort to carry on the conversation. He does not seem jealous.

37. B: Paragraph 20 states "in a terrible, slow-motion montage, Will heard the tires squeal and Puck's bark turn to a startled yelp." This means that Will is hearing and seeing what is happening as if in a film sequence. This makes choice B correct. Choice A is incorrect because this definition explains the process of creating montage films. Definition 3 is the verb form of montage, meaning to put clips together to create a whole, so choice C is incorrect. Heterogenous mixture in definition 4 means a combination of unlike things. This definition does not match what is happening in paragraph 20, so choice D is incorrect.

38. C: The last paragraph of the passage focuses on how, though many things are the same, many more will be different for Will because of Puck's passing. This is a major part of the theme of the story and should be included in the summary, so choice C is correct. Because the summary already mentions that the boys were "longtime friends," there is no need to explain that they have been friends since kindergarten. This information would be redundant, so choice A is incorrect. While it is true the boys are going to different schools, this is not a key idea of the story, so choice B is incorrect. Similarly, the fact that dogs are not allowed in the dorms is not a key idea or part of the story's theme, so choice D is incorrect.

39. A: The story begins with Troy and Will discussing a big change that is coming. They talk about the fact that they will be attending different schools and will be apart from each other for a long time. Another massive change occurs later when Will's dog, Puck, tragically dies. The passage ends with a paragraph that describes

Will's realization that things will never be the same. This is best summarized by choice A. Troy and Will do not discuss being scared or intimidated by the idea of college, so choice B is incorrect. Though Puck runs into traffic while Will is watching him, the focus of the passage is not on Will's ability to care for Puck, so choice C is incorrect. The sudden passing of Puck causes extreme sadness for Will, showing that his moment of happiness prior to the accident is over. This shows that happiness is something that comes and goes, so choice D is incorrect.

40. C: The events that happened in this story, such as Troy and Will throwing a football while discussing upcoming life changes and the accident involving Puck, are realistic and could happen to the average person. Realistic events and characters are major characteristics of realistic fiction, so choice C is the correct answer. While it is true the car in the passage seems to be a normal car that exists in real life, these cars could be used in many genres. This alone is not enough information to determine that the passage is realistic fiction, so choice A is incorrect. The characters are not able to predict what will happen to Puck until just before the accident happens. If they had an abnormal ability to see into the future, the passage would not be realistic, so choice C is incorrect. Choice D is incorrect because these facts about the setting do not show that the story is realistic fiction. This setting could also be used in other genres.

41. B: In paragraph 18, "a low, loud car careened around the corner, shattering the stupor of the summer night. Puck ran barking toward the car as it wove across the street like a wayward pinball." This creates tension and a sense of danger as Puck rushes toward the reckless driver. While Will and Puck's bond is emphasized in the passage, it is not the focus of paragraph 18. Additionally, their close bond does not directly foreshadow the accident, so choice A is incorrect. Though Puck quickly darted into traffic, he was not described as being erratic, so choice C is incorrect. Troy is portrayed as a loyal and caring friend, but this does not happen in paragraph 18 or foreshadow the accident, so choice D is incorrect.

42. D: Paragraph 22 uses the metaphor "dizzy with emotion" to portray how Will feels when he realizes that his dog has passed away. The statement that Will "wanted to wallow and writhe in the pool of sadness that was overtaking him" uses imagery to show the depth of Will's sadness, so choice D is correct. Paragraph 22 does not contain examples of irony or idioms, and the paragraph is not funny, so choice A is incorrect. Choice B is incorrect because paragraph 22 does not contain any exaggerations or contrasts. The paragraph does not contain symbolism, nor does it create conflict between characters, so choice C is incorrect.

43. C: The correct answer is C because Andy and his family were in good spirits, or happy, when he left for school at the beginning of the term. Now that he's returned, he knows something is wrong, but isn't sure what it is. Choice A is incorrect because the passage does not discuss Andy's eye color. The phrase *different eyes* is used metaphorically and does not literally mean that Andy has different eyes. For this reason, choice B is also incorrect. Choice D is incorrect because Andy is uneasy rather than happy. He knows something bad has happened.

44. A: Choice A is the correct answer because the phrase *a heavy blow* refers to the very difficult situation that Andy's father now finds himself in. The difficult situation hit him like a hammer, or heavy blow, because it was sudden and very financially painful. While it's true that Andy can't go back to school, choice B is incorrect because the sentence refers to Andy's father rather than Andy. Although losing six thousand dollars is part of the heavy blow, choice C is incorrect because the sentence does not show how much money Andy's father lost. The reader finds out the amount of money in paragraph 11, while the sentence in the question does not appear until paragraph 14. Choice D is incorrect because the sentence does not refer to Andy.

45. D: While parts of the other answer choices are correct, the best answer is choice D because it is the only choice that correctly summarizes the passage. Choice A is incorrect because Andy's father has not won six thousand dollars; he has lost that amount of money. Choice B is incorrect because Nathan Lawrence has stolen twenty thousand dollars, but only six thousand of that amount belonged to Andy's father. Choice C is incorrect because Andy is not cheerful that he doesn't have to go back to school; he likes school and is very disappointed.

46. B: The reader learns in paragraph 1 that Andy likes school. When Andy finds out he can't return to school, he is disappointed but he makes his voice sound cheerful when he's speaking to his family. Choice A is incorrect because it doesn't show Andy's feelings; it just shows that Andy knows how the family's misfortune will affect his studies. Choice C is incorrect because it simply contains Andy's new plans for the future and does not show his emotions. Choice D is incorrect even though this sentence does show Andy's emotions. However, this sentence refers to Andy's opinion about Squire Carter and not about returning to school.

Language Practice Test #1

Questions 1 – 7 pertain to the following passage:

An American Hero

(1) In the year 1912, the unsinkable Titanic sank, the United States territory of Arizona became a state, and my Great Uncle Charlie was born. (2) Charlie was born in a small town in Kentucky. (3) On a farm. (4) He grew up learning about the seasons, when to plant the seeds, and when the crops were ripe for picking. (5) His mornings were spent with his hands in dirt as he tended to the growing corps.

(6) When Charlie was only 12, his father died. (7) He had to quit school to take care of his family. (8) While other children were learning and playing at school, Charlie worked in factories to help pay for his mother and sisters to eat. (9) Irregardless of how he felt about having to work, Charlie never complained.

(10) On December 7, 1941, Japan attacked the American naval base at Pearl Harbor. (11) Charlie enlisted in the army when he was 30 years old, and went to fight in the war. (12) He fought in six major battles, including landing in Normandy on D-Day. (13) While he was in the army, Charlie joined the United States horseshoe team and became the champion of the European allies. (14) After the war, Charlie returned to Kentucky married a woman named Bethany, and had three children.

(15) Today, Charlie can still be found with his hands in the dirt. (16) He loves to work in the small garden beside his front porch. (17) The bright colors of ripening strawberries, tomatoes, and ears of corn can be seen next to the house with Charlie walking though the rows of crops with his watering can. (18) He tends to them with love. (19) Charlie watches over his family like the crops in the garden, and that is why he is my hero.

1. What is the BEST way to explain the information in sentences 2 and 3?

a. Charlie was born in a small town in Kentucky. It was on a farm
b. Charlie was born in Kentucky. In a small town and on a farm
c. Charlie was born in a small town. In Kentucky, it was on a farm
d. Charlie was born in a small Kentucky town on a farm

2. What change, if any, should be made to sentence 5?

a. Change *corps* to *crops*
b. Change *were* to *was*
c. Insert a comma after *dirt*
d. Make no change

3. What change, if any, should be made to sentence 9?

a. Change *complained* to *complains*
b. Change *irregardless* to *regardless*
c. Delete the comma after *work*
d. Make no change

4. What sentence could BEST follow and support sentence 10?

a. Pearl Harbor is a naval base in Hawaii
b. The USS Arizona was one of the battleships that sank
c. This event directly led into the United States' involvement in World War II
d. Charlie had never been to Hawaii

5. What change, if any, should be made to sentence 14?

a. Change *returned* to *returns*
b. Insert a comma after *Kentucky*
c. Insert *and* after *Kentucky*
d. Make no change

6. What change, if any, should be made in sentence 16?

a. Change *loves* to *loved*
b. Insert a comma after *garden*
c. Change *beside* to *besides*
d. Make no change

7. What change, if any, should be made in sentence 17?

a. Change *colors* to *colours*
b. Delete the comma after *strawberries*
c. Change *though* to *through*
d. Make no change

Questions 8 – 14 pertain to the following story:

The Top Deck

(1) We walked outside through the sliding glass doors and waited in line for the large, double-decker red bus. (2) My family flew to London for a week in July to celebrate my sisters graduation. (3) She wore a blue cap and gown. (4) The sky was gray, and light puddles spotted the ground. (5) As the bus pulled up against the curb, dirty water splashed our feet.

(6) The driver's seat was on the opposite side of the bus, and the driver smiled at me when I showed him my ticket. (7) I looked out the window and realised that we were driving on the opposite side of the street. (8) All around us people who were on the wrong side of the street driving from what looked like the passenger seat. (9) The bus was filled with people. (10) Almost every seat was taken, and people were even standing in the aisle holding onto handrails and poles. (11) Their was a spiral staircase directly behind the driver, and we walked up to it to try to find more seats. (12) There were two rows of seats upstairs and a large window that looked onto the streets. (13) Four seats were open near the front of the bus and we hurried to get them.

(14) The bus stopped every few seconds, and each time I had to hold onto my seat to keep from sliding into the aisle. (15) "What street are we looking for?" my dad asked my mom. (16) "Oxford" she replied. (17) I looked out the giant window. (18) We passed a large building that was shaped like an egg, and we continued to travel. (19) The bus driver's voice came over the speakers. (20) "Now approaching Liverpool," he said

(21) My mom looked at my dad. (22) I grabbed my sister's arm, but she was busy taking pictures of the buildings out the window. (23) "Liverpool," my mom whispered with a worried look on her face. (24) "We're lost, aren't we?" my dad said.

8. What change, if any, should be made in sentence 2?

a. Change *flew* to *flied*
b. Change *week* to *weak*
c. Change *sisters* to *sister's*
d. Make no change

9. What change, if any, should be made in sentence 7?

a. Change *realised* to *realize*
b. Change *street* to *streat*
c. Change *looked* to *look*
d. Make no change

10. What change, if any, should be made in sentence 11?

a. Delete the comma after *driver*
b. Change *Their* to *There*
c. Change *staircase* to *stair case*
d. Make no change

11. Which of the following is the BEST way to rewrite the ideas in sentence 8?

a. All around us people were driving from what looked like the passenger seat, and they were driving on the opposite side of the street
b. All around us people who were on the wrong side of the street, driving from what looked like the passenger seat
c. All around us people were driving on the wrong side of the street. Driving from what looked like the passenger seat
d. All around us people were driving from what looked like passenger seat, they were on the opposite side of the street

12. What change, if any, should be made in sentence 16?

a. Change *Oxford* to *oxford*
b. Insert a comma after *Oxford*
c. Insert a period after the quotation mark
d. Make no change

13. Which sentence does not belong in this essay?

a. Sentence 20
b. Sentence 6
c. Sentence 13
d. Sentence 3

14. What is the BEST transition word or phrase that could be added to the beginning of sentence 19?

a. However
b. Once in a while
c. Additionally
d. After a while

Questions 15 – 21 pertain to the following story:

Longhorn Café

(1) Last Saturday night my dad took me to watch the Longhorns play football in Austin. (2) It was a cool evening, and the orange-painted stadium was filled with screaming fans. (3) Even though we live in San Antonio, my dad has always been a dedicated Longhorns fan, and he wears his orange proudly.

(4) We arrived in Austin early. (5) "Traffic," my dad said as his only explanation. (6) He parked the truck down a small side street and motions for me to get out and follow him. (7) "I want to take you someplace," he said. (8) "I used to come here all the time when I was in college. (9) We walked up to a small building with a large patio off to the side. (10) A large tree with low branches spread across the patio and connected with the roof. (11) The leaves were beginning to change colors, and it was like sitting under a leafy canopy.

(12) We sat at a table outside on a rusting rocking bench beside an abandoned bathtub. (13) Stands of colored lights hung across the patio. (14) Wrapped around the tree. (15) "What is this place?" I asked. (16) My dad smiled and pointed to a sign bordered with colored lights. (17) "Spider Café," he said. (18) All around us, people were drinking coffee and staring at them computer screens. (19) Our waiter was named Chris, and he had a long beard, wore a dirtied apron, and carried empty coffee mugs.

(20) The waited came up to us, and my dad ordered himself a latte and a sweet drink for me. (21) My dad looked around the patio and smiled. (22) He leaned into the bench and placed his hand on the side of the bathtub. (23) He didn't even mind when he spilled coffee onto his favorite orange shirt. (24) "You'll love it here," he said, "when you are a Longhorn football player?"

15. What change should be made in sentence 6?

a. Change *parked* to *park*
b. Change *street* to *Street*
c. Insert a comma after *street*
d. Change *motions* to *motioned*

16. What change, if any, should be made in sentence 8?

a. Change *come* to *came*
b. Change *to* to *too*
c. Insert a quotation mark after *college*
d. Make no change

17. What revision, if any, is needed in sentences 13 and 14?

a. Strands of colored lights hung across the patio wrapped, around the tree
b. Strands of colored lights hung across the patio and wrapped around the tree
c. Strands of colored lights hung. Across the patio, wrapped around the tree
d. No revision is needed

18. What change, if any, should be made in sentence 18?

a. Change *them* to *their*
b. Delete the comma after *us*
c. Insert a comma after *and*
d. Make no change

19. Where is the best placement for sentence 19?

a. After sentence 22
b. After sentence 20
c. Before sentence 18
d. No change is needed

20. What change, if any, should be made in sentence 20?

a. Change *ordered* to *orders*
b. Change *himself* to *hisself*
c. Change *waited* to *waiter*
d. Make no change

21. What change should be made in sentence 24?

a. Change *Longhorn* to *longhorn*
b. Change *you are* to *your*
c. Change *football* to *Football*
d. Change the question mark to a period

Questions 22 – 28 pertain to the following story:

Strike Three

(1) As I stared down at the hitter in the batters box, I remembered what my dad had said to me. (2) "Shut everything out." (3) I focused on the glove in front of me. (4) I looked into the deep, blackened pocket, and sawed my target. (5) The batter tapped his bat against the sides of his cleats, and rested the bat on his shoulders. (6) With hard eyes, he stared back at me.

(7) I kicked the front of my cleat into the bright white rubber on the pitching mound and took a deep breath. (8) Shut everything out," he had said. (9) Slowly the noises disappeared. (10) I could no longer hear the shouts from the parents in the stands. (11) In my head, I silenced the cheers from both dugouts. (12) The umpire did not exist. (13) There were no players, no coaches, not even a catcher. (14) There was just me. (15) The ball and the glove.

(16) I took a deep breath and brought my hands together at my chest. (17) I looked over at first base, but there was no runner. (18) In one motion, my feet left the rubber and connected with ground. (19) Dirt flew in the air as my arm rotated forward and released the ball in front of me. (20) I watched as the ball spun and landed into glove with a hard crack. (21) The umpire shot up from his crouched position and pointed his finger to the right and yelled, "Strike Three!"

(22) The noises came back. (23) The crowd cheered in the stands and I could here stomping feet. (24) My teammate clapped his hand to its glove and ran toward me. (25) My coach raised a first into the air in celebration. (26) I was surrounded by my teammates, and they were patting me on the back. (27) My dad was sitting on a bleacher behind home plate. (28) He raised his thumb to me and smiled as I ran off the field with my teammates.

22. What change, if any, should be made in sentence 1?

a. Change *stared* to *starred*
b. Change *dad* to *Dad*
c. Change *batters* to *batter's*
d. Make no change

23. What change should be made in sentence 4?

a. Change *blackened* to *blacked*
b. Change *sawed* to *saw*
c. Delete the comma after *deep*
d. Change *into* to *in to*

24. What change should be made in sentence 8?

a. Change *everything* to *every thing*
b. Delete the comma after *out*
c. Change the comma after *out* to a period
d. Insert quotation marks before *Shut*

25. What is the best way to combine sentence 14 and sentence 15?

a. There was just the ball, the glove, and me
b. There was just me, the ball, and the glove
c. There was just me and the ball and the glove
d. Make no change

26. What change, if any, should be made in sentence 23?

a. Change *cheered* to *cheer*
b. Change *here* to *hear*
c. Change *could* to *can*
d. Make no change

27. What sentence could BEST follow and support sentence 22?

a. My foot was still planted hard into the ground
b. The sounds came flooding into my ears as I looked up
c. I felt good
d. The umpire took off his mask and started walking toward the fence

28. What is the BEST transition word that could be added to the beginning of sentence 26?

a. However
b. Consequentially
c. Soon
d. Therefore

Questions 29 – 34 pertain to the following passage:

Imagine a Better World

(1) My favorite song is "Imagine" by John Lennon. (2) It was released in 1971. (3) It is one of the few famous songs that John Lennon recorded and sang alone. (4) For the majority of his career, John Lennon was a member of an iconic rock band called the Beatles, a band that changed the music industry. (5) The Beatles accepted a lot of success in their career, with popular songs such as "I Want to Hold Your Hand," "Come Together," "Let it Be," and "Here Comes the Sun." (6) After the band decided to separate, John Lennon became a solo artist as well as an promoter for peace.

(7) "Imagine" tells the story of Lennons dream of peace in the world. He asks the listener to imagine different situations. (8) He says to imagine that there are no countries, religions, or possessions. (9) He says, "I wonder if you can." (10) This line strikes me the most I try to imagine such a world. (11) When talking about no possessions, he continues and says, "No need for greed or hunger." (12) It is a great line. (13) Throughout the song, he says, "Imagine all the people," and he gives examples. (14) At first he says, "living for today," and then moves on to say, "living life in peace," and finally, "sharing all the world."

(15) My favorite part of the song is the chorus. (16) Lennon says, "You may say I'm a dreamer, but I'm not the only one. (17) I hope someday you'll join us, and the world will be as one." (18) When I really listen to the words of this song, I realize that "Imagine" is so much more than something that sounds nicely. (19) Lennon is saying something very important and suggesting ways in which the world can live in peace. (20) Because of this song, I am a dreamer as well, and I join John Lennon in the fight for world peace.

29. What is the BEST verb to replace *accepted* in sentence 5?

a. Lasted
b. Liked
c. Had
d. Watched

30. What change should be made in sentence 6?

a. Change *separate* to *separated*
b. Insert a comma after *artist*
c. Change *solo* to *Solo*
d. Change *an* to *a*

31. What change, if any, should be made in sentence 7?

a. Change *Lennons* to *Lennon's*
b. Change *dream* to *dreamt*
c. Insert a comma after *peace*
d. Make no change

32. What is the BEST way to revise sentence 10?

a. This line strikes me the most as I try to imagine such a world.
b. This line strikes me the most, I try to imagine such a world.
c. This line strikes me, the most. I try to imagine such a world.
d. No revision needed.

33. What change, if any, should be made in sentence 17?

a. Insert a quotation mark before *I*
b. Move the period after the quotation marks
c. Change *you'll* to *youl'l*
d. Make no change

34. What change should be made in sentence 18?

a. Delete the comma after *song*
b. Change *something* to *some thing*
c. Change *nicely* to *nice*
d. Change realize to realized

Answers and Explanations for Language Test #1

1. D: because this sentence is the simplest way to explain where Charlie was born. A is not correct because two sentences are not necessary. The additional subject and verb are unnecessary to express the idea. B is not correct, because *In a small town and on a farm* is a fragment. C is not correct, because the sentences contain awkward wording. The sentences need to be combined in order to express the idea in the simplest form.

2. A: because in this sentence, *crops* has been misspelled as *corps*. B is not correct, because the subject of the sentence, *mornings*, is plural. Therefore, the verb also must be plural for correct subject verb agreement. C is not correct, because this sentence does not need a comma.

3. B: because irregardless is not a word. The correct word is *regardless.* A is not correct because *complains* is in the present tense, while the rest of the paragraph is in the past tense. C is not correct, because a comma is needed after an introductory clause.

4. C: because this sentence supports both sentence 10 and sentence 11. The sentence supports the cause and effect idea that the attack on Pearl Harbor prompted the United States to become involved in the war, which caused Charlie to enlist in the army. A is not correct. Although this sentence provides new information, it does not link and support sentences 10 and 11. B is not correct. Although this sentence provides new information, it does not link and support sentences 10 and 11. D is not correct. Although this sentence provides new information, it does not link and support sentences 10 and 11.

5. B: because this sentence uses commas in a series as it lists aspects of Charlie's life after the war. Both *returned to Kentucky* and *married a woman named Bethany* are events that have happened and therefore need to be separated by a comma. A is not correct. *Returns* is in the present tense, and the rest of the paragraph is written in the past tense. C is not correct. The correct sentence uses commas in a series, and therefore only uses one *and* in the sentence.

6. D: because the sentence is correct as written. A is not correct. Although the rest of the essay is written in the past tense, the last paragraph begins with *Today* and is written in the present tense. Therefore, *loves* is correct. B is not correct, because this sentence does not need a comma. C is not correct. Both *beside* and *besides* are prepositions, but *beside* means "next to" and *besides* means "in addition to" or "other than." *Beside* is used in this sentence as "next to."

7. C: because in this sentence, *through* has been misspelled as *though.* A is not correct, because *colors* is spelled correctly. B is not correct, because this sentence needs a comma after *strawberries,* since the sentence contains a list and uses commas in a series.

8. C: In this sentence, *Sister's* is possessive and requires an apostrophe. A is not correct. *Flew* is the correct past tense of *fly*. B is not correct, because *week* is a noun and is spelled correctly.

9. A: because *realized* is misspelled in this sentence. B is not correct, because *street* is spelled correctly. C is not correct, because *look* is in the present tense, while the essay is written in past tense.

10. B: because a homonym has been misused. *There* is used to indicate a physical or abstract place, while *their* is used to indicate possession. A is not correct, because this sentence has two independent clauses joined by the conjunction *and*, and a comma is used before the conjunction. C is not correct, because *staircase* is one word.

11. A: because this rewording of this sentence makes the meaning clear and is grammatically correct. B is not correct because this sentence is a fragment. C is not correct because the second sentence is a fragment. D is not correct because this sentence is a run-on sentence.

12. B: because a comma is needed before the closing quotation when the sentence is not completed with the quotation. A is not correct because *Oxford* is a proper noun and must be capitalized. C is not correct. The sentence does not end with the quotation; therefore, a comma, rather than a period, goes before the quotation mark.

13. D: because this sentence this sentence provides new information that is not important to the rest of the essay. Answers A, B, and C are incorrect, because all of these sentences present content that is important to the essay.

14. D: In the previous sentence, the phrase *we continued to travel*, suggests a passage of time. A proper transition into the next sentence would involve the acknowledgement that time has passed. A is not correct because *however* is not a good transition into the sentence. B is not correct. Although *once in a while* relates to time, it does not transition well into the sentence given the context of the previous sentence. C is not correct. *Additionally* is not a good transition into the sentence because it does not indicate a passage of time.

15. D: because *motions* is in the present tense, and the rest of the essay is written in the past tense. B is not correct because *street* is not used in this sentence as a proper noun and does not need to be capitalized. C is not correct. A comma is unnecessary because the second sentence is not an independent clause.

16. C: because a quotation mark is needed to end dialogue. A is incorrect because *come* is in the present tense, and the essay is written in the past tense. B is not correct. *Too* means "also" or an indication of excess.

17. B: because this sentence is grammatically correct as written. A is not correct. The comma is misplaced and disrupts the sentence. C is not correct because the second sentence is a fragment. D is not correct because sentence 14 is a fragment.

18. A: because *their* indicates possession; *them* does not. *Computer screens* belong to the subject, *people*. B is not correct. *All around us* is an introductory clause and needs a comma. C is not correct. *Staring at them computer screens* is not an independent clause and therefore does not need a comma.

19. B: because the sentence provides additional information about the waiter. The sentence should be placed after the waiter has been introduced in sentence 20. A is not correct. The subject of the paragraph has shifted to the father at sentence 21, and therefore a sentence involving information about the waiter would be out of place after sentence 22. C is not correct. Sentence 18 provides setting information. A sentence involving information about the waiter before this sentence would be out of place. D is not correct. This sentence provides additional information about the waiter and should not conclude a paragraph.

20. C: because *waiter* has been misspelled. A is not correct. *Orders* is in the present tense, and the essay is written in the past tense. B is not correct because *himself* is the correct word, while *hisself* is not a word.

21. D: because the sentence is a statement, not a question. Therefore, the sentence needs to be punctuated with a period. A is not correct. In this sentence, *longhorn* refers to the mascot of a sports team and is a proper noun. Proper nouns need to be capitalized. B is not correct. *You* and *are* in this sentence are used as both a subject and a verb. *Your* indicates possession. C is not correct. *Football* is not a proper noun and does not require capitalization.

22. C: In this sentence, *batter's* is possessive and needs an apostrophe. A is not correct because *stared*, the past tense of the verb, *stare*, is spelled correctly. B is not correct. In this sentence, *dad* is not a proper noun, since it is not used as a name. *My* before *dad* indicates that it is not a proper noun.

23. B: because *saw* is the correct past tense of the verb, *see*. A is not correct because *blackened* is the correct adjective. C is not correct. A comma is needed to separate adjectives when each adjective separately describes the noun. D is not correct. *Into* is spelled correctly.

24. D: It is correct because the quotation marks after *out* indicate dialogue. Quotation marks are needed before *Shut* to begin the dialogue. A is not correct. When used as a noun, *everything* is one word. B is not correct. A comma is needed before the closing quotation when the sentence is not completed with the quotation. C is not correct. The sentence is not completed with the quotation, and therefore it needs a comma rather than a period before the closing quotation.

25. A: because this sentence is grammatically correct. B is not correct. When using the pronoun, *me*, in a series, it is always placed at the end of the series. C is not correct. The repetition of *and* is not grammatically correct. The nouns need to be separated using commas in a series.

26. B: It is correct because a homonym has been misused. *Hear* indicates the act of hearing and listening. *Here* indicates location. A is not correct. *Cheer* is in the present tense, and the rest of the essay is in the past tense. C is not correct. *Can* is in the present tense, and the rest of the essay is in the past tense.

27. B: It is correct because this sentence supports both sentence 22 and 23. The preceding sentence discusses noises coming back. The next logical sentence should have something to do with noises. A is not correct. Although this sentence provides new information, it does not link and support sentences 22 and 23. C is not correct. Although this sentence provides new information, it does not link and support sentences 22 and 23. D is not correct. Although this sentence provides new information, it does not link and support sentences 22 and 23.

28. C: because a proper transition into the next sentence would involve the acknowledgement that time has passed. A is not correct. *However* is not a good transition into this sentence since it does not require a shift in ideas. B is not correct. *Consequentially* is not a good transition into this sentence since it presents no cause and effect. D is not correct. *Therefore* is not a good transition into this sentence since it presents no cause and effect.

29. C: The missing verb in this sentence must have something to do with possession since it discusses the band's success. *Had* indicates possession. A, B, and D are incorrect, because these verbs do not fit within the sentence.

30. D: It is correct because in the sentence, the article *an* is followed by a noun, *promoter*. *Promoter* begins with a consonant and a consonant sound and therefore must be followed by the article *a*. A is not correct. The verb in this sentence is *decided*, not *separate*, and therefore *separate* does not need to be in the past tense like the rest of the paragraph. B is not correct because the comma is unnecessary. C is not correct. *Solo* is not a proper noun and does not need to be capitalized.

31. A: because *Lennon* is possessive in this sentence; therefore, it requires an apostrophe. B is not correct. In this sentence, *dream* is a noun rather than a verb, so it does not need to be in the past tense. C is not correct, because a comma is unnecessary.

32. A: because the sentence is missing the article *as*. This is the simplest way to express the idea of the sentence. B is incorrect because this sentence is not grammatically correct. C is incorrect because the first sentence is grammatically incorrect.

33. D: It is correct because the sentence is correct. A is not correct. This sentence is part of a longer quotation that began in the previous sentence. Since the quotation is continuing, the sentence does not begin with quotation marks. B is not correct. In a quotation, the punctuation is placed before the ending quotation marks. C is not correct. *You'll* is the correct contraction of *you will*.

34. C: In this sentence nice is an adjective rather than an adverb. It describes the noun, *sounds*, not the verb. A is not correct. *When I really listen to the words of this song* is an introductory clause, and a comma is needed after the clause. B is not correct. *Something* is one word when used as a noun. D is not correct. Although most of the essay is in the past tense, the final paragraph is in the present tense. *Realized* is in the past tense.

Reading Practice Test #2

Refer to the passage "Like Riding a Kite" to answer questions 1-9.

Like Riding a Kite

(1) Imagine soaring high above the earth. There is no engine, no fuselage beneath you. There is only you, your glider, the wind, and the sky. It's like riding a kite with no strings attached, rising and falling on the breeze like a bird. It is freedom and thrill and ultimate pleasure. This is the world of hang gliding.

(2) While many people have a general idea of what hang gliding is all about, few really understand the sport. Most people don't realize a majestic glider can be collapsed to the size of a duffel bag. Few people know that gliders can stay aloft for hours and that the world distance record for a single glider flight is nearly 190 miles. Even fewer people realize that a hang glider can actually climb in the sky, even without an engine. In California, in the 1980s, one expert glider pilot gained more than 14,000 feet of altitude after takeoff! Hang gliders have mind-boggling capabilities.

(3) The amazing sport of hang gliding has a rich history dating back to the 1890s. In 1891, the first hang glider was invented by Otto Lilienthal in Germany. It was made of wood and cloth, weighed 40 pounds, was 23 feet wide, and could go about 35 miles per hour (mph) at an altitude of 100 feet. British inventor Percy Picher also built gliders with similar features in the late 1890s. Unfortunately, both inventors were killed in glider crashes before their designs were perfected. With the element of danger involved in early hang gliding—and with the advent of airplane flight by the Wright brothers in 1903—many people lost interest in hang gliding.

(4) After the end of World War II, however, many military-trained pilots wanted to keep flying. Airplanes were too expensive for most people, so the sport of hang gliding was reborn. Through invention and innovation, new designs for hang gliders began to emerge. These included new materials and designs for glider construction and the addition of a control bar to improve safety. The basic design for today's hang gliders premiered at a meet in California in 1971. It included a broad, flexible wing on a sturdy frame with a control bar and a seat or safety harness.

(5) Since 1971, few major design changes have been made to hang gliders, although as new materials for construction become available, minor changes are made to improve flight. Modern sails range from 13 to 28 feet across. They are made of durable, lightweight, manmade

fabric—such as nylon—and are designed to flex in shape and tension based on the wind. The sail is attached to a frame made from aluminum tubing. The frame includes a control bar that is shaped like a rounded triangle and used for steering. Suspended from the frame is a harness or seat to improve pilot comfort and safety.

(6) Another way pilots improve comfort and safety is through the use of proper gear and equipment. Pilots should wear light, protective clothing and gloves designed for hang gliding. A helmet is also an important safety component. In addition, pilots need special instruments that are used during flight. These tools help measure thermals, the warm air currents used to lift and propel gliders through the air.

(7) Thermals are important to both taking off and staying aloft, but they aren't the only factor in flight. Modern gliders weigh about 35 pounds and are specially balanced to a pilot's weight and preferences. To take off, the pilot is secured in the glider and then runs off the edge of a large hill or cliff, where thermals catch the glider and lift it into the air. If the wind is sustained at 12 mph or above, the pilot may even be able to take off without running. Once the glider is airborne, the pilot steers by shifting his or her weight and using the control bar. Each glider has its own unique feel, and a pilot must know the glider well to achieve a safe takeoff, flight, and landing.

(8) In addition to knowing the unique feel of the glider, a pilot must know the safety rules of the sky to have a safe flight. Pilots of hang gliders do not need to be licensed, but they must obey all rules and laws for flying. Hang glider pilots should never fly in bad weather or high winds. They must yield the right of way to any aircraft in distress and all hot air balloons. They must never intentionally fly into a cloud or a flock of birds. Finally, hang glider pilots should stay at least five miles away from airports during flight and at least 100 feet from buildings, telephone wires and poles, populated places, and crowds.

(9) Throughout history, mankind has looked for a way to soar with the birds across the canvas of the sky. Hang gliding offers that opportunity. With modern features and equipment, and with proper training in techniques and the rules of the sky, hang glider pilots can safely experience the thrill of flight. In a glider, the pilot is one with the breeze, the sunlight, and the world itself. Hang gliding is truly like riding a kite through the expanse of the heavens.

1. Read this sentence from paragraph 2.

Few people know that gliders can stay aloft for hours and that the world distance record for a single glider flight is nearly 190 miles.

Based on this text evidence from the passage, what is the meaning of *aloft*?

a. Motor powered
b. Suspended in the air
c. In one piece
d. Collapsible

2. Read the following sentences from paragraph 1:

Imagine soaring high above the earth. There is no engine, no fuselage beneath you. There is only you, your glider, the wind, and the sky. It's like riding a kite with no strings attached, rising and falling on the breeze like a bird.

What is the effect of the figurative language used in these sentences?

a. They help the reader understand where the inspiration for hang gliding came from.
b. They show the reader the reason for the many concerns about the safety of hang gliding.
c. They allow the reader to understand what hang gliding is like and why people enjoy it.
d. They interest the reader by presenting facts and historical events in a poetic way.

3. Paragraph 3 states "With the element of danger involved in early hang gliding—and with the advent of airplane flight by the Wright brothers in 1903—many people lost interest in hang gliding." What is the most likely reason for this change?

a. The Wright brothers did well publicizing their invention.
b. Most people had already experienced hang gliding.
c. Both were dangerous, but planes were new and exciting.
d. Planes were a safer way to fulfil the desire for flight.

4. Which sentence from the passage shows that advances in technology have made hang gliding safer?

a. Thermals are important to both taking off and staying aloft, but they aren't the only factor in flight.
b. In addition to knowing the unique feel of the glider, a pilot must know the safety rules of the sky to have a safe flight.
c. These included new materials and designs for glider construction and the addition of a control bar to improve safety.
d. It was made of wood and cloth, weighed 40 pounds, was 23 feet wide, and could go about 35 miles per hour (mph) at an altitude of 100 feet.

5. What is the most likely reason the author of this passage uses a chronological structure for paragraphs 3 through 5?

a. To help the reader create a mental image of hang gliding
b. To explain the changes in popularity and safety of hang gliding
c. To give step by step instructions for the process of hang gliding
d. To persuade readers to give hang gliding a try on their own

6. Read this summary of the passage "Like Riding a Kite":

> Hang gliding is a freeing and exciting sport that allows participants to glide with the birds and accomplish new feats. It got its start in the late 19th century. However, due to safety issues and the invention of the plane, many people lost interest in it. After World War II, hang gliding became popular again, and changes were made to hang gliding equipment and procedures to make the sport safer.

Which idea should be included in this paragraph to create a complete summary of the passage?

a. Now, pilots who follow safe practices can enjoy the sport of hang gliding.
b. Some rigs are small enough to pack down into a duffel bag.
c. The Wright Brothers can be blamed for the demise of the glider.
d. Hang gliding allows participants to get closer to nature.

7. In paragraph 3, what does *advent* mean?

a. End
b. Beginning
c. Expansion
d. Popularity

8. Which of the following statements are key ideas from the passage, and which are simply supporting details? Mark your answer for each statement below.

Statement	Key Idea	Supporting Detail
Modern glider sails are 13 to 28 feet wide.		
Glider pilots must know the rules of the sky.		
All glider pilots should wear helmets for safety.		
Modern glider design premiered in 1971.		
Hang gliding involves more than meets the eye.		

9. What was the author's main purpose in writing this article?

a. To inform readers about the sport of hang gliding
b. To entertain readers with a description of hang gliding
c. To help readers analyze the development of hang gliding
d. To persuade readers to try hang gliding

Refer to the passage "Annabel Lee" to answer questions 10-17.

Annabel Lee

by Edgar Allan Poe

It was many and many a year ago,
In a kingdom by the sea,
That a maiden there lived whom you may know
By the name of Annabel Lee;
And this maiden she lived with no other thought
Than to love and be loved by me.

I was a child and she was a child,
In this kingdom by the sea,
But we loved with a love that was more than love—
I and my Annabel Lee—
With a love that the wingèd seraphs of Heaven
Coveted her and me.

And this was the reason that, long ago,
In this kingdom by the sea,
A wind blew out of a cloud, chilling
My beautiful Annabel Lee;
So that her highborn kinsmen came
And bore her away from me,
To shut her up in a sepulchre
In this kingdom by the sea.

The angels, not half so happy in Heaven,
Went envying her and me—
Yes!—that was the reason (as all men know,
In this kingdom by the sea)
That the wind came out of the cloud by night,
Chilling and killing my Annabel Lee.

But our love it was stronger by far than the love
Of those who were older than we—
Of many far wiser than we—
And neither the angels in Heaven above
Nor the demons down under the sea
Can ever dissever my soul from the soul
Of the beautiful Annabel Lee;

For the moon never beams, without bringing me dreams
Of the beautiful Annabel Lee;
And the stars never rise, but I feel the bright eyes
Of the beautiful Annabel Lee;
And so, all the night-tide, I lie down by the side
Of my darling—my darling—my life and my bride,
In her sepulchre there by the sea—
In her tomb by the sounding sea.

10. Read lines 26-33 of the poem.

But our love it was stronger by far than the love
Of those who were older than we—
Of many far wiser than we—
And neither the angels in Heaven above
Nor the demons down under the sea
Can ever dissever my soul from the soul
Of the beautiful Annabel Lee;

Based on these lines, what can the reader predict?

a. The narrator will act rationally in laying Annabel to rest.
b. The narrator will continue to love Annabel as he did before she passed.
c. The angels will see her death was wrong and return Annabel to the narrator.
d. The angels will kill the narrator in order to reunite him with Annabel.

11. Part A: Read this information about the word sepulchre.

From the Latin sepulcrum, which means "burial place"

Based on this information, which of the following is a synonym for sepulchre?

a. Garden
b. Shack
c. Storage
d. Crypt

Part B: Which line from the poem supports the answer to part A?

a. In this kingdom by the sea
b. In her tomb by the sounding sea
c. And bore her away from me
d. Can ever dissever my soul from the soul

12. What can be concluded from lines 21-26?

a. The angels in heaven are responsible for Annabel's death.
b. The narrator is being challenged to find Annabel.
c. All men on the sea quickly knew of the passing of Annabel.
d. Annabel was killed by men of the sea on a cold night.

13. What is the most likely reason the narrator uses dashes at the end of some lines?

a. To create a break so the next line can begin
b. To emphasize the information between the dashes
c. To fully replace the use of commas
d. To make the rhythm of the poem clearer

14. How does the author's word choice impact the tone of this poem?

a. By describing the "kingdom of the sea," he creates a fantastical tone.
b. By mentioning the moon, stars, and night sky, he creates a dark tone.
c. By using words like "killing" and "tomb," he creates a sorrowful tone.
d. By conveying actions like "bore" and "shut," he creates an urgent tone.

15. Which lines from the poem best support the idea that Annabel returned the narrator's love?

a. That a maiden there lived whom you may know
By the name of Annabel Lee;
And this maiden she lived with no other thought
Than to love and be loved by me.

b. For the moon never beams, without bringing me dreams
Of the beautiful Annabel Lee;
And the stars never rise, but I feel the bright eyes
Of the beautiful Annabel Lee;

c. So that her highborn kinsmen came
And bore her away from me,
To shut her up in a sepulchre
In this kingdom by the sea.

d. And neither the angels in Heaven above
Nor the demons down under the sea
Can ever dissever my soul from the soul
Of the beautiful Annabel Lee;

16. Which of the following is the best summary of "Annabel Lee"?

a. A young couple living in a seaside kingdom loved one another with great intensity. Their love was so enviable that even the angels in heaven were jealous. Because of their jealousy, the angels killed the girl. The narrator lived on feeling forever attached to Annabel.
b. A female child in a seaside town must be married away to a royal. However, she is in love with another child in the town. In her attempt to run away with the person she loves, Annabel passes away tragically in the cold.
c. A young man who works on the sea loves Annabel deeply. He cares for her so much that he wants her to live on a ship with him. As such, he prays to angels in heaven to have her brought to him.
d. A young maiden feels as though her love for the narrator is one sided. As such, she begins to behave carelessly. One night, she is killed in a chilling wind. It is only at this point that the narrator confesses his love for the girl.

17. What is the most likely reason the narrator wrote this poem?

a. To warn others against falling too deeply in love
b. To accuse the heavens of taking his love
c. To send a final message to his love
d. To show the nature of everlasting love

Refer to the passage "More than Video Games" to answer questions 18-21.

More than Video Games

(1) The school bell rang, and it took all the self-control Reggie had not to jump up and run out of the classroom. He hurriedly swung his backpack onto his back, made his way outside to his dad's car, and got in.

(2) "Hey, Bud," Reggie's dad said with a laugh. "What are you in such a hurry for?"

(3) "Dad, remember? Alien Quest 3 came out today! And I have a whole weekend to play it."

(4) "Oh, that's right! Well, we'll start downloading it when we get home, and that should give you plenty of time to finish your homework."

(5) "I already finished all of my homework. And we preordered it, remember? It should already be downloaded."

(6) "Oh wow, alrighty then. Well, until we get home, tell me about your day. Surely there's more going on in your life than video game releases."

(7) Reggie talked about school for a few minutes, but soon began telling his dad all about Alien Quest 3. As soon as they got home, Reggie bolted inside. He yelled a quick hello to his mom and younger brother as he shut the door to his room. He turned on the game and could hardly wait as it loaded and the words "Alien Quest 3" slowly appeared on the screen.

(8) Reggie hardly noticed the first hour and a half go by. He had gotten used to the new features of the game in no time and was flying through the quests. He only stopped when his stomach began growling, and he glanced at his watch. *Oh wow*, he thought, *it's past dinner time*. Reggie paused the game and walked to the kitchen.

(9) "We saved some pizza for you," Reggie's mom called out from the living room.

(10) Reggie piled some pizza slices on a plate, but as he walked back to his room, he heard a familiar sound. He looked at his family and realized that they were all watching one of his favorite movies. He hesitated, and his dad looked up at him.

(11) "Oh, sorry, your brother wanted to watch a movie, and I didn't want to interrupt your game. I forgot how much you like this one," he explained. He turned to Reggie's brother, John, and said, "Maybe we should save this one for another day. Reggie wouldn't want us to watch it without him, and he's been waiting to play his new game today."

(12) "Okay," John said quietly, disappointed.

(13) "Wait," Reggie said. He turned toward his room, then back toward his family. He pivoted between the two for a few seconds before he finally said, "Give me a second, and I'll come watch it with you. I just need to save my progress."

(14) "Are you sure, Bud?" Reggie's mom asked. "You've been looking forward to that game for a while."

(15) "Yeah, I'm sure. I do have all weekend to play it." He looked at John and added, "After all, there's more to life than video games."

18. Which of the following statements best represents the theme of this passage?

a. You can't choose family.
b. Life is about balance.
c. Gaming is harmful.
d. New isn't always better.

19. In paragraph 7, the author explains that "Reggie bolted inside." What is the most likely reason the author used this hyperbole?

a. To demonstrate how quickly Reggie could run
b. To explain how the game was supposed to be played
c. To make the reader feel eager about the game
d. To help show how excited Reggie was

20. Read this excerpt from the passage.

(3) "Dad, remember? Alien Quest 3 came out today! And I have a whole weekend to play it."
(4) "Oh, that's right! Well, we'll start downloading it when we get home, and that should give you plenty of time to finish your homework."
(5) "I already finished all of my homework. And we preordered it, remember? It should already be downloaded."
(6) "Oh wow, alrighty then. Well, until we get home, tell me about your day. Surely there's more going on in your life than video game releases."
(7) Reggie talked about school for a few minutes, but soon began telling his dad all about Alien Quest 3. As soon as they got home, Reggie bolted inside. He yelled a quick hello to his mom and younger brother as he shut the door to his room. He turned on the game and could hardly wait as it loaded and the words "Alien Quest 3" slowly appeared on the screen.

What event is foreshadowed by this scene?

a. Reggie will not be able to play the entire weekend because he will beat the video game before then.
b. Reggie's father will want to join him and play along, but Reggie will not let him.
c. Something important will prevent Reggie from spending the entire weekend playing the video game.
d. The mother and younger brother will be upset that Reggie blew by them, and they won't speak to him.

21. Which of the following characteristics of the story help the reader identify it as realistic fiction?

a. The events are possible.
b. It is written in the past tense.
c. The setting is a modern home.
d. It focuses on a small family.

Refer to the passage "The Top Five Reasons Video Games Are Good for Your Health" to answer questions 22-25.

The Top Five Reasons Video Games Are Good for Your Health

(1) Too many people think video games are just time-wasters. They say video games are for weak-minded imbeciles. They insist that no good can come from this electronic entertainment. In contrast to these common theories, I believe video games offer numerous benefits. Let me share with you the top five reasons that video games are good for your health.

(2) First, video games improve overall coordination. Response times are quicker, attention is more focused, and awareness is heightened. When I play video games, I find myself focused and intent on my mission. Since I began playing video games, my coordination—particularly my hand-eye coordination—has improved immensely. Even my handwriting has improved! The advent of motion sensor systems, such as Nintendo's Wii, Microsoft's Xbox 360 Kinect, and Sony's PlayStation 3 Move, has further enhanced users' coordination and reaction times.

(3) In addition to improving coordination and reaction times, many games also enhance logic and reasoning abilities. Most games employ some sort of strategy, whether in sporting competitions, driving pursuits, fantasy quests, or military battles. Winning a game—even just playing a game—requires a plan and the ability to adjust that plan and adapt to changing conditions. The ability to use logic and reason to solve problems leads to the ability to think on your feet. These are all important life skills, making video games beneficial for personal development.

(4) Sometimes, however, you are not concerned about developing new skills—you just want to have fun. Video games are a great way to fill empty hours productively. They focus mental energies and allow unbridled relaxation. They entertain small children and keep older ones out of trouble. Finally, video games allow safe and fun experimentation in a variety of environments, with a plethora of tools, at a relatively low cost.

(5) Beyond creating skills and filling the hours with fun, video games also create a sense of passion and excitement. They encourage goal setting and persistence. They develop a healthy spirit of competition. When you play a game often, you develop a deep desire to accomplish a little more or go a little further each time you play. This breeds excitement, anticipation, and a constant hope for success. Setting incremental goals and working passionately toward those goals leads to achievement in video games and in life.

(6) Finally, the skills and attitudes gained playing video games often open the door for development of deep social bonds. There is a unique camaraderie among those who play games together, almost as if they were teammates. These bonds tend to be strongest when a common game is played or when individuals are members of an online community. Even without these commonalities, however, the shared universe of video games provides the foundation for social interaction, conversation, and friendship.

(7) Are video games without pitfalls? Certainly not. But many games offer life-improving benefits that are often overlooked. They improve coordination and response time, enhance logic and reasoning, fill empty hours productively, create a sense of passion and excitement, and foster a variety of social bonds among players of all types, skill levels, and backgrounds. With so many positive aspects, video games are worth checking out. Try them—you might find you like them!

22. How does the information from paragraph 3 support the author's argument?

a. By outlining the physical benefits of playing video games
b. By detailing how video games make players smarter
c. By portraying video games as an affordable form of entertainment
d. By explaining how playing games supports personal development

23. Why did the author use a rhetorical question in paragraph 7?

a. To ask the reader to consider something
b. To bring attention to a point he will refute
c. To force the reader to pause while reading
d. To provoke the reader's desire to play games

24. Why does the author present a counter argument in paragraph 7?

a. To give the reader both sides of the argument so they can make their own decision about playing video games
b. To convince readers to play fewer video games once they have developed the skills listed in the passage
c. To acknowledge the negative side of video games and explain that the good aspects outweigh the bad
d. To explain to readers that they should monitor how much time they play and make sure they are taking breaks

25. Who is likely the intended audience for this passage?

a. People who view games negatively
b. Avid and passionate gamers
c. Board of Education members
d. Video game developers

Refer to the passages "More than Video Games" and "The Top Five Reasons Video Games Are Good for Your Health" to answer questions 26-28.

26. How is the conclusion of "More Than Video Games" different than the conclusion of "The Top Five Reasons Video Games are Good for Your Health"?

a. It addresses a need for balance in gaming and other aspects of life.
b. It addresses the opposing view of the topic of video games.
c. It portrays playing video games negatively.
d. It uses an extended metaphor to make the same point.

27. How might the opinions of Reggie from "More Than Video Games" and the author of "The Top Five Reasons Video Games are Good for Your Health" be different?

a. The author of "The Top Five Reasons Video Games are Good for Your Health" would find family time more valuable than Reggie would.
b. Reggie would prioritize video games over school while the author of "The Top Five Reasons Video Games are Good for Your Health" would be eager to use his or her gaming skills to complete schoolwork.
c. The author of "The Top Five Reasons Video Games are Good for Your Health" would likely feel video games were a solution to many problems while Reggie would likely seek help from his family.
d. Reggie would feel it is important that people are educated about the benefits of video games while the author of "The Top Five Reasons Video Games are Good for Your Health" would want them to form their own opinions.

28. What is one similarity between the passages?

a. Both explain the benefits of playing video games.
b. Both portray video games as a small part of life.
c. Both depict characters that are indifferent to gaming.
d. Both discuss the enjoyment of playing video games.

Refer to the passage "Archimedes: Father of Mathematics" to answer questions 29-32.

Archimedes: Father of Mathematics

(1) Archimedes was born around 287 BC in Syracuse, which was a Greek city-state in Sicily. Throughout his life, he contributed to various fields, including mathematics, physics, and engineering, providing many concepts and devices still used today. Archimedes came from a family of scholars and mathematicians. He received a comprehensive education in philosophy,

mathematics, and science. It is believed that Archimedes studied in Alexandria, Egypt, which was a Greek center of study.

(2) Archimedes is best known for his contributions to mathematics. In his works "On the Sphere and Cylinder" and "Measurement of a Circle," he was able to use geometry to approximate the value of pi, the exact value of which is famously elusive even to this day. He is also credited with advancements in number theory and methods for calculating values in geometry, which became the foundation for calculus.

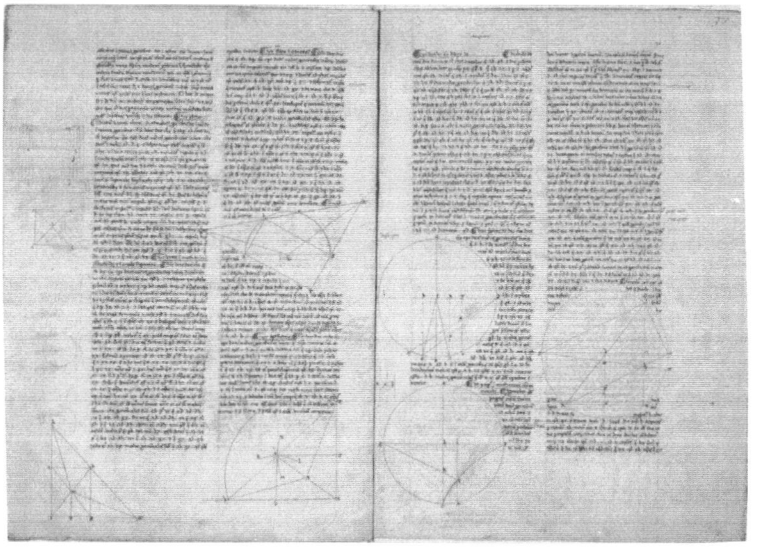

Photograph of a page from Archimedes's "On the Sphere and Cylinder"

(3) Archimedes's contributions to physics could be considered of equal weight. He defined some of the principles of statics and hydrostatics, which allowed him to help pave the way for fluid mechanics. He is the eponym for the term "Archimedes's Principle," which states that an object submerged in a fluid experiences a buoyant force equal to the weight of the displaced fluid. Though ships had made use of buoyancy long before Archimedes, the improved understanding of the underlying forces revolutionized the design and efficiency of watercraft.

(4) In addition to being a major contributor to theoretical understandings of mathematics and physics, Archimedes was also an inventor. He invented and built various machines, often manipulating common machines like screws and pulleys to great effect. One of his inventions that is still in use today is the screw pump, which consists of a simple screw inside of a cylinder. As the screw is turned, the fluids on one end of the pump are pulled to the other end, allowing for active pumping of fluids in irrigation and drainage systems. Archimedes also created many war machines to help defend the city of Syracuse from Roman invaders. Among these were the "Claw of Archimedes" and the "Archimedes Death Ray," which were intended to be used against naval invaders.

(5) One popular story associated with Archimedes is his "eureka moment." Archimedes was given the seemingly impossible task of determining whether a crown produced for the king was made of pure gold or if it was an alloy. According to legend, while Archimedes was soaking in a bath, he noticed that his body caused the water level to rise, and he realized that he could use the principle of displacement to measure the mass of the crown and find out what it was made of. He was so excited that he shouted "eureka," which is the Greek term for "I have found it!" This story and the associated term "eureka" have become commonplace in pop culture, demonstrating the lasting impact of Archimedes's innovations.

(6) As Archimedes lived in a time of great wars, his life was not all centered around peaceful discovery. In 212 BC, Rome attacked Syracuse. Archimedes was supposedly entranced by a geometric equation when the city was overtaken. Instead of stopping his work to hide or fight, he continued to work and adjured a Roman soldier to not disturb his circles. The soldier did not recognize Archimedes and killed him for resisting. Archimedes's tragic death serves as a powerful symbol of his unwavering devotion to his work. Archimedes's contributions to science and mathematics have served as an incredible legacy and foundation for future scientists and mathematicians, including Sir Isaac Newton and Carl Friedrich Gauss.

29. Which of the following best explains the controlling idea of the passage?

a. Archimedes made many profound and long-lasting contributions to society.
b. Archimedes untimely death was due to his obsession with learning.
c. Archimedes could not possibly have made these contributions on his own.
d. Archimedes would not have been as successful had he not attended school.

30. What is the most likely reason the author included the image of Archimedes's work in the passage?

a. To illustrate Archimedes's contributions to the field of physics and popular culture
b. To display the work that Archimedes did not want to abandon later in the passage
c. To help readers understand the type of work Archimedes did in geometry
d. To convey a sense of organization through Archimedes's notes and documentation

31. What key idea is supported by the details in paragraph 4?

a. Archimedes's personality has made him remain prevalent in mainstream culture throughout time.
b. The city of Rome would not have been successful in war without Archimedes.
c. Most of Archimedes's life was spent in pursuit of intellectual gain.
d. Archimedes applied his knowledge of math and physics to create experimental and proven devices.

32. What is the most likely reason that the author of this passage organized the information based on stages in Archimedes's life?

a. To help the reader understand the impact that Archimedes had on the Roman War over the course of his life
b. To give a detailed description of the time period in which Archimedes lived, went to school, and worked
c. To provide the reader with background information about Archimedes before explaining his contributions and untimely death
d. To explain the underlying cause of Archimedes death and allow the reader process potential outcomes

Refer to the passage "Charles Darwin on the Galapagos Islands" to answer questions 33-36.

Charles Darwin on the Galapagos Islands

(1) During the 1800s, Charles Darwin became known for his studies of plants and animals on the Galapagos Islands. He is often referred to as "the father of evolution[1]" because he was first to describe a mechanism by which organisms change over time.

(2) The Galapagos Islands are situated off the coast of South America. Much of Darwin's work on the islands focused on birds. He noticed that island birds looked similar to finches on the South American continent and resembled a type of modified finch. The only differences in the finches Darwin saw were in their beaks and the kind of food they ate. Finches on the mainland were seed-eating birds, but the island finches ate insects, seeds, plant matter, egg yolks, and blood.

(3) Darwin theorized that the island finches were offspring of one type of mainland finch. The population of finches was changing over time due to their environment. He believed the finches' eating habits changed because of the island's limited food supply. As the finches began to eat differently, the way their beaks worked and looked changed as well. For instance, insect-eating finches needed longer beaks for digging in the ground. Seed-eating and nut-eating finches required thicker beaks to crack the seed shells.

(4) The process by which the finches changed happened over many generations. Among the population of beetle-eating finches, those born with longer, sharper beaks naturally had access to more beetles than those with shorter beaks. As a result, the sharp-beaked, insect-eating

finches thrived and produced many offspring, while the short-beaked insect-eating finches gradually died out. The sharp beak was, in effect, selected by nature to thrive. The same thing happened in each finch population until finches within the same population began to look similar to each other and different from finches of other populations. These observations eventually led Darwin to develop the theory of natural selection.

[1] The theory of evolution is the theory that all species are descended from other species and that varied needs for survival have led to the development of new species.

33. Read this sentence from paragraph 4.

These observations eventually led Darwin to develop the theory of natural selection.

What text evidence from the story helps the reader understand the meaning of "natural selection"?

a. As a result, the sharp-beaked, insect-eating finches thrived and produced many offspring, while the short-beaked insect-eating finches gradually died out. The sharp beak was, in effect, selected by nature to thrive.
b. He is often referred to as "the father of evolution" because he was first to describe a mechanism by which organisms change over time.
c. As the finches began to eat differently, the way their beaks worked and looked changed as well.
d. Among the population of beetle-eating finches, those finches born with longer, sharper beaks naturally had access to more beetles than those finches with shorter beaks.

34. Based on information in the passage, what can readers conclude about animals other than finches?

a. Other animals take longer to evolve than the finches that were studied because they have longer life spans.
b. Evolution and natural selection only occur in land animals, so sea creatures stay the same for generations.
c. The way an animal's mouth or teeth function can be influenced by the foods available in their environment.
d. Islands are ideal places to study animals for signs of evolution because they are heavily populated by many species.

35. How does the footnote support the reader's understanding of the theory of evolution?

a. It shows that the theory of evolution is closely related to the theory of natural selection.
b. It shows that the theory of evolution is a very old idea that predates Darwin's studies.
c. It shows that the theory of evolution only applies to animals.
d. It shows that the theory of evolution does not describe an ongoing process.

36. Which of the following best describes the author's purpose in writing this passage?

a. To explain Darwin's discovery of plants and animals on the Galapagos Island
b. To explain how observing finches led to the proposal of the theory of natural selection
c. To explain the potential evidence disproving Darwin's theory of natural selection
d. To explain Darwin's contributions in the field of nature conservation

Refer to the passage "Archimedes: Father of Mathematics" and "Charles Darwin on the Galapagos Islands" to answer questions 37-39.

37. In "Archimedes: Father of Mathematics" and "Charles Darwin on the Galapagos Islands," how are Archimedes and Darwin alike?

a. Both men were able to use mathematics to their benefit.
b. Neither man enjoyed his work, but both felt it was necessary.
c. Both men made historically significant contributions to their field.
d. Neither man was able to reach his full potential due to early deaths.

38. Which two of the following ideas are suggested by both passages? Select all that apply.

a. Schooling is an important component of success.
b. Dedication to one's field can be unhealthy.
c. Observation leads to new understanding.
d. One person's work can have a lasting effect.
e. Working hard is not always rewarding.

39. What is a key difference between "Archimedes: Father of Mathematics" and "Charles Darwin on the Galapagos Islands"?

a. "Charles Darwin on the Galapagos Islands" focuses on the life of Darwin while "Archimedes: Father of Mathematics" focuses on the death of Archimedes.
b. "Archimedes: Father of Mathematics" discusses the contributions of Archimedes across his lifetime while "Charles Darwin on the Galapagos Islands" focuses on only a small portion of Darwin's contributions.
c. "Charles Darwin on the Galapagos Islands" was written with a large amount of figurative language while "Archimedes: Father of Mathematics" uses several technical terms.
d. "Archimedes: Father of Mathematics" is written to inform readers about the life of Archimedes while "Charles Darwin on the Galapagos Islands" was written to entertain readers.

Refer to the passage "Call of the Wild" to answer questions 39-46.

Call of the Wild

by Jack London

Buck did not read the newspapers, or he would have known that trouble was brewing, not alone for himself, but for every tide-water dog, strong of muscle and with warm, long hair, from Puget Sound to San Diego. Because men, groping in the Arctic darkness, had found a yellow metal, and because steamship and transportation companies were booming the find, thousands of men were rushing into the Northland. These men wanted dogs, and the dogs they wanted were heavy dogs, with strong muscles by which to toil, and furry coats to protect them from the frost.

Buck lived at a big house in the sun-kissed Santa Clara Valley. Judge Miller's place, it was called. It stood back from the road, half hidden among the trees, through which glimpses could be caught of the wide cool veranda that ran around its four sides. The house was approached by gravelled driveways which wound about through wide-spreading lawns and under the interlacing boughs of tall poplars. At the rear things were on even a more spacious scale than at the front. There were great stables, where a dozen grooms and boys held forth, rows of vine-clad servants' cottages, an endless and orderly array of outhouses, long grape arbors, green pastures, orchards, and berry patches. Then there was the pumping plant for the artesian well, and the big cement tank where Judge Miller's boys took their morning plunge and kept cool in the hot afternoon.

And over this great demesne Buck ruled. Here he was born, and here he had lived the four years of his life. It was true, there were other dogs, there could not but be other dogs on so vast a place, but they did not count. They came and went, resided in the populous kennels, or lived obscurely in the recesses of the house after the fashion of Toots, the Japanese pug, or Ysabel, the Mexican hairless,—strange creatures that rarely put nose out of doors or set foot to ground. On the other hand, there were the fox terriers, a score of them at least, who yelped fearful promises at Toots and Ysabel looking out of the windows at them and protected by a legion of housemaids armed with brooms and mops.

But Buck was neither house-dog nor kennel-dog. The whole realm was his. He plunged into the swimming tank or went hunting with the Judge's sons; he escorted Mollie and Alice, the Judge's daughters, on long twilight or early morning rambles; on wintry nights he lay at the Judge's feet before the roaring library fire; he carried the Judge's grandsons on his back, or rolled them in the grass, and guarded their footsteps through wild adventures down to the fountain in the stable yard, and even beyond, where the paddocks were, and the berry patches. Among the terriers he stalked imperiously, and Toots and Ysabel he utterly ignored, for he was king,—king over all creeping, crawling, flying things of Judge Miller's place, humans included.

His father, Elmo, a huge St. Bernard, had been the Judge's inseparable companion, and Buck bid fair to follow in the way of his father. He was not so large,—he weighed only one hundred and forty pounds,—for his mother, Shep, had been a Scotch shepherd dog. Nevertheless, one hundred and forty pounds, to which was added the dignity that comes of good living and universal respect, enabled him to carry himself in right royal fashion. During the four years since his puppyhood he had lived the life of a sated aristocrat; he had a fine pride in himself, was even a trifle egotistical, as country gentlemen sometimes become because of their insular situation. But he had saved himself by not becoming a mere pampered house-dog. Hunting and kindred outdoor delights had kept down the fat and hardened his muscles; and to him, as to the cold-tubbing races, the love of water had been a tonic and a health preserver.

And this was the manner of dog Buck was in the fall of 1897, when the Klondike strike dragged men from all the world into the frozen North. But Buck did not read the newspapers, and he did not know that Manuel, one of the gardener's helpers, was an undesirable acquaintance. Manuel had one besetting sin. He loved to play Chinese lottery. Also, in his gambling, he had one besetting weakness—faith in a system; and this made his damnation certain. For to play a system requires money, while the wages of a gardener's helper do not lap over the needs of a wife and numerous progenies.

The Judge was at a meeting of the Raisin Growers' Association, and the boys were busy organizing an athletic club, on the memorable night of Manuel's treachery. No one saw him and Buck go off through the orchard on what Buck imagined was merely a stroll. And with the exception of a solitary man, no one saw them arrive at the little flag station known as College Park. This man talked with Manuel, and money chinked between them.

40. What is the purpose of paragraphs 2-5?

a. To introduce all of the story's characters
b. To show Buck's personality
c. To introduce Buck
d. To show Buck's affection for Toots and Ysabel

41. Which sentence or phrase shows Buck's attitude about Judge Miller's place?

a. They came and went, resided in the populous kennels, or lived obscurely in the recesses of the house
b. The whole realm was his
c. He had a fine pride in himself
d. And to him, as to the cold-tubbing races, the love of water had been a tonic and a health preserver

42. The use of the word *imperiously* in paragraph four helps the reader know that Buck feels

a. Scared
b. Angry
c. Happy
d. Regal

43. The author organizes this selection mainly by

a. Describing Buck's life in the order in which it happened
b. Outlining Buck's history
c. Showing Buck's life and then showing a moment of change
d. Comparing Buck's life at Judge Miller's place to what came afterwards

44. This selection is part of a longer work. Based on the selection, what might be a theme of the larger work?

a. Change
b. Family
c. Hard work
d. Relationships

45. Which sentence from the passage foreshadows the rest of the story?

a. And over this great demesne Buck ruled
b. These men wanted dogs, and the dogs they wanted were heavy dogs, with strong muscles by which to toil, and furry coats to protect them from the frost
c. His father, Elmo, a huge St. Bernard, had been the Judge's inseparable companion and Buck bid fair to follow in the way of his father
d. But he had saved himself by not becoming a mere pampered house-dog

46. What's the most logical explanation why Buck doesn't read the newspapers?

a. He's not interested in current events
b. He's busy exploring Judge Miller's place
c. The Raisin Growers' Association takes all his time
d. He's a dog

Answers and Explanations for Reading Test #2

1. B: In the context of this sentence, *aloft* means "suspended in the sky," so choice B is correct. The sentence from paragraph 2 says that a glider can "stay aloft," so the reader knows that *aloft* is a state that the glider can be in or out of. This sentence also discusses the world record for a single glider flight, which shows that *aloft* must be related to the glider's flight. Choice A is incorrect because gliders are not motor powered, and being motor powered is not a state they can be in and then out of. Choice C is incorrect because this sentence does not discuss the glider being split into pieces, and neither does the rest of the passage. Choice D is incorrect because the glider is always collapsible. It does not stay collapsible for just a few hours at a time.

2. C: The imagery and similes used in paragraph 1 allow the reader to understand the appeal of hang gliding. They show that the sport allows pilots to soar through the air and experience the freedom and excitement of flying. Though readers most likely have not experienced hang gliding, this figurative language helps them understand how it feels and highlights its most attractive effects. Choice C is correct. Choice A is incorrect because the passage does not make it clear that the experience of flying like a bird or freely soaring through the air inspired the first inventors of hang gliders. Choice B is incorrect because the unsafe parts of hang gliding are not described in paragraph 1. Choice D is incorrect because this excerpt does not give the reader facts or describe events from the past. It only describes a positive hang-gliding experience.

3. D: Because of the death of early hang gliders, hang gliding was not seen as safe. These hang gliders' deaths occurred during the same time that airplane flight was becoming possible. After both of these factors came into play, people lost interest in hang gliding. From this, it can be inferred that the general public felt planes were a safer alternative for those who wanted to experience flight. The sentence does not suggest that the Wright Brothers publicizing their invention made people less interested in hang gliding and more interested in flight by planes, so choice A is incorrect. Choice B is incorrect because very few people had experienced hang gliding at this time. While it is mentioned that hang gliding had an element of danger, the passage does not suggest that planes were also dangerous. Furthermore, hang gliders were also new at this time, so choice C is incorrect.

4. C: Choice C explains that new technology and changes to the design of hang gliders increased safety for people who hang glide. Choice A only addresses the use of thermals, currents of warm air, in flying. Because choice A does not refer to safety, it is incorrect. Choice B is incorrect because it mentions safety as it relates to knowing rules, not changes in technology. Choice D explains the build of early gilders, not advanced ones, so it is incorrect.

5. B: The chronological organization of these paragraphs helps readers understand when hang gliders first became popular, why the interest in the sport later declined, and how their popularity grew again along with their safety. It provides a timeline of the progression of hang gliding and the public's interest in it. Paragraph 1 helps provide readers with a mental image of hang gliding, but does so with descriptive writing that is only used in this paragraph, so choice A is incorrect. While a chronological order could be used to give step by step instructions, no instructions are given in these paragraphs, so choice C is incorrect. Choice D is incorrect because this passage is not written to persuade readers, as the passage does not present an argument or a call to action.

6. A: The summary includes ideas about the start of hang gliding and its growth in popularity and safety. Adding choice A after the last sentence would best complete the summary by showing that, with safe practices, hang gliding can be enjoyed as a sport today. Choice B explains how small hang gliders can break down, but this is a small detail from the passage. It does not make the summary more effective, so it is incorrect. Adding choice C would be redundant, so it is incorrect. The summary already explains that the invention of the plane contributed to the loss of interest in hang gliding. Choice D is incorrect as this idea is given in the first sentence of the summary.

7. B: Paragraph 3 mentions "the advent of airplane flight by the Wright brothers in 1903." The Wright brothers created the first successful motored airplane. This means that the Wright brothers brought on airplane flight and allowed it to begin. The word *advent* means "beginning," so choice B is correct. The passage supports the idea that airplane flight was an available option for those who wanted to fly. This means that airplane flight was occurring, not ending, so choice A is incorrect. The passage does not support the idea that airplane flight was clearly increasing in 1903, only that it was made possible, so choice C is incorrect. In paragraph 4, the passage states that airplanes were expensive and used during World War II. This does not show that airplane flight would have been popular in 1903 or soon after, so choice D is incorrect.

8.

Statement	Key Idea	Supporting Detail
Modern glider sails are 13 to 28 feet wide.		X
Glider pilots must know the rules of the sky.	X	
All glider pilots should wear helmets for safety.		X
Modern glider design premiered in 1971.		X
Hang gliding has had a dynamic history.	X	

The passage mentions the safety concerns involved in hang gliding many times. It also supports the idea that the sport is popular today because it is safer now, but only when pilots know and follow the rules. The passage's description of the many events and challenges that occurred throughout the history of the sport show that it has had a dynamic history. These are both key ideas. The passage does not focus on the specific physical characteristics of gliders. The size of glider sails today is just a supporting detail. The passage also does not focus on specific safety rules, so each rule is a supporting detail. While a large portion of the passage explains the history of hang gliding, specific events are supporting details for the larger key idea.

9. A: The author's main purpose for writing this passage is to tell the reader about hang gliding. The author explains how long hang gliding has been taking place, how it got started, how it works, and some rules and safety guidelines pilots must follow. The author does not describe hang gliding throughout the passage, so choice B is incorrect. The author does not provide an analysis of the development of hang gliding. He or she instead uses a few paragraphs to give the reader a brief history of hang gliding, so choice C is incorrect. The author does not write in a persuasive manner or use persuasive methods, so choice D is incorrect.

10. B: In these lines, the speaker explains that their love was strong and that his soul cannot be separated from Annabel's. Based on these ideas, the reader can predict that the narrator will continue to love Annabel as he did before she died. Because of the intensity of the narrator's feelings, the reader cannot predict that the speaker will behave rationally when laying Annabel to rest, so choice A is incorrect. In these lines, the narrator explains that the angels cannot make him stop loving Annabel. In lines before this, it is suggested that the angels caused her death. There is no suggestion that the angels will decide that separating them wrong, so the reader cannot predict that they will return her to him. This makes choice C incorrect. Similarly, these lines do not suggest that the angels will kill the narrator to reunite them, so choice D is incorrect.

11. Part A: D: *Sepulchre* is used twice in this poem. It is first used to name a place where Annabel is "shut up" in line 19 and is later used to describe her "tomb" in line 41. Knowing that information as well as the fact that *sepulcher* comes from a word meaning "burial place," *crypt* is the best synonym, as it also means a burial place or vault. This makes choice D correct. Gardens, shacks, and storage rooms are not typical places where bodies are laid to rest, so choices A, B, and C are incorrect.

Part B: B: The last line of the poem, "In her tomb by the sounding sea," repeats and gives more information about line 40, "In her sepulchre there by the sea." Line 41 clarifies that the sepulchre is a tomb, which supports the correct answer to Part A. Choice A is incorrect because it is repeated throughout the poem to show the reader the larger setting. It does not show the meaning of *sepulchre*. Choice C is incorrect because, while Annabel was taken from the speaker and laid in her sepulchre, this line does not show the reader what kind of place a sepulchre is. This line does not eliminate the incorrect answer choices in Part A. Choice D is incorrect because it only describes the speaker's view of his love for Annabel. It does not show what kind of place she has gone to.

12. A: The narrator portrays the angels in heaven as being unhappy and envious of the love he and Annabel share. He implies that they caused the "chilling wind" that killed Annabel, so choice A is correct. Lines 17-20 say "that her highborn kinsmen came and bore her away from me, to shut her up in a sepulchre in this kingdom by the sea." The highborn kinsmen, who can be interpreted as literal relatives or as angels, have separated Annabel from the narrator. However, there is no mention or evidence of this being a challenge for the narrator, so choice B is incorrect. Lines 23 and 24 explain that all men of the sea are aware that the angels' envy is the reason for Annabel's death. However, this does not mean that they quickly knew of Annabel's passing. In fact, the beginning of the poem shows that her death could have occurred long ago, so choice C is incorrect. Line 26 explains that a wind sent by the angels was responsible for "chilling and killing" Annabel, not a person, so choice D is incorrect.

13. B: The dashes used in this poem emphasize certain statements from the narrator. They create a visual break that highlights the writing between them. For example, in lines 9 through 11, the dashes are used to draw attention to "I and my Annabel Lee" to emphasize that it was the two of them that loved so intensely. They are also used in lines 22 and 23 to emphasize the author saying "yes!" as though he had an epiphany that the angels killed Annabel. Choice A is incorrect because these dashes are not meant to create a break. This is not necessary, and a new line can begin without the use of a dash, as most of the lines in the poem do. While commas can be used where the dashes are, there are commas throughout the poem, so choice C is incorrect. Because dashes are read like commas, they do not change the rhythm or make it clearer, so choice D is incorrect.

14. C: The author uses words like *killing* and *tomb*, along with *chilling* and *sepulchre*, to create a sad and sorrowful tone as he morns the loss of his love. The use of kingdom of the sea tells the reader the setting of the poem. It is not used as an element of fantasy, so choice A is incorrect. The way the moon, stars, and night sky are used in the poem does not create a dark tone. The author uses them in the last stanza to explain how he mourns at night, so choice B is incorrect. *Bore* and *shut* are not used to create an urgent tone. They are only used to describe the separating of Annabel from the narrator, so choice D is incorrect.

15. A: The last two lines in choice A show Annabel's love for the narrator. She could not think of anything other than loving and being loved by the narrator. The lines in choice B explain that the narrator cannot go a night without seeing Annabel in his dreams. This shows the narrator's never-ending love for Annabel, but not Annabel's love for the narrator, so choice B is incorrect. The lines in choice C explain Annabel's separation from the narrator, not her love for him, so it is incorrect. The lines in choice D explain how the narrator feels his soul can never be disconnected from Annabel. This reflects his love for her, not her love for him, so choice D is incorrect.

16. A: Choice A summarizes the poem most accurately. The narrator and Annabel were young lovers, and their love made the angels jealous. The narrator explains that the angels killed Annabel for this reason. He also explains that he will continue to love and feel attached to Annabel. Choice B says that Annabel was to be married to a royal. This is not true, so choice B is incorrect. Choice C claims that the narrator worked on the sea and wanted Annabel on the ship with him. The poem does not suggest that the narrator worked on a ship. It only shows that they were in a seaside kingdom. The narrator also blames the angels for killing Annabel. He does not pray to them, so choice C is incorrect. Choice D is incorrect because Annabel and the narrator are in love throughout the poem, and they return each other's love.

17. D: This poem shows an example of everlasting love as the author continually mourns the death of his love and portrays their love as eternal, so choice D is correct. Even after her death, the narrator has not stopped loving or forgotten Annabel. Choice A is incorrect because this poem is not a cautionary tale. It does not explain the downside of falling in love. It only recounts the narrator's story. While the narrator is certain the angels killed Annabel because they were jealous, the poem only focuses on this briefly. The primary focus is on the way her death made the narrator feel, so choice B is incorrect. The poem is not written as a message or letter to Annabel, so choice D is incorrect.

18. B: Reggie was incredibly excited about playing his new game and became so engrossed that he missed dinner and was going to miss a movie with his family. He realized that the game was taking up all his time and that there were other important things, like family time, that he could be doing. This caused him to recognize that there was more to life than games and that he needed to balance how he spent his time, so choice B is correct. Choice A is incorrect because Reggie does not express frustration with his family or the desire to choose different family members. Even though Reggie missed family dinner while playing, games are not portrayed as harmful in his passage. Reggie saw that he needed to play less so he could spend time with family, not give up video games altogether, so choice C is incorrect. Reggie was excited about the new game, but the passage does not include any comparison between this new game and an old one, so choice D is incorrect.

19. D: By saying that Reggie "bolted inside," the author demonstrates that Reggie ran into the house very quickly so he could play the game. This demonstrates his excitement, making choice D correct. As his quick pace was due to excitement, not necessarily his usual running speed, the statement is not meant to show how quickly Reggie can run, so choice A is incorrect. Reggie was running so he could start playing the game. He was not yet playing it, so choice B is incorrect. The hyperbole is used to show Reggie's excitement, not to make the reader excited. This would be done with descriptive writing that explained the details of the game in an enticing way, so choice C is incorrect.

20. C: Reggie tells his father that he has all weekend to play his new game, to which his dad says "there's more going on in your life than video game releases." This foreshadows, or hints at, Reggie's later realization that there is more to life than video games and his decision to prioritize time with his family. While the passage does suggest that Reggie will play through the game quickly, this is not foreshadowed, especially by this excerpt, so choice A is incorrect. Reggie's father does not show or mention that he wants to play the game himself. Instead, he suggests the opposite in this conversation by explaining that he thinks there is more to life than games, so choice C is incorrect. Choice D is incorrect. There is a brief mention of Reggie quickly greeting his mother and brother, but neither of them acts in a way that suggests that they are upset by his behavior.

21. A: The events that occur in this story, such as Reggie being excited to play and being so interested in his game he forgets about dinner, are very possible. Being picked up from school and spending time with family are parts of many people's days. This makes the story an example of realistic fiction. Though the story is written in past tense, the tense does not make it realistic. Many genres can be written in past tense, so choice B is incorrect. Similarly, stories within other genres can be written with modern homes as the setting, so choice C is incorrect. Though the story does focus on a small family, this is not an element that is specific to realistic fiction. Stories in many genres could focus on a family, making choice D incorrect.

22. D: Paragraph 3 focuses on the benefits of video game play that relate to strategy, logic, and reasoning. It also refers to these as important life skills, so choice D is correct. Choice A is incorrect because the physical benefits, such as coordination, of video game play are outlined in paragraph 2. Though paragraph 3 focuses on the mental aspect of games, the author does not claim that video games make an individual smarter, so choice B is incorrect. The author does not discuss the affordability of games, so choice C is incorrect.

23. B: In paragraph 7, the author poses the question "are video games without pitfalls?" and acknowledges that they are not. The author then explains why video games are still beneficial, in spite of this fact. The rhetorical question is used to bring attention to an argument that others may make before going on to prove that the benefits outweigh the pitfalls. Choice A is incorrect because, since the author immediately answers the question, he or she is not really asking the reader to ponder whether or not video games have pitfalls. There are many ways to force a reader to pause while reading, such as using punctuation. Question marks are not the only form of punctuation that would cause a reader to pause, so choice C is incorrect. Because the question brings attention to the downside of video games, the author is most likely not using it to make the reader want to play. This makes choice D incorrect.

24. C: In paragraph 7, the author states that playing video games comes with pitfalls. However, the author also explains that the positive effect of the aspects mentioned in the passage is greater than the negative effect of those pitfalls. This passage is persuasive, so it is meant to convince readers that video games are beneficial and should be played. This means that the counterargument is not included in order to give readers information to make their own decision. The writer still wants readers to support the playing of video games and try it themselves. This makes choice A incorrect. The passage does not suggest that the number of games played should be reduced once the reader has developed the skills mentioned in the essay, so choice B is incorrect. The author of the passage does not mention time limits or playing in moderation, so choice D is incorrect.

25. A: This passage is persuasive and written to convince people that there are benefits to playing video games. This means that it is most likely written for people who view games negatively, as the author wants to change their minds. Avid gamers are people that play video games often and enthusiastically, so they would not need to be convinced to play, and choice B is incorrect. The passage does not mention how gaming impacts learning in schools, so it is unlikely that this passage is written for members on the Board of Education. This means that choice C is incorrect. Choice D is incorrect because the passage neither suggests improvements for games nor praises game developers, so it is unlikely that they are the intended audience.

26. A: "More Than Video Games" highlights the importance of doing things outside of playing video games. "The Top Five Reasons Video Games are Good for Your Health" does not. These conclusions differ, so choice A is correct. The conclusion of "More Than Video Games" does not address an opposing view or counterargument. "The Top Five Reasons Video Games are Good for Your Health" does, so choice B is incorrect. Neither passage portrays playing video games as something negative, so choice C is incorrect. The conclusion of "More Than Video Games" does not make the same point as "The Top Five Reasons Video Games are Good for Your Health," so choice D is incorrect.

27. C: The author of "The Top Five Reasons Video Games are Good for Your Health" makes it clear that video games have several benefits, including making players more coordinated, better at reasoning and logic, and more social. Reggie realizes family is more important than video games and acts in a way that shows that he has heeded his father's words. Because of these conclusions, it is likely that the author of "The Top Five Reasons Video Games are Good for Your Health" would view games as a solution to a problem while Reggie would ask his family for solutions. Choice A is incorrect. Based on the passage, it is more likely that Reggie would find family time valuable. It is unlikely that Reggie would prioritize games over schoolwork, as he completed his homework before playing the game and realized that there is more to life than games. This means that choice B is incorrect. Because "The Top Five Reasons Video Games are Good for Your Health" is written to persuade people to play games, it is unlikely the author would simply want people to form their own opinions. It is also likely that Reggie would want people to understand the benefit of balance in life over gaming, so choice D is incorrect.

28. D: Both passages portray video games as being fun and exciting. "More Than Video Games" portrays this through Reggie's excitement, while "The Top Five Reasons Video Games are Good for Your Health" explains it more blatantly. Choice A is incorrect because only "The Top Five Reasons Video Games are Good for Your Health" explains the benefits of playing video games. Only "More Than Video Games" portrays video games as being a small part of life, so choice B is incorrect. Both Reggie and the author of "The Top Five Reasons Video Games are Good for Your Health" are excited about gaming, not indifferent, so choice C is incorrect.

29. A: This passage explains the many contributions Archimedes made to the fields of mathematics and physics. It also describes his inventions. This is done to highlight how significant his contributions to society have been, so choice A is correct. While the passage does suggest that Archimedes died because he refused to halt his work and leave the city, this is not the controlling idea of the passage. It is only a detail, so choice B is incorrect. The passage mentions several of Archimedes's contributions to many fields, but it does not suggest that he could not have done this on his own, so choice C is incorrect. The first paragraph explains that Archimedes came from a well-educated family and that he was also well educated. However, this is only mentioned in the first paragraph, and the passage does not suggest that his success was due to his education. The reader could draw this conclusion, but it is not the controlling idea, so choice D is incorrect.

30. C: The image of Archimedes's "On the Sphere and Cylinder" follows a paragraph detailing his work in geometry. The image displays examples of his work in that area. These examples show circles and triangles with lines and points drawn on them. These drawings show the reader the type and depth of work Archimedes was doing in geometry. Because the image focuses on his work in geometry and not physics or his impact on culture, choice A is incorrect. Choice B is incorrect because the passage does not support the idea that this is the work Archimedes was focused on at the time of his death. If it were, it would be more logical for the image to be located after the last paragraph. The passage does not describe Archimedes as an organized individual. Therefore, it cannot be concluded that this image is meant to convey organization, so choice D is incorrect.

31. D: Paragraph 4 explains that Archimedes was an inventor as well as a mathematician and physicist. He used his knowledge of physics to create the screw pump. He also created war machines, like a claw and a death ray. Since the screw pump is still used today, the reader can conclude that it is proven to work well. Archimedes's devices were original because he invented them, so they were also experimental, and choice D is correct. Paragraph 5 discusses that Archimedes is known for making "eureka" a common phrase in pop culture. Since this is not discussed in paragraph 4 and Archimedes's personality is not a key idea of the passage, choice A is incorrect. Paragraph 4 outlines how Archimedes tried to help Syracuse during a war, not Rome, so choice B is incorrect. Paragraph 4 does not focus on how Archimedes spent his time throughout his life or his pursuit of knowledge, so choice C is incorrect.

32. C: The passage starts with information about Archimedes's family and education. His background equipped him to have the successes and make the contributions that are explained in the body of the passage. The final paragraph explains how Archimedes died. This chronological order describes the life of Archimedes, starting with his early years and then describing his career and his death. Though the passage mentions a war with Rome, this was not the purpose of the passage's organization. A chronological structure is not necessary for explaining his contribution during war, so choice A is incorrect. Choice B is incorrect because the passage does not give a detailed description of the period Archimedes lived in. Archimedes died as a result of refusing to flee his invaded city. The use of chronological organization does not support the reader's understanding of this event. Readers may speculate what happened as a result of his death, but that is not the purpose of the passage, so choice D is incorrect.

33. A: Natural selection is the idea that animals who thrive in an environment are more likely to reproduce and pass down their genes than animals who do not thrive, as they will likely die before they can do so. As a result, the genes better suited for the environment become more common. This is best explained when the text states that "the sharp-beaked, insect-eating finches thrived and produced many offspring, while the short-beaked insect-eating finches gradually died out. The sharp beak was, in effect, selected by nature to thrive." Choice B is incorrect. The sentence in this choice explains evolution, not natural selection. The description is too broad and does not capture the specific meaning of "natural selection." Choice C explains that changes occurred, but it does not explain the process by which the changes happen or clearly link this change to the idea of natural selection. This makes it incorrect. Choice D describes the advantages of the long, sharp beak that eventually became common among the finches. However, it does not explain the process by which it became common, which supports the idea of natural selection, so it is incorrect.

34. C: The passage explains that the finches' beaks changed as the foods that were available to them changed. Based on this, the reader can conclude that the way an animal's mouth and teeth function is impacted by the foods available in their environment, so choice C is correct. The passage does not discuss the natural length of any animal's life, so the influence of this factor on evolution cannot be concluded from the information in the passage. This makes choice A incorrect. The passage focuses on the evolution of the finch and does not address how it applies to other animals. However, this does not suggest that only land animals or animals like the finch evolve. The passage only focuses on the finch because it led Darwin to form his theory, so choice B is incorrect. The passage states that Darwin did his studies in the Galapagos Islands, but does not explain why, so choice D is incorrect.

35. A: The footnote explains that the theory of evolution suggests that the resources different beings needed in order to survive led them to adapt and give way to new species over time. The passage explains that natural selection is the idea that in a group of organisms that are of the same species but have different traits, those with a trait that promotes survival are more likely to reproduce and pass the trait to the next generation. These ideas are closely related, as they both focus on the traits an organism needs to survive and the possibility that changes to an organism's needs may result in generations that are different from previous generations of the same organism. Choice A is correct. The passage states that Darwin is "the father of evolution" and that he was the first to describe evolution, so choice B is incorrect. Choices C and D are incorrect because neither the footnote nor the passage suggest that only animals undergo evolution or that evolution does not still occur. In fact, the theory of evolution also applies to plants and is believed to be ongoing today.

36. B: The author of this passage provides information about who Charles Darwin is and then explains how his observation of finches on the Galapagos Islands led him to propose the theory of natural selection. The primary focus of the passage is the characteristics of the finches and how Darwin interpreted those characteristics, so choice B is correct. The Galapagos Islands is where Darwin went to study plants and animals, but the passage does not mention any new species that Darwin discovered there. This means that choice A is incorrect. Choice C is incorrect because the passage does not mention a counterargument or any evidence that would disprove the theory of natural selection. The passage explains Darwin's contributions to the study of the theory of evolution, not nature conservation, so choice D is incorrect.

37. C: Both Archimedes and Darwin made significant contributions to their field. Archimedes remains well known for his work in mathematics and physics and Darwin's theories are still widely studied by scientists. Based on the passages, only Archimedes used mathematics in his work, so choice A is incorrect. Neither passage directly addresses how the men felt about their work. "Archimedes: Father of Mathematics" explains that Archimedes died as a result of not wanting to leave his work, so it can be assumed that he valued it. This makes choice B incorrect. Darwin's life and death are not addressed in "Charles Darwin on the Galapagos Islands." This means that the reader cannot conclude that they both had untimely deaths that stopped them from working to their full potential, so choice D is incorrect.

38. C, D: In both passages, a new understanding results from observations. Archimedes observed that his body displaced water and realized that he could use a similar method to measure the mass of the king's crown. Darwin observed finches and realized that they have different traits. He concluded that the birds evolved so that they would be better suited to surviving in their environment. Both men applied their observations to create new understandings. Additionally, both men created theories and principles that have made a lasting impact on the fields of math and science. Choices C and D are correct. Schooling is only mentioned in the passage about Archimedes, so the idea that schooling is an important component of success is not supported by both passages. This makes choice A incorrect. Only the passage about Archimedes features an unhealthy outcome to dedication, making choice B incorrect. Both men worked hard in their fields and were rewarded with great knowledge, so choice E is incorrect.

39. B: "Charles Darwin on the Galapagos Islands" focuses only on Darwin's theory of natural selection. "Archimedes: Father of Mathematics" discusses Archimedes's early life, his contributions to math and physics, and his death. Choice A is incorrect because, while the death of Archimedes is mentioned, it is not the focus of the passage. Additionally, the passage about Darwin does not focus on his life, it only focuses on how he developed his theory of natural selection. Both passages are informative, and neither passage contains much figurative language. This makes choice C incorrect. Choice D is incorrect because "Charles Darwin on the Galapagos Islands" is informative and not intended to be entertaining.

40. C: The correct answer choice is C because paragraphs 2-5 introduce Buck and the setting in which he lives. The paragraphs accomplish this introduction by giving many detailed facts, such as the detail in paragraph 5 about the times he escorted Mollie and Alice on walks. Choice A is incorrect because two new characters, Manuel and the stranger, are introduced in paragraphs 7 and 8. While aspects of paragraphs 2-5 show Buck's personality, choice B is incorrect because the paragraphs also give other details about Buck, such as information about his parents and appearance. Choice D is incorrect because Toots and Ysabel are only mentioned in paragraphs 3 and 4. Furthermore, paragraph 4 says that he utterly ignored Toots and Ysabel, not that he is affectionate towards them.

41. B: The correct answer is choice B because the sentence indicates that Buck felt as if he owned or ruled over Judge Miller's place. The word *realm* indicates that the sentence is referring to everything. Choice A is incorrect because it talks about other dogs that came and went but does not show Buck's attitude towards them or Judge Miller's place. Choice C is incorrect because it shows Buck's opinion of himself but not his opinion of Judge Miller's place. Choice A is incorrect because it describes something that Buck enjoys, but does not give his attitude about the house and grounds at Judge Miller's.

42. D: Choice D is correct because the sentence indicates that Buck considers himself to be like a king. Kings or royalty are often considered regal. Choice A is incorrect because nothing in the paragraph indicates that Buck is scared; in fact, Buck is like a king, which makes him unlikely to be scared of the other dogs. Choice B is incorrect because Buck doesn't indicate anger, which could be shown by barking or growling. Choice C is incorrect because *regal* is referring to Buck feeling like a king, which is unrelated to his happiness.

43. C: Choice C is correct because the first part of the passage mostly describes Buck's life, but the passage ends in a moment of change when the stranger wraps a piece of rope around Buck's neck. Choice A is incorrect because the passage does not describe a sequence of events as they happen. Instead the passage gives an overview of how Buck lived before the moment of change. Although part of the passage describes Buck's history, the passage also describes the moment in which his life changes, making choice B incorrect. Choice D is incorrect because the passage only describes life at Judge Miller's place but doesn't describe what came afterwards.

44. A: The best answer is choice A because the passage begins by setting up Buck's life and then showing a moment where his life is about to drastically change. Choice B is incorrect because only paragraph 5 refers to family; this is not a big enough portion of the passage to imply that the larger selection is about family. Although Buck might need to work hard in the future, choice C is incorrect because the passage does not have that many clues about upcoming hard work. Choice C is incorrect because the passage does not spend time showing that Buck strongly values relationships. The end of the passage indicates that Buck is about to experience a moment of change.

45. B: The correct answer is choice B because the sentence talks about how the men want dogs; the sentence foreshadows that Buck may be the type of dog that the men want. Choice A is incorrect because it refers to Buck's attitude around Judge Miller's place but does not hint at what might be coming next. Although part of the sentence indicates that Buck hopes to follow in Elmo's footsteps, the rest of the sentence simply describes Buck's father. Choice B better foreshadows what's going to happen in the story because it more closely relates to the events in paragraph 7 and 8. Choice D is incorrect because the sentence describes Buck's personality and interests without giving clues about what's going to happen next.

46. D: The best answer is choice D because, as a dog, Buck can't read. Although Buck may not be interested in current events, choice A is incorrect because choice D is a more logical answer. Choices B and C are also incorrect because the logic that Buck doesn't read the newspapers is drawn from the fact that dogs can't read.

Language Practice Test #2

Questions 1 – 7 pertain to the following story:

The Greek Festival

(1) Every October my family attends the Greek Festival at the Greek Orthodox Church close to our house. (2) We were first invited four years ago by one of my friends, Amelia. (3) Her family attends the Greek Orthodox Church and works several booths at the festival each year. (4) They telled us that everyone was welcome.

(5) When we first arrived at the festival, we could hear the music from the parking lot? (6) It was music that I had never heard before, and some of it was in another language. (7) Amelia told me later that it was traditional Greek music. (8) We also noticed the smells that seemed to come from all over the festival grounds. (9) All around us, there were signs for meat, pastry, coffee drinks, and other side dishes. (10) My mom's favorite were the grape leaves, and my dad loved the Baklava. (11) It is a dessert that is made up of baked thin sheets of pastry dough covered in a sweet sauce like honey. (12) Amelia suggested us eat it with ice cream and chocolate sauce. (13) As much as I liked the baklava, my favorite was the gyro pita. (14) Gyro is lamb meat in a warm pita with tomato, lettuce, onion, and a Greek sauce. (15) I ate two pitas and it was deliciously!

(16) After we had eaten, everyone gathered around the dance floor and watched as people from all different age groups danced traditional Greek dances. (17) The dancers were dressed in special clothing and black dress shoes.

(18) Amelia danced in the second group of dancers, and her mom tossed money toward her. (19) Soon, the dance floor was covered in dollar bills from all of the dancers families. (20) The food was great, the music was fun, and the dancing was even better. (21) We had a great time at the greek Festival, and now I look forward to it every year!

1. What change, if any, should be made in sentence 4?

a. Change everyone to every one
b. Change telled to told
c. Change welcome to welcomed
d. Make no change

2. What change should be made in sentence 5?

a. Change arrived to arrive
b. Change festival to Festival
c. Delete the comma after festival
d. Change the question mark to a period

3. What change, if any, should be made in sentence 10?

a. Change were to was
b. Change mom's to moms
c. Change loved to loves
d. Make no change

4. What is the BEST way to revise sentence 12?

a. Amelia suggested, us eat it with ice cream and chocolate sauce.
b. Amelia suggested to us eat it with ice cream and chocolate sauce.
c. Amelia suggested us eat it, with ice cream and chocolate sauce.
d. Amelia suggested that we eat it with ice cream and chocolate sauce.

5. What change, if any, should be made in sentence 15?

a. Change ate to eat
b. Change deliciously to delicious
c. Change two to too
d. Make no change

6. What change, if any, should be made in sentence 19?

a. Change covered to cover
b. Change from to form
c. Change dancers to dancers'
d. Make no change

7. What change, if any, should be made in sentence 21?

a. Change had to have
b. Change look to looked
c. Change greek to Greek
d. Make no change

Questions 8 – 14 pertain to the following passage:

Dogs in the Park

(1) On Saturday, my mom took me to a dog show at a park by our house. (2) The sun was out, and it was a really warm day. (3) I ride my bike to the park almost every day in the summer. (4) The dogs were all lying in the grass when we arrived, and they looked warm in the sun. (5) One of my mom's friends, Mary, is a dog trainer, and she invited us to watch the dog show after my mom told her how much I love dogs.

(6) Their were all kinds of dogs at the show. (7) Some were really little, some were big, and some had really long hair. (8) My favorite were the dogs in the toy category and the sporting category. (9) The dogs that were waiting to be shown were with their trainers at different areas of the park getting ready. (10) Some trainers brushed its dog's hair, and some gave treats.

(11) We sat on the grass and watched the show. (12) The trainers were all dressed up. (13) The men wore suit pants and jackets, and the women wore dress skirts, stockings, and blazers. (14) All of the dogs were lined up and stood still wile the judges walked down and looked closely at all the dogs. (15) The judges looked at the dogs' hair, paws, and teeth. (16) Then it was time for each dog to show off. (17) Each trainer ran with their dog and held the leash high in the air. (18) The judges watched as the dogs ran, and judged how good they turned corners and listened to their trainers.

(19) At the end of the show, the judges awarded prizes. (20) The dogs and their trainers gathered in a line, and the judges presnted the winners with large ribbons. (21) Mary's dog won first place, and she was given a purple ribbon that was bigger than most of the small dogs in the toy category. (22) We left the park, and I told my mom that I want to learn how to train dogs.

8. What change, if any, should be made in sentence 6?

a. Change Their to There
b. Change dogs to dog's
c. Change were to was
d. Make no change

9. What change, if any, should be made in sentence 8?

a. Change were to was
b. Insert a comma after category
c. Change favorite to favorites
d. Make no change

10. What change should be made in sentence 10?

a. Change its to their
b. Change its to it's
c. Change brushed to brush
d. Change dog's to dogs

11. What change should be made in sentence 14?

a. Insert a comma after up
b. Change walked to walk
c. Change wile to while
d. Insert a comma after down

12. What change, if any, should be made in sentence 20?

a. Change dogs to dog
b. Change presnted to presented
c. Change their to its
d. Make no change

13. Which sentence does not belong in this essay?

a. Sentence 18
b. Sentence 11
c. Sentence 7
d. Sentence 3

14. What is the BEST transition word that could be added to the beginning of sentence 22?

a. However
b. Later
c. Otherwise
d. Consequentially

Questions 15 – 21 pertain to the following story:

First Party

(1) Today my brother turned one year old. (2) We had a big party to celebrate, and a lot of people came. (3) My ant came to the house early to help my mom hang streamers. (4) My cousin helped me make party favors for both the big kids and the babies. (5) We packed the little bags with candy, pencils, whistles, and noisemakers. (6) My parents invited a lot of people. (7) Soon the house was filled with family, friends, and even some babies for my brother to play with.

(8) My grandparents on my dad's side flew even flew in from California the day before to help. (9) My dad lighted the barbeque in the back yard and took orders from the guests. (10) He made hamburgers, turkey burgers, hot dogs, chicken wings, and sausages. (11) My aunt sliced strips of onion, tomato, pickles, and lettuce. (12) She also cuts up an avocado because she knows that it is my favorite topping on my hamburger. (13) My cousins, friends, and I all played in the backyard after we ate.

(14) My brother slept through most of the party, he was awake by the time he had cake. (15) He don't know he was missing his party by napping. (16) My mom put him in his high chair, and we all sang "Happy Birthday," to him. (17) There was one candle in the center of the large cake, and my mom blew it out since he was two little.

(18) My brother sat in his chair and ate cake. (19) Soon there was cake everywhere. (20) It was all over his hands, his face, his tabletop and chair. (21) There was blue icing everywhere. (22) He even lifted up his arms and grabbed pieces of his hair. (23) His big, blue eyes looked at everyone as they smiled and laughed. (24) He stuffed some more cake into his mouth and smiled. (25) I think he knew he had a good first birthday.

15. What change should be made in sentence 3?

a. Change hang to hanged
b. Change ant to aunt
c. Change help to helped
d. Change came to comes

16. Where is the best placement for sentence 8?

a. After sentence 2
b. After sentence 4
c. After sentence 5
d. No change is needed

17. What change, if any, should be made in sentence 9?

a. Change took to takes
b. Change barbeque to BBQ
c. Change lighted to lit
d. Make no change

18. What change, if any, should be made in sentence 12?

a. Change know to knew
b. Change cuts to cut
c. Change an to a
d. Make no change

19. What is the BEST transition word that could be added to the beginning of sentence 14?

a. Later
b. Therefore
c. Although
d. However

20. What change, if any, should be made in sentence 15?

a. Change don't to didn't
b. Change was to is
c. Change napping to nap
d. Make no change

21. What change should be made in sentence 17?

a. Change There to They're
b. Delete the comma before and
c. Change blew to blowed
d. Change two to too

Questions 22 – 28 pertain to the passage:

Dinner is Served

(1) Every year my friend and I celebrate each other's birthdays by going out to dinner because our birthdays are three weeks apart. (2) On my birthday, my family took us to Aribba, my favorite mexican food restaurant. (3) For Annmae's birthday, she chose a Japanese restaurant called Tomo where the food is cooked at the table.

(4) I had never eaten Japanese food before and didn't know what to expect? (5) When the hostess brought us to our table, I was surprised to see that there were four extra seats. (6) That was not the only thing that was strange. (7) The table was not a regular restaurant dinner table. (8) It was a half circle and there was a giant sheet of metal in the center. (9) The hostess came back with other people and sat them with us at our table.

(10) We filled out cards that said what kind of food we wanted. (11) We had to pick between chicken, beef, shrimp, and pork. (12) A man then came to our table and lit the metal sheet. (13) He laid out rice and vegetables, and started cutting and cooking. (14) He worked very fast it was almost hard for me to see his hands. (15) After the rice, he cooked each of the different meats and started serving plates. (16) While things were cooking he would take his spatula and fling a piece of bell pepper or carrot at someone at the table. (17) He toss the most at Annmae since it was her birthday, but they all hit her chin and slid down onto her shirt.

(18) It was really exciting watching our food cooked right in front of us. (19) The chef was nice and the food is delicious. (20) I even liked having other people sit at our table because it was like being at a party at dinner. (21) I am really glad that my friend chose Tomo and I can't wait to see where we try next year!

22. What change, if any, should be made in sentence 2?

a. Change birthday to birth day
b. Delete the comma after birthday
c. Change mexican to Mexican
d. Make no change

23. What change should be made in sentence 4?

a. Change had to have
b. Change Japanese to japanese
c. Change didn't to don't
d. Change the question mark to a period

24. What sentence could BEST follow and support sentence 9?

a. Now I understood why there were extra seats
b. The hostess smiled at us as she left
c. The woman worse a blue dress and he hair was tied back
d. I wondered how many times she was going to come back

25. What is the BEST way to revise sentence 14?

a. He worked very fast it was almost hard for me, to see his hands.
b. He worked very fast, and it was almost hard for me to see his hands.
c. His hands worked very fast it was almost hard for me to see.
d. Make no revision.

26. What change, if any, should be made in sentence 16?

a. Change were to are
b. Insert a comma after cooking
c. Change take to took
d. Make no change

27. What change, if any, should be made in sentence 17?

a. Delete the comma after birthday
b. Change hit to hitted
c. Change toss to tossed
d. Make no change

28. What change should be made in sentence 19?

a. Change is to was
b. Change was to is
c. Change delicious to deliciously
d. Change chef to Chef

Questions 29 – 34 pertain to the following passage:

History's Unsinkable Lessons

(1) In Ruth Campbell's book Exploring the Titanic, the events of the famous ship's only journey and sinking are brought to life. (2) In 1912, Titanic was built and was the largest passenger steamship at the time. (3) On what would be its first and only journey, the ship departed from Southampton in England and was supposed to arrive in New York City. (4) The ship hit an iceberg late at night on April 14, 1912, and sunked less than three hours later.

(5) Titanic was designed by some of the best engineers and had the latest technology of the time. (6) The ship was made to carry over three and a half thousand passengers and crew members, but had only twenty lifeboats. (7) There were not enough lifeboats for all of the people onboard, and as a result, only seven hundred six people survived.

(8) One interesting thing about Titanic, is that the ship was divided into classes. (9) The most expensive tickets were first class, and first class passengers had the biggest and much luxurious rooms. (10) The first class rooms were the closest to the ship's deck. (11) Because this the majority of survivors came from first class. (12) They were able to reach the deck fastest to get a seat on a lifeboat. (13) Additionally, the third class rooms were located the farthest below deck, and the majority of the third class passengers did not survive.

(14) Ruth Campbell's book was very interesting but also sad because the story of Titanic is true. (15) However, Campbell ended the book by talking about the positive things that have happened because of this tragedy. (16) Most importantly, experts now recommend that ships' carry enough lifeboats for all passengers onboard. (17) This would have saved a lot of lifes. (18) It was a good book, and it displayed a good message in history that lessons should be learned from mistakes.

29. What change should be made in sentence 1?

a. Change ship's to ships
b. Insert a comma after book
c. Change are to is
d. Change brought to bring

30. What change, if any, should be made in sentence 4?

a. Change sunked to sank
b. Delete the comma after 14
c. Change hours to hour's
d. Make no change

31. What change, if any, should be made in sentence 8?

a. Change was to were
b. Delete the comma after Titanic
c. Change divided into divide
d. Make no change

32. What is the BEST way to revise and combine sentence 11 and sentence 12?

a. Because, the majority of survivors came from first class as they were able to reach the deck fastest to get a seat on a lifeboat
b. Because of this, the majority of survivors came from first class, as they were able to reach the deck fastest to get a seat on a lifeboat
c. Because this, the majority of survivors came from first class, they were able to reach the deck fastest to get a seat on a lifeboat
d. Because of this, the majority of survivors came from first class as they were able to reach the deck fastest to get a seat on a lifeboat

33. What change should be made in sentence 16?

a. Change most important to importantist
b. Change found to find
c. Insert a comma after important
d. Change ship's to ships

34. What change, if any, should be made in sentence 17?

a. Change would have to would
b. Change a lot to a lot
c. Change lifes to lives
d. Make no change

Answers and Explanations for Language Test #2

1. B: because told is the correct past tense of the verb tell. Telled is not a word. A is not correct. When used as a noun, everyone is one word. C is not correct. Welcome is not a verb in this sentence and therefore does not need to be in the past tense like the rest of the essay.

2. D: because this sentence is a statement rather than a question. As a result, it should be punctuated with a period and not a question mark. A is not correct. Arrive is in the present tense, and the rest of the paragraph is in the past tense. B is not correct. Festival is not used in this sentence as a proper noun and therefore does not need to be capitalized. C is not correct. When we first arrived at the festival is an introductory clause, and a comma is needed after the introductory clause.

3. A: because the subject of this sentence is favorite. Favorite is singular; therefore, the verb also must be singular in order for the subject and verb to agree. Were is plural. Was is singular. B is not correct. Mom's in this sentence is possessive and an apostrophe is needed. C is not correct. Loves is in the present tense, and the rest of the essay is in the past tense.

4. D: because it is the simplest way to express the idea in a grammatically correct sentence. A, B, and C are incorrect because these sentences are not grammatically correct. This sentence is not grammatically correct.

5. B: because deliciously is an adverb rather than an adjective. It describes the noun, pitas, not the verb. A is not correct. Eat is in the present tense, and the rest of the essay is in the past tense. C is not correct. Two is spelled correctly and indicates the number. Too means "as well" or an indication of excess.

6. C: because in this sentence dancers' is possessive and needs an apostrophe. Since dancers is plural, referring to more than one dancer, the apostrophe comes after the s. A is not correct. Cover is in the present tense, and the rest of the essay is in the past tense. B is not correct. The correct word is from, and it is spelled correctly.

7. C: It is correct because Greek is a proper noun and needs to be capitalized. A is not correct. Have is in the present tense, and the rest of the essay is in the past tense. B is not correct. A shift has occurred in the last sentence, and the second half of the sentence shifts into the present tense. The writer explains that she looks forward to the festival every year. Look in the present tense is therefore correct.

8. A: It is correct because a homonym has been misused. There is used to indicate a physical or abstract place. Their is used to indicate possession. B is not correct. In this sentence, dogs does not indicate possession and does not need an apostrophe. C is not correct. Was is in the present tense, and the rest of the essay is in the past tense.

9. C: It is correct because the verb in the sentence, were, is plural, and the subject must be plural for subject-verb agreement. A is not correct. Was is in the present tense, and the rest of the essay is in the past tense. B is not correct. A comma is not needed because and the sporting category is not an independent clause.

10. A: It is correct because there is plural and displays possession. Its is singular. The subject, trainers, is plural; therefore, the possession is plural as well. B is not correct. It's is only used as a contraction for it is, not for possession. C is not correct. Brush is in the present tense, and the rest of the essay is in the past tense. D is not correct. Dog's is possessive and needs an apostrophe.

11. C: It is correct because a homonym has been misused. Wile means to trick or fool, and while indicates a period of time. A is not correct. A comma is not needed. No introductory clause or independent clauses need to be joined by a comma and conjunction. B is not correct. Walk is in the present tense and the rest of the essay is in the past tense. D is not correct. A comma is not needed. An independent clause does not follow the conjunction.

12. B: It is correct because presented has been misspelled. A is not correct. Their trainers indicates that dogs should be plural, not singular. C is not correct. Their is plural and its is singular. The subject, dogs, is plural.

13. D: It is correct because although this sentence provides new information, the content is not important to the rest of the essay. A, B, and C are because these sentences are important to the essay.

14. B: It is correct because the opening phrase, We left the park, indicates a time lapse from the earlier events of the essay. An appropriate transition word would indicate time. A is not correct. However is not a good transition because sentence 22 is not contradicting anything in the previous sentence. C is not correct. Otherwise is not a good transition because sentence 22 does not suggest an alternate to something that occurred previously. D is not correct. Consequentially is not a good transition because the content of the sentence is not cause and effect from the previous sentence.

15. B: It is correct because a homonym has been misused. Ant refers to an insect, and aunt refers to the sister of one's mother. A is not correct. Hang is not the verb of this sentence and does not need to be in the past tense. C is not correct. Help is not the verb of this sentence and does not need to be in the past tense. D is not correct. Came is the verb of this sentence. Comes is in the present tense and the rest of the essay is in the past tense.

16. A: It is correct because the sentence discusses the grandparents traveling from California to help with the part. Therefore, this sentence should be placed after the description of the party and that a lot of people came. B is not correct. Sentence 4 discusses the cousin helping with party favors, and therefore a sentence about the grandparents' travel would not follow well.

C is not correct. Sentence 5 discusses the party favors, and therefore a sentence about the grandparents' travel would not follow well.

17. C: It is correct because lit is the correct past tense for the verb light. A is not correct. Takes is in the present tense and the rest of the essay is in the past tense. B is not correct. Barbeque is spelled correctly. BBQ is an abbreviation, not a word.

18. B: It is correct because cuts is in the present tense, and the rest of the essay is in the past tense. Cut is in the past tense. A is not correct. Even though the essay is in the past tense, the act of the aunt knowing is a present and ongoing action and should be in the present tense. C is not correct. In this sentence, the article an is followed by a noun, avocado. Avocado begins with a vowel and a vowel sound; therefore, it needs to be introduced with the article an.

19. C: It is correct because although means "in spite of" and is appropriate within the sentence. A is not correct. Later is not an appropriate transition word because it contradicts the beginning of the sentence. B is not correct. Therefore is not an appropriate transition word because there is no cause an effect from the previous sentence. D is not correct. However is not an appropriate transition word because sentence 14 does not contradict anything from the previous sentence.

20. A: It is correct because don't is the conjunction of do not. Do not is in the present tense, and the rest of the essay is in the past tense. The past tense of do is did. B is not correct. Is is in the present tense, and the rest of the essay is in the past tense. C is not correct. Napping is a verb in this sentence, not a noun.

21. D: It is correct because a homonym has been misused. Two is the number. Too indicates "also," "excessively," or "very." A is not correct. There indicates location. They're is the contraction of there are. B is not correct. The sentence has two independent clauses joined by the conjunction and. A comma needs to be before the conjunction. H is not correct. Blew is the correct past tense of blow. Blowed is not a word.

22. C: It is correct because Mexican is a proper noun, and proper nouns need to be capitalized. A is not correct. Birthday is one word. B is not correct. A comma is needed after an introductory clause.

23. D: It is correct because the sentence is a statement, not a question, and needs a period as punctuation. A is not correct. Have is in the present tense, and the rest of the essay is in the past tense. B is not correct. Japanese is a proper noun and needs to be capitalized. C is not correct. Didn't is a contraction of did not and is in the past tense, like the rest of the essay. Don't is a contraction of do not and is in the present tense.

24. A: It is correct because the sentence both supports the previous sentences and provides additional information. Sentence 5 states that extra seats were available at the table. This sentence provides additional information that supports sentence 5 as well as sentence 9. B, C, and D are incorrect. Although these sentences provide new information, they do not link and support the previous sentences.

25. B: It is correct because it is the simplest way to express the idea in a grammatically correct sentence. A and C are not correct because these sentences are not grammatically correct.

26. B: It is correct because While things were cooking is an introductory clause, and a comma is needed after the clause. A is not correct. Are is in the present tense and the rest of the essay is in the past tense. C is not correct. Take is part of would take and is in the past participle, not the present tense.

27. C: It is correct because tossed is in the past tense, like the rest of the essay. Toss is in the present tense. A is not correct. A comma is needed before the conjunction when two independent clauses are joined by a conjunction. B is not correct. Hit is the correct past tense of hit. Hitted is not a word.

28. A: It is correct because was is in the past tense, like the rest of the essay. Is is in the present tense. B is not correct. Is is in the present tense and the rest of the essay is in the past tense. C is not correct. Delicious is an adjective, not an adverb. It is used in this sentence to describe the noun, not the verb. D is not correct. Chef is not a proper noun and does not need to be capitalized.

29. B: It is correct because a comma is needed to separate the interjection of the book title. A is not correct. Ship in the sentence is possessive and requires the apostrophe. C is not correct. Are is the plural of is. The subject, events, is plural and therefore the verb needs to be plural in subject-verb agreement. D is not correct. Are brought is in the past participle, and bring is in the present tense.

30. A: It is correct because sank is the correct past tense of the verb sink. Sunked is not a word. B is not correct. A comma is needed to separate dates of the month from the year. H is not correct. Hours is not possessive and does not require the apostrophe.

31. B: It is correct because there is no need for a comma. As it stands, the comma disrupts the normal flow of thought in the sentence. A is not correct. The subject, ship, is singular, and the verb also must be singular in subject-verb agreement. C is not correct. Was divided is in the past participle. Divide is in the present tense, and the rest of the essay is in the past.

32. B: It is correct because it is the simplest way to express the idea in a grammatically correct sentence. Because of this refers to the content of the previous sentence. A is not correct. This sentence is not grammatically correct. C is not correct. This sentence is not grammatically correct. D is not correct. This sentence is not grammatically correct and needs a comma after class.

33. D: because in this sentence, ships is plural rather than possessive and does not require the apostrophe. A is not correct. Most important is correct. Importantist is not a word. B is not correct. Find is in the present tense and the rest of the essay is in the past tense. C is not correct, because the sentence does not need a comma. A comma would disrupt the normal flow of thought in the sentence.

34. C: It is correct because lives is the correct plural of life. Lifes is not a word. A is not correct. Would have is in the past participle, and would is in the future tense. B is not correct. A lot is correct. Alot is not a word.

Online Resources

Due to our efforts to try to keep this book to a manageable length, we've created a link that will give you access to all of your online resources:

mometrix.com/resources719/terranextg8rl

It's Your Moment, Let's Celebrate It!

Share your story @mometrixtestpreparation